CASTRATION
AND THE HEAVENLY
KINGDOM

Skoptsy icon: Lambs of God. Color plate from [Nikolai Nadezhdin], *Issledovanie o skopcheskoi eresi* (n.p.: Ministerstvo vnutrennikh del, 1845).

CASTRATION
AND
THE HEAVENLY
KINGDOM

A RUSSIAN FOLKTALE

Laura Engelstein

CORNELL UNIVERSITY PRESS

Ithaca and London

First published 1999 by Cornell University Press

Printed in the United States of America

Library of Congress Cataloging-in-Publication Data

Engelstein, Laura.

Castration and the heavenly kingdom : a Russian folktale / Laura Engelstein.

p.   cm.

Includes bibliographical references (p.   ) and index.

ISBN 0-8014-3676-1

1. Skoptsy—History.   I. Title.

BX9798.S47E44   1999

289.9—dc21   99-16167

Cornell University Press strives to use environmentally responsible suppliers and materials to the fullest extent possible in the publishing of its books. Such materials include vegetable-based, low-VOC inks and acid-free papers that are recycled, totally chlorine-free, or partly composed of nonwood fibers. Books that bear the logo of the FSC (Forest Stewardship Council) use paper taken from forests that have been inspected and certified as meeting the highest standards for environmental and social responsibility. For further information, visit our website at www.cornellpress.cornell.edu.

Cloth printing 10 9 8 7 6 5 4 3 2 1

To the memory of George L. Mosse (1918–1998)
AND
Lawrence Stone (1919–1999)

We are made a spectacle unto the world,
and to angels, and to men.

1 Corinthians 4:9

These are they which came out of great tribulation,
and have washed their robes,
and made them white in the blood of the Lamb.

Revelation 7:14

CONTENTS

X

CONTENTS

PREFACE

This book is about a community of mystical Christians that came to light in the central provinces of the Russian Empire during the reign of Catherine the Great and lasted well into the Soviet era. Similar in their ascetic practices and horror of procreation to the Shakers, who emerged at roughly the same time in a very different context, the Russian mystics went so far in their search for purity and eternal life as to adopt the practice of ritual self-castration. Following the call of a charismatic vagrant who claimed to embody the reincarnated Jesus Christ, the believers subjected themselves to pain and mutilation in the expectation of redemption. Disconcerting to its neighbors, abhorrent to church and secular authorities, still the community managed to sustain a coherent culture and attract new adherents across 150 years, surviving even the advent of a new political order.

Such devotional hyperbole is fascinating, there is no doubt. But what can a historian derive from studying an example of spiritual extravagance that diverges so sharply from the cultural norm as to evoke contempt, disgust, and continuous persecution for decades? How to get beyond morbid curiosity or simple revulsion? How to discover in the enactment of extremes some link to the host environment or to the basic human condition? These were the questions I asked myself as I stumbled onto the literature, mostly a century old, concerning this reviled group and found I could not pull myself away. What was I doing with this subject?

I had written a book about the cultural meanings of sexuality in turn-of-the-twentieth-century Russia, which examined a world of entirely secular discourse. Here was an occasion to explore the meanings attached to the absence of sex and to enter a world with an otherworldly perspective. Yet the more I read and the more closely I encountered the believers' own version of what they believed, the less I thought sexuality was actually the subject at issue. The subject at issue was faith: a faith so resistant to reasonable explanation as to stand for the very mystery at the heart of why people choose to believe at all.

There is nothing particularly Russian about the potential for established confessions to sprout unorthodox sects, which violate the fundamental tenets of the faith and challenge its authority to constrain them. Nonconformity has been endemic to English history. In North America, Shakers, Oneidans, and Mormons have all combined special versions of Christian doctrine with particular forms of sexual self-regulation. In more recent times, the public has recoiled at examples of collective enthusiasm ending in dramatic acts of self-destruction. In 1978 the Reverend Jim Jones convinced his followers to sacrifice their children and take their own lives in the Jonestown massacre. In 1997 the members of Heaven's Gate, in search of salvation, committed mass suicide. A few had submitted to castration. We would like to think such people are mentally deranged, dismissing David Koresh, leader of the Branch Davidians who came to grief in Waco, Texas, in 1993, as psychotic. But these cases show that spiritual eccentricity can afflict the ordinary citizens of even the most advanced and science-minded of nations.

Yet, how many books have been written about Grigorii Rasputin's charismatic ministry to the throne as though it encapsulated the fatal immaturity of both the ruler of Russia and his Russian subjects? Keeping the American example in mind should prevent us from jumping to conclusions about national psychology on the evidence of marginal types and exotic figures. This book will not use the example of the self-castrators to make an argument about the basic character of Russian politics or culture—proving either that Russians are predisposed to projects of radical self-transformation, or that stunning achievements in science and the creative arts were but a thin membrane spanning the chasm of ignorance and tradition. My purpose rather is to make these puzzling believers comprehensible in relation to the culture from which they emerged but of which they are not the ultimate expression.

Nor can they be viewed as exemplars of timeless spiritual primi-tivism. Like the many sects that continue to dot the American religious landscape, the self-castrators were not the remnants of a remote past but features of an increasingly modern setting. For imperial Russia, in the years before 1917, embraced many of the changes associated with progress in the Western sense. The final decades of tsarism witnessed the emergence of a secular elite that aspired to constitutional forms of gov-ernment, civil rights, individual self-fulfillment, and the rule of reason in public life. The last tsar presided over a land in the throes of industrializa-tion, urban growth, social transformation, expanding literacy and higher education, and cultural innovation.

In the tumult of changing times, bureaucrats and intellectuals, despite their differences, looked to elements of cultural continuity and folk authenticity for ballast. The self-castrators, with their violent literal-mindedness, seemed as far as possible from the modern age, but this ver-sion of folk sensibility offered little comfort. The historian must, however, reach beyond the distress of contemporaries and the discomfort such practices continue to evoke and attempt to see these mystical virtuosi in human terms. Their desire to escape the common lot—both social and existential—took a form which is not unheard of today. People refuse procreation, reject the family, conjugal bonds, or sexual relations with the opposite sex, finding different satisfactions; some alter their bodies by sur-gical means; others renounce joys and connections whose absence they later come to regret. The effort to find a place on earth is both a personal and a cultural quest, often as hard to understand in oneself as in others.

The central characters in this book belonged to a community that cre-ated its own archive. The papers they assembled are housed in the State Museum of the History of Religion in St. Petersburg, formerly the State Museum for the History of Religion and Atheism in Leningrad. Thanks to the professionalism of the staff, the material has been well preserved and organized. Scholars are welcome to work in the museum holdings, under the expert supervision of the chief archivist, I. V. Tarasova. Gener-ous with help and information, Irina Viktorovna guided me through her treasures, shared her knowledge, and facilitated my work in many ways. I value her wisdom and friendship greatly. I am also grateful to S. A. Kuchinskii, the museum director, for graciously allowing me to copy archival material. The illustrations are reproduced courtesy of the museum. In addition, I am thankful for the cooperation of the staff in the Russian State Historical Archive and the Archive of the Academy of Sciences, also in St. Petersburg.

The project enjoyed generous institutional support, which I am pleased to acknowledge. Princeton University provided travel grants and generous leave time. Research time and resources were also funded by fellowships from the Woodrow Wilson International Center for Scholars, the National Humanities Center (with the support of the Lilly Endowment), the John Simon Guggenheim Memorial Foundation, and the Rockefeller Foundation Study and Conference Center in Bellagio, Italy. I was fortunate to be able to develop and present my ideas on several rewarding occasions. In 1995 Lucette Valensi invited me to discuss some of this material at the Ecole des hautes études en sciences sociales in Paris, where I benefited from the comments of Sergio Claudio Ingerflom. Andrei Lebedev generously gave me a copy of his unpublished manuscript and bibliography, "Kondratii Selivanov i russkaia sekta skoptsov." In 1996 I was invited to give the Eugene Lunn Lecture at the University of California at Davis, and a year later I presented the Donald M. Kendall Lectures in Russian history at Stanford University. The audiences there and elsewhere asked challenging questions, and I appreciate their collective thoughtfulness.

In tussling with this troubling subject, I have profited from the wisdom of colleagues and friends. Heather Coleman told me about her research on Baptists in the Museum for the History of Religion. Nicholas Breyfogle, whom I encountered in the museum, taught me about the Molokans and the situation of Russian sectarians in general. Richard Trexler asked provocative questions, as is his wont, which pushed me in new directions. Numerous conversations with Peter Brown helped me get my bearings in the peculiar spiritual world into which I had strayed. His reading of the manuscript assured me that I'd managed to make some sense of that world in the end, and his suggestions improved what I'd written. I am glad the Skoptsy gave me a chance to know him better. John Ackerman, a most unusual editor and a loyal friend of thirty years, encouraged me in the desire to write differently from how I had before and guided me through the process.

The Skoptsy believed in resurrection. As the secular custodian of their afterlife, I confess at the end that I do too. Alvin Mesnikoff and Sergey Horujy will know what I mean by that, and their names belong in this book.

LAURA ENGELSTEIN

Princeton, New Jersey

TERMS AND ABBREVIATIONS

Note on Terms

There is no adequate English term with which to designate the practitioners of the faith discussed in this book. The word "eunuch" (of which there exists the Russian "evnukh") does not convey the specificity of this case. Castrati are singers; castrate is a verb. Self-castrator is awkward and ambiguous. I have therefore chosen to use the Russian names "Skoptsy" (plural), "Skopets" (masculine singular). In violation of Russian grammar, I use the word "Skoptsy" not only as a noun but as an adjective (as, for example, in the phrase "the Skoptsy way of life"). The name of the faith as a whole is "Skopchestvo."

Skoptsy authors make frequent mistakes of grammar, spelling, and punctuation, of which they were themselves painfully aware. In translation, I have tried to convey the expressive quality of their prose but cannot always preserve their errors.

Abbreviations

Archival citations use the conventional abbreviations: collection (fond = f.), inventory (opis' = op.), carton (karton = k.), file(s) (delo, dela = d. or edinitsa khraneniia = ed. khr.), sheet(s) (list, listy = l.), and verso (oborot = ob.).

The following abbreviations are used in the notes:

ARAN   Arkhiv rossiiskoi akademii nauk (Archive of the Russian
        Academy of Sciences), St. Petersburg
GMIR   Gosudarstvennyi muzei istorii religii (State Museum of
        the History of Religion), St. Petersburg

TERMS AND ABBREVIATIONS

OR-RGB	Otdel rukopisei, Rossiiskaia gosudarstvennaia biblioteka (Manuscript Division, Russian State Library), Moscow
RGIA	Rossiiskii gosudarstvennyi istoricheskii arkhiv (Russian State Historical Archive), St. Petersburg
Chteniia	*Chteniia v imperatorskom obshchestve istorii i drevnostei rossiiskikh pri Moskovskom universitete*

CASTRATION
AND THE HEAVENLY
KINGDOM

INTRODUCTION
❧ THE ARCHIVES OF ETERNITY

. . . c'est qu'une lettre arrive toujours à destination.

JACQUES LACAN, *Ecrits*

And before him shall be gathered all nations: and he shall separate them one from another, as a shepherd divideth his sheep from the goats: And he shall set the sheep on his right hand, but the goats on the left. Then shall the King say unto them on his right hand, Come, ye blessed of my Father, inherit the kingdom prepared for you from the foundation of the world.

MATTHEW 25:32–34

And they sung as it were a new song before the throne, and before the four beasts, and the elders: and no man could learn that song but the hundred and forty and four thousand, which were redeemed from the earth.

These are they which were not defiled with women; for they are virgins. These are they which follow the Lamb whithersoever he goeth. These were redeemed from among men, being the firstfruits unto God and to the Lamb.

REVELATION 14:4

I N 1938, Nikifor Petrovich Latyshev, a seventy-five-year-old resident of the "Red Partisan" invalid home in the Dnepropetrovsk region of the Ukrainian Republic, fearing he had not long to live, wrote to thank Joseph Stalin for assuring his welfare in old age. The Leader's beneficence had allowed the pensioner to spend his declining years in the company, as he put it, of "two or three ardent partisans, several nut cases, a few cripples, and some completely healthy lazybones."[1] The former peasant and retired factory watchman, who now styled himself a "true son of the proletariat," was not the only Soviet citizen to write directly to Stalin himself.[2] His letter is not the only one to have ended up in archival collections. But Latyshev was not the usual writer. He was one of the many

1

spiritual enthusiasts who had populated the religious landscape of imperial Russia and survived to see the advent of a new regime. Among these
spiritual dissenters, the community to which Latyshev belonged occupied a special place in the hierarchy of deviation, as the most stigmatized
of them all. Decried by civil and ecclesiastical authorities in tsarist times
and by the militant atheists who replaced them, the fellowship was persecuted throughout the 150 years of its existence.

The feature that so disturbed the guardians of orthodoxy and of
public order under two very different regimes was not the fact of spiritual error (until 1917) or the fact of devotion itself (thereafter). The
feature that set the group apart was the strange and shocking practice of
ritual castration. The way to achieve salvation in this world, the group's
members believed, was through a covenant with God and the physical
impossibility of carnal connection. Like other born-again zealots, they
called themselves True Christians or the Godly, but they were known as
"the castrated ones" or "self-castrators" (in Russian, Skoptsy), a tag they
came to adopt as their own.[3] Mostly peasants from the Russian heart-
land, they were ordinary Russian folk, but instead of celebrating the fruit
of the womb as well as the fruit of the earth, they gathered in the warm
huts where the harvest bounty was lovingly dried to slice their genitals
off at the root and cast the unwanted bits into the burning oven!

Hounded for decades, the community was dispersed once and for all
in the 1930s. Then why was Latyshev grateful to Stalin? And how did his
expression of gratitude survive until the present time? The two questions
are connected, for the very regime that succeeded where the autocracy
had failed, in eliminating unwanted forms of belief, also provided the
veterans of tsarist oppression with an unexpected haven. Through the accident of personality as much as ruthless iconoclasm, the Bolsheviks enabled Latyshev and his fellows to establish a monument to their own fate.
The man who provided the personal link was the old-time Bolshevik
Vladimir Bonch-Bruevich (1873–1955). Lenin's close associate and administrator of the Council of People's Commissars from 1917 to 1920,
Bonch-Bruevich in 1938 was head of the State Museum of Literature in
Moscow. It was he who received the pages of regular script, composed in
unschooled Russian, in which Latyshev poured out his heart. "Knowing
that among humanity I am nothing in comparison to others," Latyshev
wrote Bonch-Bruevich, "I hesitated to send [my letter] to the addressee.

I beg you to accept it for the State Museum, to preserve as a document. In 100 or 200 years it will speak of how the common folk understood the Greatness of the Great."[4]

Latyshev's letter finally ended up in the Museum of the History of Religion and Atheism, established in 1932 in the desecrated Cathedral of Our Lady of Kazan in Leningrad, which Bonch-Bruevich directed from 1947 until his death.[5] With the end of the Soviet Union, the cathedral returned to its original function, but the archives of what is now the State Museum of the History of Religion in St. Petersburg still occupied the damp, stone-walled cubbies beneath the dome, awaiting new, post-Communist quarters. That is where, in 1996, I discovered Latyshev's outpouring to the Greatest of the Great, among many other pages he had written.

There was an ideological logic to this outcome. From the beginning of his career as a Social Democrat in the 1890s, Bonch-Bruevich had made a specialty of the sectarian question, seeking in such spiritual dissenters as Latyshev the kernel of defiance that might have inclined them to rebellion of a political kind. In 1903 the Party endorsed the project of recruiting followers among these groups, which it imagined to be democratic as well as nonconforming. "The Russian sectarian movement," the Party congress declared, "in many of its aspects, is one of the democratic currents directed against the established order."[6] Knowledge and trust were the preconditions of success. Bonch-Bruevich had already begun the process of contacting believers, offering to present their case in a sympathetic light, if they sent him the necessary information. He had used his experience as the son of a publisher to print edifying texts for the common folk. Now he invited the folk to participate in the production of material about themselves. The sectarians, for their part, valued his indifference to doctrinal matters and his principled animosity to church and state. True to his promise, he published some of the material they sent in a series of volumes depicting them as the heroic victims of tsarist oppression.[7]

Latyshev was among those whose trust Bonch-Bruevich earned. This was no mean feat, for the Skoptsy were secretive and distrustful in proportion to the intensity of their persecution. This fervor reflected the degree to which their actions disturbed the world they came from—for the Skoptsy were extremists. Bold and cautious in different domains, they both joined and disjoined the sacred and profane, the divine and the embodied. They cut the thread of mortality, halted the succession of generations, opted for physical ruptures and spiritual resurrections. Spurning the family's bloody ties, they fixed the familial bonds in pre-Oedipal amber. Physically marked, feared and despised, they lived at the margins and acted as go-betweens. They pursued the logic of Orthodoxy to the point of incoherence, an alchemy of folkloric immanence and dualistic hyperbole. Radically different and ruthlessly excessive (thorough, literal, and fantastical), they nested in the landscape of common peasant life. Exiled to Siberia, they domesticated the rigors of climate and isolation. They emerged, in all their archaic charisma, at the height of the Russian Enlightenment and endured into the modern era, faith intact.

For all the discomfort it engendered, religiously motivated castration drew on expressive means common to the culture. It was "readable" from the outside. And despite its primitive aura, recalling an age of blood sacrifice, the ritual was adopted in the late eighteenth century, at the onset of cultural modernity. It appeared, it is true, among elements of the population least affected by such change. Yet it did not develop in isolation from elite culture or from the symbolic and disciplinary practices of the state. The castration cult was not, moreover, the only form of seemingly old-style religion that acquired a new vitality at this time. The tradition of spiritual eldership (starchestvo) reappeared in the late eighteenth century and reached the zenith of its development in the nineteenth.[8] Furthermore, the Skoptsy faith was not static. The defining elements of worship, including castration, survived the decades of social and cultural transformation that took the faithful into the twentieth century. Believers nevertheless engaged in fruitful interaction with the outside world, adapting its resources for their own ends. This is a story of the archaic (or naïf) in its encounter with the modern.

In their unavoidable interaction with the surrounding culture, the brethren were no different from ordinary villagers, whose daily lives brought them into contact with markets, manufacturing, and the printed page, no matter how hard they tried to preserve traditional patterns of existence. The very meaning of the Skoptsy faith was all along fashioned in relation to the responses and interventions of outsiders. At the end, believers assumed the task of recording the story in their own terms, using instruments from the secular arsenal: literacy, publishing, and the archive. Latyshev's relationship to Bonch-Bruevich belongs to the last stage in the community's history of self-representation. His legacy offers the historian an insight into one person's spiritual journey and into the psychology and social experience of those whose lives took this unusually dramatic turn. The texts he produced and the documents he collected, along with similar papers contributed by his confreres, also provide the historian with that rarest of evidence: testimony to how members of the common folk thought about themselves.

Latyshev's part in this archival creation constitutes a secularized version of his original quest: the search for truth and transcendence. His expression of gratitude to the Greatest of the Great was filled not only with rhetorical extravagance but also with the heartrending pain of a spiritual eccentric and social pariah, so despised of men as to be "unworthy of attention," yet unwavering in his sense of mission and of self.[9] Deprived of his genitals as a boy of ten, at the behest of parents who considered the loss his ticket to salvation, Latyshev embraced the outcast fellowship with a fervor that lasted a lifetime. Diverting his message to Stalin into the keeping of a Soviet museum was not, as the posture of self-effacement might seem to suggest, an act of humility. It reflected, rather, Latyshev's grand spiritual ambition: to create an archive for eternity. The letters and notebooks that Latyshev sent Bonch-Bruevich between 1912 and 1939 appealed not only to the bureaucrat's populist sympathies and custodial designs. They were also Latyshev's appeal to the judgment of History.

For the historian who, at last, sixty years later, fulfills Latyshev's desire by reading what he struggled to express, the question is: why go to extremes? On the one hand, how to understand a ritual practice so consistently, and trans-historically, disturbing to outsiders. On the other, how to justify the scholar's own choice of such an apparently aberrant theme: peasants, merchants, and lowly townsfolk who removed the male genitals, as well as women's nipples, breasts, and outer vaginal parts, using red-hot iron or crude cutting instruments and suffering acute bleeding and pain, in hopes of salvation. The question is one of belief, but also of vocabulary. Extremity belongs to the repertoire of religious expression. The extravagance of Skoptsy devotion set them off from their neighbors; but the distinguishing ritual can be understood only in its close relation to

Nikifor Petrovich Latyshev (1863–1939?). March 18, 1904?. GMIR, f. 2, op. 5, d. 261, l. 60. (Copyright © GMIR.) This studio portrait seems to be dated 1904. It is included in a manuscript written in 1910. At the time of the sitting Latyshev was about forty years old and living with his family in Siberia. He wears the formal Skoptsy overcoat but also the high felt boots of the settler exiles. On his lap is a white cloth concealed behind an issue of the popular illustrated magazine *Niva* (The Grainfield). The objects represent the two components of Latyshev's identity: devoted to Skoptsy purity, he was also an intellectual of the people. Latyshev wished to see his own writing in print and supplied Bonch-Bruevich with a self-portrait to include with the text. Letter to V. D. Bonch-Bruevich (December 7, 1914). GMIR, f. 2, op. 5, d. 31, l. 60b.

the ambient religion of the Orthodox folk. These mystical ascetics considered themselves to be the lambs of God, the sheep that stood at the Savior's right hand. They were the "redeemed from among men, being the firstfruits unto God and to the Lamb" (Revelation 14:4). Yet they spent their daily lives in the midst of the benighted—the goats that stood at the Savior's left and did not qualify for admission to heaven. For all that they set themselves apart, they were commonplace, as well as extreme. Occupying the cultural margin, they engaged in agriculture and trade—the central occupations of rural Russia. They lived both in and beyond time, at once creatures of convention and beings of spiritual transcendence. The historian must pursue them in both their worlds.

Their own writing makes this possible, but the initiative was not solely theirs. From the beginning, the community's self-consciousness was tightly linked to the production of records about it. Indeed, its founding narrative registers the moment at which the group was first discovered by outsiders. This and later episodes of persecution imposed physical suffering easily transmuted into tales of holy martyrdom. Officials repeatedly elicited and transcribed explanations and excuses, serving both prosecution and defense. The self-definition of members and of the group as a whole, in both symbolic and practical terms, was thus from the start associated with violations of secrecy and with the generation of written accounts. The faithful responded by redefining the violations as triumphs (as in the sacred tale of martyrdom) but also by silence and ritualized narrative evasion. Fearing the dangers of exposure (arrest and exile), some nevertheless came to feel the need to represent themselves. From iconic and mythic tropes, they moved to photography and eventually to print. Alive to the culture around them, they incorporated, while reshaping, the image first reflected in the unfriendly glass. They compiled family histories, counted livestock, drew local maps, assembled photo albums, and recorded their thoughts. Eager to correct their enemies' distortions, they hoped the atheistic Bonch-Bruevich would present their case with scholarly dispassion. They hoped their insider views would survive until a more impartial time.

The process of mirroring themselves in the outsider's eye and turning the reflection to their own account replicates the double configuration of Skoptsy life. It also allows the historian to balance external and internal and to weigh the subjective and social meanings of this particular extremity, so transcendently transgressive, yet so tightly bound to the situation they found themselves in. The sources that reveal this self-protective world are of three kinds. First, the observations of outsiders, none disinterested, include the reports of official commissions and bureaucrats, the fieldnotes of folklorists, the evaluations of political radicals and of representatives of Orthodoxy. Some, relying on archival papers, reproduce at one remove material or testimony allegedly derived from the sect itself. The second kind consists of the records of police searches and interrogations, kept in the files of the Ministry of Internal Affairs and the Ministry of Justice. These contribute to the picture generated by the first group, but in their detailed intrusion into personal and communal circumstances they also go "beyond the looking glass" into the lived world of those they pursue. The third kind is to be found largely in the files of the Museum of the History of Religion. The Skoptsy do not figure in this material as objects of investigation, the distant and timeless projection of an observer's fascinated (and horrified) regard, or the vilified targets of indignation. The collection records, instead, their own active engagement with the surrounding world and also the dynamics of a changing and intensely personal relationship: that between Bonch-Bruevich and his contacts in the field.

There is an irony in this exchange. Bonch-Bruevich was ultimately unable to control the ambiguous implications of his ethnographic and conservatorial tasks. The otherwise ruthless old Bolshevik, truculent about his secular views, hewing the Party line, yet respectful of the common folk despite the error of their ways, devoted himself to destroying the old world but also to preserving its remains.[10] The museum was to conserve and display the remnants of the past: spiritual illusions reduced to so much grist for scientific truth. For Latyshev and his kind, bent on spiritual transcendence, the production and preservation of this-worldly testimony was expected to confirm an otherworldly truth. Yet time has witnessed the collapse of the Bolshevik vision, while Latyshev's hope of surviving in the gleam of history's tolerant eye has come to pass in ways he could not have expected but which might not perhaps have surprised him in the end.

It is the story of Latyshev's stigmatized community and of a handful of his articulate brethren that I endeavor to tell in this book. My medium is the mass of written and pictorial documentation accumulated in various modes: indictment, analysis, defense, and self-explication. While hoping to delineate a three-dimensional world beyond the looking glass, I focus on the testimony elicited by Bonch-Bruevich in establishing his monument to misguided faith. Intent on plotting a graveyard of social martyrdom and intellectual delusion, marking the preeminence of the material over the sign, Bonch-Bruevich instead built an archive of transcendence and self-creation for subjects who do not usually get to map their own lives or leave their own portraits in the gallery of time.

Yet the meanings the Skoptsy attributed to themselves cannot be the last word on the subject. Following their traces, we must discover mean-

Vladimir Dmitrievich Bonch-Bruevich (1873–1955). Frontispiece, V. D. Bonch-Bruevich, *Izbrannye sochineniia,* vol. 1: *O religii, religioznom sektantstve i tserkvi* (Moscow: Akademiia nauk, 1959).

ings of our own. We must offer a perspective inaccessible to them or to the other actors who participate in their story. This vantage point need not reduce them to a single narrow focus, rendering them coherent or making them fit a particular type, whether universal or specifically Russian. They belong, of course, to the culture from which they diverge, but setting themselves apart was of the very essence of their self-conception, and they cannot, therefore, be taken as icons of the whole. Just as their identity emerged through a process of refraction, so the facets of their experience and their world bend the rays of the cultural spectrum. Knowing them may perhaps let us see the larger picture in a more vivid light. We can bring out colors whose intensity and power to move us across the years we might not have imagined.

The pathos of this tale revolves around the process of self-exclusion, by which inspired mortals tried to exempt themselves from the timetable of ordinary human existence. Born despite themselves and destined to die, they are born again by deliberate intention. That rebirth is also a foretaste of death, in which death's power to annihilate is thwarted. Those who make the journey into the Light experience the reward. Those who are saved are joyful. We must not cast the shadow of our own distress on the contours of their story. Their physical suffering was something they willingly embraced (except in the case of children). But the psychological pain of living on the edge, of enduring persecution and contempt, of being cut off, most literally, from the general condition is something even the most loyal convey between the lines. Having renewed his dedication to the faith as an adult, Latyshev allowed himself no further doubt or regret. Yet his attachment to Bonch-Bruevich has all the intensity of a soul longing for connection. Self-expression enabled him to survive, in the process of defining an identity he had not chosen. But even after he had rejected the world, he needed someone "out there," beyond the closed circle of the elect, to whom to disclose the contents of his heart. Through the process of writing he reestablished contact with the flux of time, acknowledging the power of death, even as he insists, in making this connection, that he will emerge triumphant in the end. In the last instance, Latyshev talks to God, the guardian of time and timelessness, by addressing the faceless man of science who does not share his faith and the historian and reader with the patience to listen.

1 ❧ MYTHS AND MYSTERIES

*There are some eunuchs, which were so born from their mother's
womb: and there are some eunuchs, which were made eunuchs of men:
and there be eunuchs, which have made themselves eunuchs for the
kingdom of heaven's sake.*

MATTHEW 19:12

THE Skoptsy earned their standing as the most objectionable deviation from the norm in a world in which the question of true belief was far from simple. Eastern Orthodoxy was the established religion of tsarist Russia. It had the backing of imperial authority, which
endorsed the church's monopoly on the propagation of Christian truth.
But the religious landscape of the empire was not as flat and even as the
wide steppe. It was pitted with ravines and gullies. Its roads took unexpected turns. Its vegetation varied. The vast lands under the imperial
throne were inhabited by a multitude: pagan animists among the nomads
of Siberia and in the northern lands; Muslims in the south and southeast;
Jews and Catholics in the Polish provinces; Protestants on the Baltic Sea.
The law placed non-Orthodox Christians second on the scale of spiritual value, although Catholics were considered unreliable in political
terms. Judaism was acknowledged as a legitimate creed, but the Jews
lived with special limitations.

Even within the Orthodox fold, there were differences and distinc-
tions. A fateful break occurred in the mid-seventeenth century, when the
church hierarchy imposed liturgical reforms and some clergymen refused to accept them. Known as Old Ritualists or Old Believers, they
and their followers withdrew from the fold. Fervent in their conviction
of righteousness, they took to the forests and founded their own communities, some with the help of renegade priests, some without benefit

11

of clergy. Under a regime in which offenses to Orthodoxy were a crime against the state, the defectors incurred displeasure from both sides. Leaders were executed, followers beseiged. When threatened by military attack, some barricaded themselves in their villages, preferring to burn alive, every last man, woman, and child, rather than compromise with the Antichrist in league with the throne. Beginning with Peter the Great (reign 1682–1725), at the start of the eighteenth century, successive rulers varied as to how far they accommodated or attempted to repress the movement. By the mid-nineteenth century the practice of self-immolation had died out. Old Believers kept to their convictions but made peace with the world. By the end of the empire they may have numbered at least 10 million—hard-working, sober, entrepreneurial.[1]

The core of traditional believers never broke with the church, but the imprint of standard Orthodoxy often wore thin in remote villages, where styles of popular worship assumed a local tinge. Throughout the nineteenth century the hierarchy complained of the inadequate hold of dogma among the common folk.[2] The vast majority of Russian peasants, of course, knew the difference between innocent variation and deliberate rejection of the rules. Once the authority of the church was questioned, however, in the name of true faith, the process of fragmentation was set into motion. New beliefs and practices continued to emerge. Not all the groups that set themselves apart were off-shoots of the Schism (raskol) that produced the Old Belief, though a number shared their sobriety, industriousness, and entrepreneurial flair. Lumped together with the "raskol´niki" in the legal statutes, as "harmful to the faith," the so-called sectarians exhibited a variety of practices and convictions.[3]

The term "sectarian" was tendentious but apt: the nonconformists dismissed the authority of established institutions. That was the point. There was no limit to the changes they could ring on the basic elements of Christian faith. One cleric's guide, published in 1915, listed twenty-eight distinct groups, and seven others less well defined. Specialists divided the spectrum into the rationalists and the mystics. The first category included the Baptists in their various guises; the followers of Lev Tolstoi; the Dukhobors, made famous by Tolstoi's adoption of their cause; the Molokans; the Judaizers; the Jumpers and Skippers; and the Seventh-Day Adventists. Among the mystics were numbered the Little

Doves (Golubchiki), Gray Doves (Serye golubi), and White Doves (both the Christ Faith, also known as Khlysty, and the Skoptsy.)[4]

The Skoptsy did not therefore emerge on a barren field. They sprouted like wildflowers in grass already tangled with many-colored growth. That they stood out against the heretical blur testifies to the extremity of their transgression. They were not ordinary footsoldiers in the "Salvation Army," as Latyshev called the myriad of fellow sectarian groups, none of which, he lamented, had shaken off the ties of the flesh.[5] Perhaps the original impulse was to make just such a compelling distinction, to attract attention in the welter of other variations. Someone may have wanted to raise the stakes and create an aura of excitement, to arouse wonder and awe.

Castration was also convenient. It was an operation every peasant was able to perform on his cow or horse, a strategy available to every man, and even every woman, all endowed with the thing they might determine to lose. Males submitted to the removal of their testicles in a ritual called the "minor seal" (malaia pechat'). The operator tied the scrotum at the base, sliced through the skin, cauterized the wound or applied a salve, and pronounced: "Christ is risen!" To achieve a higher level of purity, the penis itself was severed. This was the "major" or "royal" seal (bol'shaia or tsarskaia pechat'). For women the rite entailed the removal of nipples, breasts, or protruding parts of the genitals. Not all who chose the faith undertook the ordeal. Not all could withstand the pain; not all wished to incur the penalties inflicted if you were caught: the exile and hard labor. But all who joined the community of salvation were disciplined by tactics and tales that set them apart and protected them from the world outside. They pledged secrecy and practiced secrecy's arts. In proportion to the degree to which the community broke with the norm, it tried to camouflage the defection.

The Skoptsy inherited both the need for discretion and everything but the act of castration itself from the sect known as the Christ Faith (Khristovshchina). Slightly distorted, the name became "Khlystovshchina," from the verb "to flagellate." The followers were called "Khlysty." They called themselves the People of God (Liudi bozh'i). Whether they flagellated themselves or not is a matter of conjecture. It is clear, however, that the sect's other practices originated early in the eighteenth century among the peasants and lowly townspeople of central Russia. Its prophets, claiming to reincarnate Jesus Christ, led congregations known as "ships" (korabli): vessels of salvation, driven by the Holy Spirit, with Jesus at the helm, afloat on the evil waters of the world. The believers renounced meat, alcohol, tobacco, profanity, and sex. They observed an ecstatic form of worship: fervid singing of spiritual verse accompanied by swirling dances. They gathered in separate groups of men and women, clad in white. "He that overcometh, the same shall be clothed in white raiment," it was written (Revelation 3:5). Chanting, clapping, exhausting themselves in hectic motion, until the sweat gushed from their pores (what the Skoptsy called a "spiritual bath"), purging them of sin, they experienced the presence of the Holy Spirit and emerged white as doves.[6]

Around the mid-eighteenth century some followers took the logic of renunciation to unforeseen conclusions, translating sexual abstinence into physical dismemberment. Through this feat they "achiev[ed] victory over nature," as Latyshev explained, making themselves outcasts and "leaving themselves nothing for the comfort of the flesh." "Fear of the eternal torments of gehenna drives them to sacrifice themselves completely." After the Fall, humankind "was condemned by God's anger to the agony of life, some to sweat and toil to feed themselves, others in agony to give humankind more and more weak-willed sinners, inclined to the Fall."[7] The Skoptsy had withdrawn from the postlapsarian world, moving "in the direction of God." Thus to be reborn one must "break with nature." "The Skopets who embarks on the barren life, so shameful to the world, disfiguring and mortifying himself, by this alone shows that he seeks God, strives for God.... The Skopets sacrifices himself to obtain mercy for the time spent in darkness.... The Skopets is a corpse among the living, a living being among the corpses."[8] In "his death to nature and life for the sake of his soul, [the Skopets] is forever separated from the lascivious sin of nature. He has conquered in himself the animal instincts once and for all and gone over to serving God, sacrificing himself to God."[9]

These are the meanings castration acquired for those who remade themselves through the act. The first to do so derived the technique from animal husbandry. They were not squeamish about flesh and blood. As one of them later explained, "they perform castration, the way they take

the knife and cut the chicken."[10] But where did they get the idea of applying these skills to themselves? There is no direct answer to this question. Nowhere else has a self-proclaimed Christian community organized its existence around this feat. Eunuchs have appeared, for reasons
both spiritual and mundane, in various societies, including ancient
Byzantium, but these examples did not impinge on eighteenth-century
Russian peasants.[11] Closer to home, among both Muslims and Jews,
peasants might have encountered the rite of circumcision, a lesser alteration of the penis for sacred ends. The Skoptsy were aware that Christ, as
a Jew, had been circumcised, and they drew the comparison themselves,
claiming that he had actually been castrated (and sometimes calling castration circumcision).[12] Circumcision, however, was understood by the
Jews not as a spiritual exercise but as a mark of connection to God. It was
rejected by Christianity, which distinguished itself in relation to the body
not by imprinted signs but by practices of renunciation and affliction.

Christian asceticism involved bodily discipline and self-imposed deprivation, including sexual restraint. There was, however, a moment, in
the third and fourth centuries, while the new religion was still young,
when some Christians embraced the "radical option" of destroying their
capacity to reproduce. They justified the choice with reference to
Matthew 19:12, where Christ seems to endorse the case of men becoming eunuchs in search of spiritual perfection, "for the kingdom of
heaven's sake."[13] Once the Skoptsy had established their faith, some of
the more educated cited the example of Origen, the third-century
church father thought to have practiced castration on himself.[14] But his
example was unknown to the peasants who first performed the act and,
moreover, did not conform to Orthodox doctrine. The church had rejected this reading of Matthew and condemned Origen's teachings as an
example of dualistic anthropology.[15]

Dualism is characterized by hostility to the flesh, which is viewed as
inherently evil, an obstacle to salvation. In rejecting dualism, the church
confirmed the positive meaning of corporality in Christian teaching.
Christ was God incarnate. He represented not only the spiritual element
in human nature but also the possibility of mortal beings' aspiring to the
divine. Properly conceived, Christian asceticism was not so much an attempt to destroy the flesh, which impedes the progress of the spirit, but

Skoptsy icon: Lambs of God. Color plate from [Nikolai Nadezhdin], *Issledovanie o skopcheskoi eresi* (n.p.: Ministerstvo vnutrennikh del, 1845). "The next day John seeth Jesus coming unto him, and saith, Behold the Lamb of God, which taketh away the sin of the world" (John 1:29). The Skoptsy Redeemer was pure as the Lamb of God and washed away the sins of man. "These are they which came out of great tribulation, and have washed their robes, and made them white in the blood of the Lamb" (Revelation 7:14). Castration, which bathed the sufferer in blood, an effort to enlist the body in the project of transcendence. Released from its own imperatives, the body can dramatize the all-encompassing power of spiritual transformation.[16] To some extent, such an understanding of self-mortification can be detected in the pride with which the Skoptsy viewed the loss of organs, whose absence signaled the presence of salvation even in corporeal terms. Yet repugnance for the desires and sensations associated with procreation, abstinence from rich food and alcoholic drink, and the celebration of physical pain all underscore the negative impulse toward the flesh at work in the Skoptsy practice of castration. To them, lust was an instrument of the devil, and the penis the "key to the abyss," which they identified with the vagina.[17]

If the example of the church fathers was remote from the consciousness of ordinary believers, the ascetic and mystical traditions of the Eastern Orthodox church were preserved in the practices and texts of Russian monastic culture, with which the common folk were in direct contact. Lay Orthodox spirituality bore their mark, as did, in distorted form, the uncanonical varieties of sectarian faith. Wandering holy men, who went from monastery to monastery, transmitted this culture to the villages, by preaching and example. The founding figures of the Skoptsy faith exercised this same charisma of renunciation, leaving hearth and home, living on the road, and freeing themselves from all worldly connection, loosening the ties and breaking the cycles embedded in family and agricultural life. They came bearing the Word and inviting men to follow. But the call to self-remaking of a biological kind was their own invention.

The enactment of castration also involved a radical distortion of the meaning of Orthodox Christian belief. The Skoptsy sought in their cen-

---

left him pure and eternal. In the "Passion," Selivanov recalls the effects of flogging, which left "his little shirt all soaked in blood, from little head to little toes: all drenched in blood, as in berry juice. And thereupon my sweet children asked for my dear little shirt and clothed me in their own dear little white one." The blue of the lower half of the icon, in the Byzantine tradition, signifies the boundary between life and death, which was the liminal position of those castrated for purity's sake, anticipating salvation and the heavenly life (shown in the top half) but still with their feet planted on earth.

tral rite not only the transformation of the flesh—and with it, salvation—but also the kind of agony associated with the time on the cross. Like the flagellants of medieval Europe, the Skoptsy wished to relive the Savior's pain. They saw themselves practicing the "imitation of Christ." But insofar as they imagined, in an entirely idiosyncratic inversion, that the Crucifixion was itself a castration, they believed that their own "imitation" replicated the precise torment that Christ had supposedly endured. Identifying their self-administered suffering with Christ's own, they believed it reproduced the miraculous triumph over death, turning mortals into angels, the sinful into the saved. Castration thus had more than one level of meaning. It was a covenant, or sign of connection with God: the Skoptsy called it the "seal" and cited the "hundred and forty and four thousand" (Revelation 7:4) who accompanied the Lamb and "had his name and his Father's name written on their foreheads" (Revelation 14:1). These they were "which were not defiled with women; for they are virgins. These are they which follow the Lamb whithersoever he goeth. These were redeemed from among men" (Revelation 14:4). Castration was a feat of salvation and also a moment of communion with the divine. It was the Holy Spirit that visited the faithful in their ecstatic worship and presided over the moment of physical exaltation induced by the loss of blood and sudden shock of pain. Involving as it did a spiritual visitation, castration was not a requirement for membership in the community; one could choose one's time.

The direct accessibility of the divine and the timelessness of the Savior's presence were not features that in themselves distinguished the teachings of the Khlysty or the Skoptsy from more conventional versions of folk Orthodoxy. Perhaps relying on the Old Church Slavonic text of Matthew 2:4, in which Herod asks "where Christ is being born" (gde Khristos razhdaetsia), the Khlysty may have concluded that the incarnation was an ongoing process.[18] Such a misreading can hypothetically be connected with some aspects of Byzantine theology and in particular of the Eastern Orthodox mystical tradition, which emphasize the interdependence of the spiritual and the physical, the transcendent and the contingent.[19] The experience of godliness in everyday life, including a vivid sense of converse with the saints, marked all folk adaptations of Orthodoxy.[20] Yet this same tendency could lead to rupture with official belief.

One aspect of the Old Believer protest against the reforms initiated by the seventeenth-century church concerned the sense that holy rite and sacred images did not merely communicate through an earthly medium but actually embodied the divine in themselves. Altering them in any way was a form of sacrilege.[21]

The Skoptsy, like other self-designated spiritual communities deviating from established doctrine, considered themselves true Christians and thought themselves faithful to holy writ. Like the self-castrators of Origen's time, they cited the passage from Matthew 19:12, which they believed to sanction more than sexual abstinence. Other relevant passages included Matthew 18:8–9, in which Jesus says to cut out the eye that offends you, and Luke 23:29, in which he tells the sorrowing women, "blessed are the barren, and the wombs that never bare, and the paps which never gave suck." Whether exposure to these words inspired the first Skoptsy prophets or whether they were invoked only in retrospect we cannot tell. Their attitude toward the authority of the printed page was in any case ambivalent. True believers, they said, put aside "the black book" of Scripture for the "white book" of spiritual prophesy.[22] Only those "holy in the Holy Spirit" could "penetrate God's secret," Nikifor Latyshev said; for "the majority of people on the globe," the Bible was "but a dead letter, nothing more."[23] Though the Gospels affirmed what the Skoptsy believed, another wrote, nevertheless "he who pronounces the glory of the Lord, for the saving of souls and in the service of God, needs not a single book." Yet this same writer confirms the holy man's autonomy by reference to the very text he is authorized to ignore. Quoting from the Second Epistle of Paul the Apostle to the Corinthians, he says that the "secret church [of the Skoptsy] preserves 'the new testament; not of the letter, but of the spirit: for the letter killeth, but the spirit giveth life.'"[24]

In fact, books were not the primary avenue through which the Gospel entered the lives of unlettered peasants. They listened to prayers read aloud and heard the verses sung by wandering beggars, transmitting a genre dating back several centuries. These verses represented a reworking of sacred texts by monks or semieducated folk with access to the Bible or to saints' lives and other narratives.[25] The first Skoptsy prophets began as just such mendicant singers. The language in which they couched their beliefs mixed the scriptural and the folkloric, as we shall have further occasion to learn. Fruitfulness was not of the flesh, they said, for "a man without the Holy Spirit is empty and sterile." If the faithful "abandoned fleshly consolations, the honors and glory of the world," they "would receive the glory that is heavenly and eternal, and their flesh would be incorruptible." Men were to avoid the "magnetic stone" (mag-nit-kamen´) of "female sensuality" (zhenskaia lepost´) and "renounce all kith and kin," "run from fathers and mothers, wives and children." Like St. George, who thrust his sword into the evil dragon, the Skoptsy were invited "to sit on a white horse" and spear the snake of sexual desire, pleasure, and reproduction.[26] Having received the spirit, they were to cross themselves with both hands at once, because a bird (the white dove, the Holy Spirit) does not fly with one wing alone.[27]

Although influences and genealogies are hard to fix, the Skoptsy can thus be situated in the field of available and analogous religious forms. At a further remove, they can be—and were—likened to the Shakers, who came into being in exactly the same decades of the eighteenth century, also renounced sexual connection, engaged in ecstatic forms of worship, followed the lead of inspired prophets, and were industrious and sober.[28] Comparisons do not, however, illuminate the subjective dimension of this particular choice. Why, in psychological terms, some people resorted to the harrowing extreme of physical desexing may be impossible to ex-plain. To label self-castration a psychopathology or call the Skoptsy re-pressed homosexuals, even *avant la lettre,* does not make historical sense.[29] To imply that individual Russians enact some alleged national tendency to self-imposed torment is equally absurd.[30] Yet spiritually motivated cas-tration was indeed a collective impulse, and though its practitioners scan-dalously offended some cultural norms, they closely followed others. De-spite their participation in everyday life, however, they intentionally put themselves beyond human society and not just beyond the bounds of their own culture. There is no point in pretending that these were not drastic measures. They were radical by design. As in other apocalyptic styles of belief, Skoptsy extremism reflected the conviction that the end was near. It also, quite literally, brought that end into being: stopped time became a fact of individual biography, when maturation ceased; in social terms, the present cohort was always the last in line of biological succession.

If the Skoptsy could not bear the uncertainties of earthly existence and the worrisome indeterminacy of salvation, their quest must be taken with utter seriousness as the deeply religious experience it was: believers sought connection with the divine and felt themselves visited by the Holy Spirit. But Skoptsy practices, even though they drew on elements of the Orthodox canon and shared some of the vocabulary of conventional lay spirituality, nevertheless violated the core principles of Orthodox belief. And in this sense the condemnations of the church must be taken no less seriously than the claims of those who defied it. Deviation from the norm was part of Skoptsy intention. The real question is why, given the range of potential languages and cultural forms, some inhabitants of the late Russian Empire chose to express themselves in this particular way.

It is an explicitly historical question. In addition to mapping the Skoptsy belief system against the adjacent spiritual landscape, one must therefore also address the issue of time. Why did the charismatic vagrants exercise such appeal at just this moment? Why might extravagant efforts to free oneself of the seemingly inexorable pull of natural urges through self-inflicted pain capture the imagination of ordinary women and men at this particular juncture? Here, again, no links can be firmly established, but the frame is suggestive. The practice of castration among defectors from the Khlysty first came to light in 1772. In central Russia the year 1771–72 was propitious for the crystallization of mystical, apocalyptic moods. During the twelve months before the Skoptsy were discovered in Orel province, bubonic plague raged in and around Moscow, not far to the northeast. There a crowd of anxious common folk gathered at St. Barbara's Gates in an appeal to the wonder-working icon. When forcibly dispersed, they seized Archbishop Amvrosii and battered him to death. Aside from stirring popular emotion, the plague had deeper consequences as well: "The epidemic," writes the historian John Alexander, "prolonged the Turkish war that nurtured it, aggravated the chaos in Poland that led to that country's partition in 1772–73, and burdened the Russian economy with additional pressures that exploded into the

Pugachev Revolt of 1773–74."[31] This bloody uprising encompassed the empire's entire southeastern frontier and succumbed only to full-scale military repression. It expressed a level of rage and brutality lurking in the common breast at which the St. Barbara's riot had only hinted. In punishing the defeated rebels, Empress Catherine the Great (reign 1762–96) applied methods of corporeal revenge ill-befitting her enlightened image. Quartering, dismembering (mercifully after death), the gibbet, public execution and display of body parts: such was the response of power to the ferocity of the weak.

Of these events only the plague preceded the Skoptsy impulse to work violence upon themselves and somehow domesticate the awful unpredictability of the Last Judgment. But even though they were in no sense causal, these circumstances remind the modern reader of the forceful presence of extremity in the lives of ordinary people in that place and time. Furthermore, some of the principal historical elements were later incorporated into Skoptsy mythology: corporal punishment and the charismatic Pugachev both appear in their story of origins. Christ's crucifixion itself had transformed the brutality of secular punishment into divine drama. This was an old Christian motif. For Russian peasants of Catherine's time, however, the knout, which was sometimes the cause of death, was not a distant memory or metaphor but a reality many had felt on their own skins.[32] This immediacy reinvigorated the original miraculous connection: crucifixion and flogging were forms of pain and violence imbued with moral and spiritual meaning. Castration was an equally meaningful torment, this time inflicted on oneself.

The impulse to appropriate the symbols of moral authority also characterized the behavior and self-representation of the rebel Pugachev, who claimed to embody the late tsar Peter III (reigned briefly in 1762), supposed to have survived his purported death and returned to save his people. Pugachev was personally unknown to the Khlysty, but he represented a familiar type: one in a chain of folk charismatics claiming to embody departed emperors, allegedly more just or legitimate than the one on the throne and devoted to the popular welfare. As self-professed tsar, moreover, Pugachev inflicted on enemies and traitors punishments no less cruel than those eventually practiced on him. The choice of castration as a signifying act may have expressed a similar urge to master fears and threats by actuating them oneself. The dread of emasculation may not be a cause of alarm for all men in all times and places, as Freudian theory may suggest, but traditional peasant societies made no secret of their care to safeguard the male reproductive potential. One of the charges frequently leveled against witches by seventeenth-century Russian peasants concerned their power to induce sexual incompetence.[33] French peasants of the same period so feared the evil wishes of their neighbors in this regard that they often married in secret, lest enemies render them impotent on their wedding night. The spell was cast by knotting a ligature in the presence of the intended victim. In the gelding of livestock, such ligatures were used to pinch the scrotum, blocking the production of sperm.[34] In the case of humans, the effect was supposed to result from magical mimesis.

Folklore, husbandry, endemic violence, anxiety about disease, pain, and sexual performance, as well as an intimate familiarity with biological reproduction, provided the cultural material with which to recast old Christian archetypes in local terms. But what kinds of people were drawn to the new faith that so dramatically mixed the common with the exalted, the physical with the divine? A profile emerges from the records of the investigation that followed the discovery of 1772, which sheds some light on the social composition of the group and on the strategies it developed in relation to the outside world. As we shall see, the faithful fashioned modes of storytelling and self-representation that in part responded to the circumstance of continuing persecution. The allusive imagery of whiteness and purity allowed the nature of the central ritual to be obscured even as its meaning was transmitted.

The community's devious, secretive ways were not, however, simply strategic. They also expressed the central dynamic of the creed, that the flesh was the surface upon which to inscribe one's dedication to higher things, one's preparation for the beyond, one's rejection of the merely apparent ("iavnoe," in their terms) in favor of the invisible or absent; it was the palpable form in which salvation became immanent and was experienced in this life. Yet the body and its appurtenances (separate attire for women and men, according to the normal fashion) must retain their connection with the transient and unredeemed, in order to echo the miracle of God incarnate, in which divinity is present but veiled.

The conjoining of opposites—flesh and spirit, obvious and concealed, fact and figuration—governs the community's entire story. It characterizes the sect's first interaction with the forces of repression. And repression itself feeds this dynamic, as we shall see. Fortunately for the historian, it also provides evidence of the community's embodied existence. The first records were produced by the investigatory commission formed by the Holy Synod in 1772 and reinforced by a special emissary appointed by Catherine the Great. Its proceedings document the stories and personalities of the first generation to adhere to a novel version of what officials called the "impious schismatic Quaker heresy," or in Catherine's words, "a new kind of some sort of heresy."[35] Although converts pledged not to reveal secrets of the faith, habits of circumspection had not yet taken root. At this early stage, they seem to have told their tales readily.

Orel

Trouble with the authorities began as the result of an insignificant everyday event. Sometime in the summer of 1771, Trifon Emel'ianov, from the village of Maslov in Orel province, went to the river to bathe. There he encountered fellow villager Mikhail Petrov and noticed something amiss. Mikhail had castrated himself ("sam sebe skopil"), so he explained, to avoid having sex with his wife. His father, Petr Vasil'ev, as well as their neighbor, Kondratii Porfenov, had done the same. When Trifon threatened to denounce them, the three promised to have him called to the military draft, and he was in fact inducted. On Good Friday 1772, almost a year after the alleged meeting, Trifon's lonely wife told this tale to the local priest, who relayed the story to his superiors.[36]

The bathing incident as reported may never have occurred. The characters, however, appear on the official lists of villagers interrogated in connection with the case, and the story was taken at face value. Other sources suggest that it was not perhaps this tale which sparked the inquiry, but rather the complaints of a landowner who discovered thirteen castrated peasants among his serfs. The thirteen in question also appear on the official lists. Trifon's experience, if it happened at all, may demonstrate an attempted recruitment gone awry. Perhaps the account was invented to crystallize a less dramatic process of discovery, in which neighbors had agreed to ignore what was hidden, as long as there was no cause for offense. Perhaps Trifon belonged to the heretical Khlysty from which the castrated ones had broken away.[37] He might have wished to divert suspicion from himself by unmasking those still more egregious. He might have thought to enlist the authorities in squelching the competition, as a way of keeping the original fellowship intact.

Though Trifon either felt or professed disapproval of what he claimed to have seen, those whose parts were missing viewed the absence as no loss: what was gone was old and in its place was something new, something better. "Therefore if any man be in Christ, he is a new creature: old things are passed away; behold, all things are become new" (2 Corinthians 5:17). Because none was in his first youth, they all had pasts to reckon with. Mikhail Petrov, now thirty-two, had been married twice; his first wife and three of six children had died. Not long ago, when visiting an uncle in a nearby village, he had looked in on a neighbor, then recovering from the consequences of castration, which, the latter explained, he had undergone for "purity's sake." When Mikhail learned the nature of the other's "special faith," he told his own father. Under cover of darkness, the two had themselves castrated by a certain Andrei, who did the same for their neighbor Kondratii. Kondratii, at thirty-seven, was that rare bird in the Russian countryside, an unwed middle-aged male. Mikhail's father, Petr, was closer to the norm: now fifty, he had started a family thirty years before. At the time of his wife's recent death, he had joined the Christ Faith as the "best way to salvation." It was his son who first took the next, more radical step.[38]

The Skoptsy were enjoined to "renounce all kith and kin." As Jesus had said to follow him, so the prophets of the new faith called for a break with the mundane and its affective entanglements. Yet, as the case of Petr and his son suggests, it was precisely the ties of the heart that pulled many a man and woman into the new fellowship. In the course of the inquest, almost two hundred villagers were sought for questioning about their faith. Many were married, either elderly or in middle age, and had reaped the fruits of a lifetime of labor.[39] About a quarter were female. Among the large number apprehended, a core of forty men and thirty women, from twenty-four separate villages and estates almost all in the district nearest the city of Orel, had gathered around the prophet Akulina Ivanova, a runaway serf of great personal appeal. Over half of these, like

Trifon Emel'ianov and the uncle's neighbor recovering from his wounds, belonged to the category of "single homesteaders" (odno-dvortsy), the descendents of minor servitors given small parcels of arable land in return for military service. Intermediate in the rural social hierarchy, homesteaders could own serfs but were themselves subject to tax, a mark of subordinate status.[40] The rest of Akulina's followers were the serfs of local landowners. In the larger group, a handful were serfs attached to a linen factory; a quarter were homesteaders. In the end, the inquest identified the most active members to be thirty-nine men and four women (twenty-four peasants, eighteen homesteaders, one retired soldier). These included ten men and one woman from Akulina Ivanova's original following, among them the father and son who had encountered Trifon Emel'ianov in the stream. Of the thirty-nine men, thirty-two were castrated (twenty-one peasants and eleven homesteaders).[41]

The process of disaffection from the Christ Faith was some years under way at the moment the new tendency came to light. The break involved the conversion of whole families and friendship networks under the charismatic influence of a few restless figures with no families of their own. The inspired company included more serfs than independent farmers but did not represent the destitute fringe of village life. The prophets to whom the villagers flocked, by contrast, were notable both for their poverty and marginality. At the moment of exposure the principal "master" and teacher was the fugitive peasant Andrei Ivanov Blokhin.[42] When finally arrested on May 28, 1772, Blokhin told investigators that he had been born and raised on the estate of the late General Stepan Apraksin. Now thirty years old, Blokhin had fled the village of Brasov when he was fourteen for life on the road. Accompanying a pair of blind beggars, he had made the rounds of the marketplaces for six years, living on handouts, until he encountered the serf Mikhail Nikulin, belonging to General Sergei Naryshkin. A good twenty years older than Andrei, Nikulin was a Christ Faith preacher, who explained how to gain eternal life and salvation ("kak pritti v zhivot vechnyi i spastisia"). From Nikulin, Blokhin told the commission, he learned the new creed: not only the renunciations common to the Khlysty—alcohol, meat, profanity, and sex—but also the need for castration ("skopittsa").

Perhaps four years before the discovery and inquest, Blokhin had been searching for a sure means of curbing the demands of the flesh. Re-calling the effect of gelding on livestock, he had decided to practice the measure on himself, cauterizing his own testicles with a red-hot iron ("sam sebe skopil, raskolennym zhelezom te tainye udy sebe otzheg sam"). His example was followed by a comrade from his vagabond days, one Kondratii Trifonov (also called Nikiforov), an escaped serf from the Kantimirov estate in the Sevsk district of southern Orel province. Whether Trifonov was too timid to press the iron to his own flesh, as Blokhin maintained, and whether his friend did it for him, we have only the latter's word. Once the two had healed, they set out to perform the service for a host of other serfs and homesteaders in the neighboring vil-lages, perhaps as many as sixty-two in all.[43]

The daisy chain of inspiration was complex. Nikulin, who instructed Blokhin, claimed that he himself had been converted by yet another Christ Faith teacher, Kuz'ma Prokhorov, since deceased, who had been succeeded by Akulina Ivanova. Like Blokhin, Akulina had escaped the life she was born to. As an unmarried girl, she had fled the same estate to which Nikulin also belonged. Her spiritual talents soon attracted an im-pressive following among adherents of the Christ Faith. Leading the faithful in songs of prayer, she appealed to the Virgin Mary: "All my hopes I place on Thee, Mother of God, guard me under Thy roof." Scolding those who had sex with their wives, she kept pregnant women from meetings. She also wielded the power of foresight: "When the heart is bright with light," she declaimed, "a person can know what is happen-ing in Moscow and Kiev, whether the harvest will be good or bad, who is rich or poor, and everything that befalls humankind." She would circle the company, stopping at each person in turn. For Nikulin she predicted a good harvest; until now wanting, he would soon be rich in grain and livestock. More exalted even than Akulina herself was a certain Pavel Petrov, a peasant from the Sheremetev estate, whom she revered as Jesus Christ.[44] Crossing herself with two fingers (the Old Believer way), she exhorted the rest to bow before him and kiss his hand.

Most recruits to the new castration faith, when questioned by inves-tigators, mentioned Andrei and Kondratii as preachers and castrators; most had also encountered Akulina and Pavel Petrov.[45] Their stories re-veal a limited circle of contacts and a fairly predictable sequence of events. Some examples give a sense of how acquaintance and proximity and the habits of daily routine provided avenues for recruitment. They also demonstrate how deeply questions of faith and the search for meaning were embedded in the private lives of ordinary people. The homesteader Andrei Pavlov Liamin, twice married, with five children, knew the three men said to have menaced Trifon Emel´ianov. Already an adherent of the Christ Faith, Liamin had joined the breakaway group under Akulina Ivanova's influence and been castrated (in a drying barn warmed by a stove) at the hands of Andrei Blokhin. The forty-five-year-old widow Dar´ia Feoktistova, a serf belonging to Prince Dmitrii Sontsov-Zasekin, had been "lured" in the new direction in the local church of St. George the Great Martyr.[46] During holy services, the unmarried Anna Iakovleva Polovinkina, a peasant on General Vasilii Nashchokin's nearby estate, told her of special gatherings in her brother Ivan's house. There Dar´ia met Akulina Ivanova, who led the faithful in prayer and song, holding aloft the Life-Creating Cross (Zhivotvoriashchii krest) and swearing them to secrecy. All prayed before the icon candles, then, sitting in place, joined in singing verses "through which the Holy Spirit entered their hearts."[47] Making the rounds, Akulina foretold to each the day of their death and their chances of wealth and good fortune. They called her Spiritual Mother.

In the same church of St. George the Great Martyr, the homesteader Stepan Antonov Sopov had met Anna Polovinkina's brother Ivan, with similar results. After joining prayers led by Akulina Ivanova, Sopov allowed himself to be castrated by Andrei Blokhin in the drying barn. Sopov was a married man of forty-two, wealthy enough to possess some peasants of his own, at least one of whom was castrated along with him. He was also well enough educated to recognize some of the phrases as distortions of the Kiev Prayerbook (Kievskii molitvennik), which he owned. He himself recorded the words to various spiritual songs.[48]

Under questioning, people told stories that revealed the contours of their social world and the character of personal ties. They show the variety one would expect in any human company. And despite the ubiquity of patriarchal mores, spiritual enthusiasm and initiative were not the monopoly of either sex. One confession tells of loyalty, and no doubt also submission, as dominant family themes. The serf woman Akulina

Savel´eva Panikhidina, now fifty years old, had married at seventeen. Before leaving for the army, her husband had heeded the word of his own father and joined the Christ Faith. His wife had done the same. Their teachers were Kuz´ma Prokhorov and Akulina Ivanova. In her husband's absence, Akulina Savel´eva's religious ardor had waned, but upon his return after more than twenty years' service, they reentered the fold and renounced conjugal relations. By then Akulina Ivanova had followed Blokhin in the direction of castration.[49]

For another couple, intensified faith proved as much a cause of conflict as a bond. At the time of the investigation, Tat´iana Nikiforova, aged sixty, and her husband, the retired soldier Nikita Vasil´ev Akinin, aged sixty-five, had been married for over forty years. Originally serfs on local estates, they had soon moved to the city of Orel. There, after two decades of childless marriage, they were introduced to the so-called Quaker sect by the merchant's widow, Solomonida Kharitonova Tarakanova. Its leader was Kuz´ma Prokhorov. Eventually the couple lost interest, but three years previous Tat´iana had been recruited anew by their neighbor Akulina Savel´eva Panikhidina, her own fervor recently revived. This time Tat´iana's husband had tried to stop her, beating her more than once, in the time-honored manner of bringing a wife to heel, but she had persisted nonetheless. Boasting (for it spoke in his favor) that he had indeed tried to deter his wife, Nikita Vasil´ev admitted that he had not denounced her. Despite their wavering and uncertain faith, all three whose spiritual paths had crossed—Akulina Savel´eva and Tat´iana and Nikita Akinin—were among those detained as culprits.[50]

In the enlightened reign of Catherine the Great, what crime or transgression had these miscreants been charged with committing? Because secular and ecclesiastical authority were tightly entwined, it is not surprising that grounds for prosecution were mixed.[51] The clerical investigators based their actions on decrees of July 16, 1722, and December 9, 1756. The Synod had enacted the first of these to condemn the Old Believer practice of collective self-immolation. No heretic could achieve sanctity through resistance, it declared. To martyr oneself in the name of "false belief" was a form of political insubordination, akin to soldiers' rushing into battle without an officer's command. Deliberately to pursue suffering and death even for the sake of the true faith showed an impious willfulness.[52] The power to inflict martyrdom belonged to God; the right to inflict "salutary" pain, to the sovereign. The second decree, citing an earlier ruling on sorcerers, penalized heretics for trying to hide.[53]

But times had changed. Heretics were no longer burned at the stake.[54] Catherine preferred to emphasize the social rather than doctrinal character of this deviation. In doing so, she set the tone for the sect's subsequent treatment. Having involved the state in the investigation and judgment, the empress insisted that the problem be seen as strictly secular and also, nonpolitical. Nothing was "more important," she said, ". . . than extinguishing the very first signs of such irrational nonsense," which she also termed "the insanity of immature minds." Downplaying the religious element, she insisted that the "new kind of some sort of heresy" be treated as "an ordinary civil case," to be be prosecuted with all due haste but without the use of torture.[55]

Following Catherine's instructions to spare the "simpletons" who "blindly submit to the insanity of their leaders," almost all the guilty parties were released to the keeping of landlords, priests, or officials.[56] Only three, the supposed ringleaders, were punished: for performing castrations, Andrei Blokhin was flogged with the knout in his native village and exiled in perpetuity to Nerchinsk, near the Chinese border; for spreading the idea, Mikhail Nikulin was beaten with a cudgel in the city of Orel, and the peasant Aleksei Sidorov likewise, in his home village. The latter were also sentenced to hard labor. Meanwhile, the provincial authorities dedicated themselves to the search for Kondratii Trifonov, called Nikiforov, who had eluded all efforts to track him down.[57]

Facts and Figurations

Who was the elusive Kondratii? While on the lam in 1772, he was identified by the authorities as a vagabond serf from the village of Stolbishche, or Stolbov, on the Kantemirov estate in the Sevsk district of Orel province.[58] Even on the record, however, his name was uncertain—Trifonov-Trofimov-Nikiforov; later some thought he was the same as Andrei and that Andrei's companion was not Kondratii but Martyn Rodionov, or that Martyn and Andrei had shared the name Kondratii. At various times Kondratii may have answered to Andreian, Foma, or Ivan, and finally Andrei.[59] Various members of the Rodionov family appear in the 1772 lists, but no such Martyn. Syllables were in any case slippery: perhaps the peasant Sofon Avdeev Popov, of later accounts, was really the homesteader Stepan Antonov Sopov of archival record.[60] Commoners of the period were easily confused: family names were unstable (sometimes that of the village) and patronymics informal. Combinations repeated themselves: in 1772 Ivan Emel´ianov is listed as the serf of a local landowner;[61] the Sosnovka village priest, who in 1775 reported the whereabouts of the fugitive "Kondratii," was also Ivan Emel´ianov.[62] In eluding arrest, Kondratii would no doubt have feigned identities on purpose.[63] But indeterminacy suited his position between the social and the otherworldly. As befitted a prophet, he would have spurned earthly ties, assuming a name that could not be taken literally but, as one scholar put it, was only "an arbitrary sign."[64] In a similar spirit, monks changed their names when taking vows to signal their spiritual calling.[65]

Portrait of Kondratii Selivanov. Color plate from [Nikolai Nadezhdin], *Issledovanie o skopcheskoi eresi* (n.p.: Ministerstvo vnutrennikh del, 1845). This engraving was circulated by the Skoptsy. The prophet wears a white neckerchief and holds a white cloth on his knee, both symbols of purity. He must have been castrated as an adult, since he has a beard. The portrait clearly dates from the so-called Golden Age, between 1802 and 1820, when Selivanov lived among wealthy followers in St. Petersburg. In his youth he had wandered from market to market, begging for alms, but this definitive portrait shows him to be a man of wealth and culture (the armchair, the fruit).

In 1775 someone called Kondratii was run to ground, sentenced to the knout, and marched off to Siberia. His punishment, when it came, was not unlucky: it established the conditions for the identity he eventually assumed, that of Kondratii Selivanov.[66] Under this name, he figures as the central character in the community's defining narrative of exposure and survival. The "Passion of Kondratii Selivanov" describes his trials and tribulations while evading pursuit, his capture, flogging, and road to exile, and also the acquisition of loyal followers eager to serve the cause.[67] By subjecting him to bodily torment and public degradation and thrusting him even further beyond the bounds of the social order than he had voluntarily driven himself, the state offered the former vagrant the conditions of deification.

In the tradition of the Christ Faith prophets, Selivanov considered himself the reembodiment of the original Redeemer.[68] The inquest of 1772 reported a similar description of someone called Pavel Petrov, but no such person was found. When the story of origins was finally told, Selivanov is the one honored by Akulina Ivanova as "Lord and Beloved Father" (Gosudar′ batiushka) and "Father Redeemer" (Otets iskupitel′). Proclaiming Selivanov the "one teacher you own—your Father Redeemer alone," she declares him the sole claimant to the position.[69] "I did not come to you on my own," he tells his followers, "but was sent by my Heavenly Father."[70] "What happened to me is what happened to the former Lord Jesus Christ, Son of God."[71] He was the "helmsman" (kormshchik) sent by the Lord to pilot the ships and steady the masts.[72]

When exactly the "Passion of Kondratii Selivanov" was formulated and by whom can be debated, as we shall see. But two things are certain: first, that the narrative reworks the events documented in the archival records of 1772; and, second, that it was accepted by the community as authentic. Along with another text, called the "Epistle," it established a particular mode of expression and articulated the sect's basic beliefs. It also performed a transformative function, wresting victory from defeat. Relating the trauma of disclosure, the narrative converted sacrilege to sanctity: Selivanov's earthly sufferings confirmed the actuality of the returned Christ. Persecution and expulsion, translated into the idiom of spiritual transcendence, echoed the double nature of the embodied God.

Unlike the testimony offered in 1772, when the faithful ignored the

pledge of secrecy and openly described their beliefs, the narrative composed after the events adopts the mode of allegory and evasion to refor-
mulate the material of everyday life. The confusion of literal and symbolic enacted in narrative terms was a central component of the faith.
The confusion worked in both directions. In reading holy Scripture, the
Skoptsy rendered metaphor—or what church doctrine construed as
metaphoric—concrete. In representing their faith, they operated in reverse, draping the substantial in allusive figures of speech. If castration
translated the symbolic language of Scripture into palpable bodily signs,
the sacred tale transformed the literal and embodied into the figurative
and symbolic. Castration appears in the "Passion" as purity, begging for
alms, felling of trees, and the "flaming crown."[73] The "ferocious snake"
stands for the force of evil; more specifically it also represents the penis,
the invidious organ that leads the bearer to the "abyss" of hell (the
vagina) and eternal damnation.[74] And on yet another level, the narrative
uses the language of materiality to represent, while concealing, matters of
the soul: converts to the true faith are called "goods" or "wares"; surgical
removal and scarring becomes God's seal (pechat'), a word already enjoying a confusion of registers: the convenant with God, the palpable impression.[75]

In this linguistic universe, meaning often hangs on the slippage between signs: sounds join words in spiritual connection. In folk Orthodoxy saints' names, by virtue of phonetic likeness, sometimes determined
their particular attributes. Ideas of redemption and castration may have
been linked by similar echo-effects: "iskupitel'" (redeemer) and "oskopi-
tel'" (castrator) are but vowels apart, and neither far from "ochistitel'"
(purifier).[76] Similarly, "wares" (tovar) may evoke the "creature" (tvar')
whom Christ transforms in spiritual rebirth (2 Corinthians 5:17): "Itak,
kto vo Khriste, tot novaia tvar'" (Therefore if any man be in Christ, he is
a new creature). But the slippages were not accidental: they represented
the fusion of divine and created in the landscape of folk Orthodoxy, an
experiential rendering of the mystery of Christ.

This Son of God assumes his role in a story modeled upon Scripture
and the lives of the saints. The hero that emerges from the script is a
mythic persona, a holy figure who asserts his personality against all odds
and expresses himself in the rhythms of folk idiom. These rhythms echo

the movement of the sacred verses sung by the faithful as they engaged in the whirling figures of the ritual dance, following the prescribed patterns of crossing and crisscrossing in a woven tapestry of radiant souls. The Jesus Prayer, too, which the worshipers uttered in unison, was a matter of repetition, a low muttering moved by the spirit and directed to God. "Lord Jesus Christ, Son of God, have mercy on us" (Gospodi, Iisuse Khriste, Syne Bozhii, pomilui nas).[77] The goal was silent communion in which no unscripted syllables broke the concentration. Thus cadences of the body, of the breath, and of the Holy Word swept the believers upward and out of themselves. Sounds, motions, and emotions produced the release of sacred ecstasy.

The "Passion" conveys the mighty power of egotism in archetypal phrases, the tools of a collective art.[78] In tone a mix of prayer and fairy tale, it recounts actual events and mentions real places and specific persons by name. Selivanov claims that, like Jesus, he has been "sent by the Heavenly Father" and by a virgin mother, the prophet Akulina Ivanova, "of the pure womb, free of sin," to "gather up souls on the road to salvation and uproot all sin" (134). Pursued by the authorities, he is concealed beneath the floorboards in the huts of sympathetic peasant neighbors, but eventually the Khlysty, angry at his defection, hand him to "the Hebrews for crucifixion" (134). At various times fettered, interrogated, insulted, and flogged, he is at one point received by his followers, his white shirt, symbol of Skoptsy purity, "soaked in blood, as in berry juice." In a veritable descent from the cross, his disciples cradle him in their arms and exchange the bloody shirt for an unsullied white one to signal the purifying outcome of pain. Unlike Jesus, Selivanov then requests "a bit of fresh milk from the cow," which "the evil ones" allow him to drink, restoring his spirits (137).

On the road to Siberia, a journey that lasts "for a year and a half, by land and by water" (139), Selivanov is kept under strict watch, sometimes beaten to within an inch of his life, but also regarded by his captors with awe as a "great charmer" who "can enthrall anyone, even the Tsar." Wherever he goes, he reports, "the people followed me by the legion [polki polkami]" (136–37). Along the way, he claims to have encountered fellow charismatic Emel′ian Pugachev, who captained the massive popular uprising against landowners and the regime that began shortly after

the Skoptsy first came to light. The Orel trial occurred in 1772, the rebellion in 1773–74, Pugachev's execution in January 1775, and Selivanov's
sentencing six months later. Although Selivanov could not, therefore,
have met the famous outlaw, his story not only has them crossing paths
but establishes a parallel between them. Of this imagined Pugachev, Selivanov says, "People followed him by the legion, and he was also kept
under heavy guard. But my guard was twice as large and extremely strict.
And the people who followed me began to follow him, and those following him followed me" (138).

Pugachev had claimed to embody the late tsar Peter III, the husband
that Catherine the Great had dispatched in order to succeed him. Her
unlamented spouse had become an object of popular veneration, especially among the Old Believers, because he had softened penalties against
them.[79] The tradition of pretendership, in which a common man claimed
to embody a displaced or even imagined ruler more just or legitimate
than the one on the throne, dated at least as far back as folk incarnations
of Jesus. Listeners whose belief system centered on marvelous reappear-
ances would thus not have balked at mention of the late Pugachev in a
narrative of supposedly true events. In the realm of allegory and eternal
return such discrepancies only intensified the power of truth over con-
tingency, of spirit over the flesh. But Selivanov does not limit himself to
the use of real figures for allegorical purposes. He also disguises actual
people in mythic garb. The "Turk" who tries to lure him from the path of
virtue (138) represents not only the devil but also the enemies of the
faith.[80]

The narrative's fairy-tale quality helps blend the literal and the fantastic. In a series of picaresque flashbacks, Selivanov recounts his adventures as an itinerant beggar and prophet. At one point he describes himself in the role of sacred minstrel.[81] In real life, he did not disclose his
place of origin or given names, refusing all markers of social belonging.
The details of the story emphasize his actual marginality, as well as miraculous powers that include the ability to survive on air and water and talk
to wild beasts. "Wandering from city to city, for I had nowhere to rest my
dear little head, I dressed as a beggar and often changed my clothes. Once
for three days I lay without food or drink in a pit of offal. I hid for ten
days in the fields of rye. Exhausted, I lay down and fell asleep; and when

I awoke I saw a wolf was lying beside me and looking at me. But I said to him: 'go to your place.' He obeyed and left. Then I spent twelve days in the hay, when all I had to keep me was a small jug of water, from which I drank a spoonful a day" (142).[82]

Freed by his ordeal from the claims of the body, endowed with the miraculous spiritual powers associated with saints, the Selivanov figure achieves the attributes of the divine. For the ordinary mortal, the physical ordeal of castration achieves the results associated with Christ's suffering on the cross. Selivanov assures a convert, "Do not fear, you will not die, but on the contrary your soul will be resurrected and you will be lighthearted and joyous and fly as if on wings: the [Holy] Spirit will inhabit you and your soul will be renewed" (145–46). That same horribly human and miraculously transcendent event is replicated in the passion tale by Selivanov's experience of flogging. Christ himself had been punished as a common criminal, an act designed to mock his spiritual pretentions. The use of bodily torment and public shaming to teach a moral lesson, in the form of corporal punishment, was still defended by tsarist officials as late as the mid-nineteenth century.[83] No doubt for practical reasons, the prisoner being flogged was sometimes positioned before the executioner as though pinned to a cross.[84] In administering their own ceremonies of dismemberment, the Skoptsy also used the suffering and marked body as a moral sign, reversing the significance of pain and submission, as Christ had done in his time. Having interpreted the original crucifixion as Christ's castration, they reenacted the tragedy of social annihilation and moral abasement as the triumphant drama of salvation. They were taking agony into their own hands.

Castration, like corporal punishment, was never a solitary act. Performed in the company of the faithful, it both defined and cemented the community. To prove his sacred credentials, Selivanov claims he has been invested with divine authority by the "Heavenly Father." He demonstrates his miraculous powers and the force that emanates from his own personality—the ability to deflect evil (the wolf, the Turk), charm his enemies, and attract a popular following (those who follow "by the legion"). But he also needs the endorsement of figures of established moral authority with a following of their own. In the narrative this role is fulfilled by the prophet Akulina Ivanova, a character who seems to corre-

spond to the woman of the same name sought by the investigating commission. The narrative also mentions a woman called Anna Romanova,
supposed to be Akulina's associate, who is not named in the inquest and
may not have existed at all. Anna resembles the actual Akulina as described by the villagers questioned in 1772. In particular, we are told,
Anna was famous among the Khlysty for her ability to predict the future:
when the rivers will run with fish, the fields be heavy with grain. In the
narrative it is Anna who announces, as Selivanov enters the congregation, that "God himself has arrived!" To Selivanov, she says: "Though you
be sent far away and irons shackle your hands and feet, after suffering
great deprivation you will return to Russia, summon all the Prophets,
and pass judgment upon them. Then all the Tsars and Kings and Bishops
will bow before you and honor you greatly and come to you by the legion." He remembers her telling him further that "a bird had left me and
flown off to circle the entire universe and proclaim to everyone that I
was the God of Gods, Tsar of Tsars, and Prophet of Prophets" (146–48).

By the time the "Passion" was composed, Selivanov had indeed returned from Siberia.[85] For almost two decades thereafter, he resided in
St. Petersburg, where he had acquired some wealthy followers who cared
for his needs, and where he was venerated by high-society figures fascinated with his charismatic charm. It was a period in which spiritual enthusiasm was fashionable in court circles, but it is not clear how Selivanov came to the attention of the capital's elite. In 1820, Alexander I
(reign 1801–25) moved to curtail the prophet's influence by having him
confined to a monastery. In confinement Selivanov was treated with respect. He is said to have died in 1832, at an advanced but indeterminate
age. As befits a man dedicated to eluding the power of death as well as
the encumbrances of social definition, his final resting place is unknown.[86] Before his mysterious disappearance from among the living,
Selivanov was supposed, by many nineteenth-century accounts, to have
met in person with emperors Paul I (reign 1796–1801) and Alexander,
seeming to fulfill the prophecy of the holy tale, which would have appeared after these encounters, if they occurred at all. The Skoptsy themselves memorialized the occasions in verses that imagine Selivanov
counseling Alexander on the eve of the anti-Napoleonic campaign and
offering spiritual patronage:

When God's cause thou receive,
And in me come to believe,
Rewards will I thee serve,
And thy crown preserve.[87]

Selivanov was clearly the hero of the sacred narrative, but who was its author? The founder was described by most later sources as illiterate, and it was part of his posture of innocence and social exclusion to bear the mark of cultural humility as well. Some sources, however, insist that he could write.[88] A similar ambiguity attends Selivanov's close associate Aleksandr Shilov, said to have been unlettered and also to have written sacred chants.[89] Whatever the case may be, some early brethren were at least partly educated men. In 1772, Stepan Sopov, the well-to-do home-steader, transcribed, in his own hand, the text of sacred songs. Selivanov, however, was unlikely to have composed the text that bears his name. In it he summons his "dear beloved children" to "pay close attention to the words uttered by my lips."[90] He may indeed have recited such a story to disciples, who then took it down, in the manner, as they believed, of Christ's Apostles. Some version was read aloud at gatherings of the faithful.[91] The text, however, first appeared in print as part of the report of an investigative commission appointed by the Ministry of Internal Affairs under Nicholas I (reign 1825–55). A similar composition was purport-edly found among documents collected by the superior of the Solovet-skii monastery, in which various Skoptsy were incarcerated in the 1820s and 1830s. Because Selivanov had access to St. Petersburg high society when mystical religion was all the rage in the beau monde, it is not im-possible that the literary version of his story was the invention or elabo-ration of an amateur of folklore. It may have benefited from the creative efforts of the eminent folklorist Vladimir Dal' (1801–72), who wrote the first draft of the official report.[92] What is certain is that scholars and offi-cials considered the "Passion" an authentic product of the folk mind.[93] At the same time, however, most used it as a historical source, drawing on the narrative for details of Selivanov's early years as leader. The Skoptsy themselves were on firmer ground in asserting the authenticity of this tale, for, unlike scholars who spoke in the voice of scientific reason, they willfully confused the actual with the symbolic.

In addition to the founding myth, the Skoptsy produced two other genres: historical narratives that relocated spiritual events, past and future, on human ground, and sacred verses that did the opposite. Like the "Passion," the verses embedded real-world events in a web of spiritualized meaning. They share the naive, picturesque tone of the prose account, accentuating the repetitious, incantational quality suited to dancing and chants. The reinvention of Russian imperial history was even less stable than the passion tale. No fixed version emerged but only the general outlines of an accepted script. Variations were recounted to officials and church authorities in the course of investigations conducted during the reigns of Alexander I and Nicholas I. The stories concern the founder's claim to embody not only the Redeemer but also, on the model of Pugachev and other folk pretenders, the emperor Peter III. Nowhere in the "Passion" is the expression "Tsar of Tsars" more than a turn of phrase, no doubt echoing the scriptural "blessed and only Potentate, the King of Kings, and Lord of Lords" (1 Timothy 6:25). Perhaps this is yet another example of metaphor taking on flesh, for Selivanov seems to have adopted the new identity on returning from exile, in more or less the same period that the "Passion" itself took shape. Some commentators believe that the imperial claim preceded the purely spiritual one, but the two dimensions are hard to separate, since the former tsar was himself considered a miraculous being.[94]

The resulting brew provoked indignant responses from defenders of imperial dignity. In the words of one hostile commentator: "The Skoptsy developed this demented nonsense into a vast fairy tale, in which Gospel about the true Christ the Savior mixed, in garbled form, with historical legends about the true emperor Peter III, until they constituted a fable of fantastic proportions."[95] This mélange of the actual and the spiritual indeed followed the same rules as the rest of Skoptsy belief, reinforcing the original blasphemy. First, that beings of superior status and moral stature should descend among common mortals in some shape recognizable as their own. Thus the vagrant Kondratii felt himself the vessel of the Holy Spirit and, as such, a new embodiment of the Son of God. Second, in the reverse direction, that the lived experiences of the humble should be reflected upward and associated with characters of a higher order. Thus peasants who committed the unthinkable act of physical self-castration imagined that the original Savior, along with his Apostles, had been castrated, too. The identification of Kondratii with Peter III, himself allegedly castrated, fits both these models.

The fables about Peter III do not, however, separate the two modes of return, the commonplace escape from death and the unique and extraordinary resurrection after death. Like the "Passion," these narratives combined details of the lived world with particulars of the transcendent.[96] The Skoptsy, in this vein, considered Empress Elizabeth (reign 1741–62) the true virgin Mother of God. Elizabeth was not Peter III's actual mother, but the Skoptsy believed that she was and had conceived him through the intercession of the Holy Spirit. The sense of holy calling prevented her from remaining long on the throne, which she was said to have vacated in favor of a woman who resembled her exactly. Elizabeth then departed for Orel province, where she assumed the name Akulina Ivanova and settled among the Skoptsy. After a lifetime spent in prayer, she was buried in a garden.

When her son Peter married the future Catherine the Great, the Skoptsy explained, the bride was dismayed to discover his castration and decided to have him killed. Peter was supposed to have learned of her intentions in time to assume the uniform of one of his guards and flee in the guise of a common soldier, leaving the obedient servant to be murdered in his stead. In some versions, the guard is described as a Skopets, who voluntarily martyrs himself for the emperor's sake. Peter escapes not only to save his own skin but also to save the human race. Catherine was understood to have noticed the switch but to have buried the guard without comment, while continuing to pursue her fugitive spouse. Like the fabled Selivanov in his Christ-persona, Peter was also forced to hide from his enemies, subsisting without food for days on end. In a pattern of echoes and repetitions, the emperor, again like Selivanov, wandered his homeland, preaching castration—the "fiery baptism"[97]—and introducing himself as the true Christ.

The Golden Age

When Paul succeeded his mother on the throne, he released Selivanov from Siberian exile. The Skoptsy believed that the emperor had intended to restore the old man, his true father, to his rightful place. They also believed that the prophet had refused to recognize Paul as his son unless the tsar submitted to castration. It was the emperor's anger at this demand which explained, according to them, why Paul had confined the prophet to a madhouse, where he remained until freed by Alexander I. The faithful refused to admit that Selivanov had ever actually died, predicting that he would appear again, in all his "power and glory." Then they would follow him "by the legion," from Siberia to Moscow, where he would be met by the ringing of bells in the Uspenskii Cathedral. Gathering his children "by the million and billion," the Redeemer would ascend the imperial throne and sit in judgment on the living and the dead, the castrated and uncastrated.[98] The rulers of the earth would bow down, while missionaries set about converting the world and castrating the human race. Among the converts of special note were Alexander I and his spouse and the emperor Napoleon, allegedly the illegitimate son of Catherine the Great, whom she had educated in the Russian Imperial Academy before sending to France, where he pursued his later notorious career. Alive, well, and castrated, Napoleon had taken refuge in Turkey but would appear in Russia for the Last Judgment. In other versions, Napoleon is less benign, appearing as the Antichrist, spawn of Catherine and the devil.[99] In the end, those spared in the Last Judgment would live to all eternity; those already dead would enjoy eternal beatitude in heaven.

The naive rendition of the imperial past through Skoptsy eyes was vague about the mechanisms of eventual triumph. A more sophisticated narrative, in written form, outlined a more elaborate vision of the Skoptsy future. It was the work of Aleksei Elenskii (or Elianskii), a courtier of Polish origin who had joined the Russian imperial service after the third partition of his homeland, when he also converted to Orthodoxy. In the early decades of the century, the center of St. Petersburg high society's fascination with Western mystical belief was the so-called spiritual union formed around Ekaterina Tatarinova, a court dame related by family ties to the highest officials of the realm. She and her associates were intrigued by the forms of worship practiced by the Khlysty and the Skoptsy, but it is unlikely that they went as far as castration.[100] Elenskii, however, may have done so. While under scrutiny himself, he managed to have Selivanov released from confinement in the Smol´nyi monastery only a few months after he was transferred there from the madhouse in 1802.

Two years later, Elenskii outlined a plan for theocratic rule under Skoptsy domination. Writing before the onset of the anti-Napoleonic campaigns, Elenskii explained that Russia's victory would depend on the leadership of what he called the true church: Alexander would continue to rule, but Selivanov, inspired by the Holy Spirit, would become the power behind the throne. The spirit of the apostolic church, preserved by the Skoptsy, would guarantee Russian domination over the rest of the world. For having composed this fantastical plan, however patriotic, Elenskii was declared insane and confined to the Spaso-Evfim'ev monastery in Suzdal, where he died in 1813 and where the actual Selivanov later ended his days.[101] No doubt influenced by the constitutional plans and political projects that circulated in the corridors of power during the early years of Alexander's reign, Elenskii transposed the Skoptsy vision of the Last Judgment and heaven on earth into worldly terms. Elenskii's memo became known to the reading public once it was published in the 1860s. There is no evidence, however, that his fantasy of theocratic domination was shared by the humble brethren.

Ordinary Skoptsy expressed their sorrows and expectations more readily in the form of holy verse. These redundant cadences convey the fundamental circularity and timelessness of the Skoptsy vision. They often repeat the tale of exile, torment, and return, as if it were in fact never-ending. An example transcribed in 1822 strikes a plaintive note:

> Hark, oh you beloved,
> You students of the Lord,
> Sons of God, tormented:
> How he was crucified on the cross,
> tormented everywhere and worse.
> sitting on that very chair
> after questions answered there
> in Tula
> in Morshchansk he was beaten with a sword
> on the back by Pilate, hard
> Beaten to the quick

Laying it on thick
He implored the one on high
the highest in the sky
but they didn't spare his hide
blood gushed out from his side
the prophets sang his song
of his torments, long,
and his light
his passion and the sight
of gardens drowned in blood
the lips of Jesus, lips of Christ
sealed tight. . . .[102]

Other verses, however, had a bolder tone:

From the white dawn, the mount of Zion,
From the East, Irkutsk, the land,
From Irkutsk, from France,
by the million and the billion
fly in droves white doves
in droves, the suffering cross aloft
all the castrated, traded
in the land of Greece
helmsmen,
moneybags
of renown,
well known,
banners flown,
in chains restrained
the bells chime
hailed, the falcon
toward him flies
the Holy Spirit glides
God of Gods, Tsar of Tsars,
Spirit of Spirits: he is with us
through the burning flame,

to the imperial town
approaching approaches imperial
places paradaisical
fulfilling the secret sacraments
sacred and Davidical.[103]

In official St. Petersburg, there were men who feared the practical consequences of such extravagant beliefs. Who could be sure that the vector would always point from the actual to the symbolic and that myths of imperial conquest would remain myths, in view of the appalling fact that allegories of chastity had indeed resulted in physical mutilation? A leader who could persuade his flock to impose unthinkable horrors on themselves might lead them in other, equally extreme directions, and no threat on earth would be dreadful enough to hold them back. How, moreover, could a regime that anchored its own ship on the rock of spiritual submission tolerate a community founded on deception, for whom appearances must, by definition, mask the inner truth?

Whenever possible the authorities tried to remove the Skoptsy from circulation, sending them to remote corners of the empire, where Orthodox believers were few and far between. But the terms in which the regime framed its response shifted with the changing political idiom of successive reigns. In the spiritual atmosphere of Alexander I's early years, the attempt to turn the Skoptsy from the error of their ways relied mainly on influence and persuasion. Nicholas I preferred to induce conformity by bureaucratic means, using information to facilitate repression. Alexander II favored science and modernized the courts of law, which then demanded the knowledge of forensic experts. Persecution made the Skoptsy all too aware of the rules that governed their existence, and they adapted their conduct in response. The attention of outsiders also influenced the way believers thought about themselves and how they presented themselves to the world. To understand who they were and what they became one must discover what the Skoptsy saw in the cultural glass.

2 ❧ REPORTS AND REVELATIONS

REVELATION, betrayal, and persecution were constant threats to the Skoptsy community's existence. Siberian exile caused physical and mental hardship, rupturing family and economic ties, altering the structure of households and congregations. To evade the force of the law, the Skoptsy kept abreast of edicts and decrees. Defendants were called on to testify in court. Sworn to silence, some managed to guard their precious secrets; others failed. If the faithful strove to keep the metaphorical veil intact, their enemies tried as hard to expose what was hidden. Investigators gathered and published information that revealed the inner sanctum of Skoptsy spiritual life. Defectors, for their part, eagerly breached the bounds of discretion in hopes of personal advantage or psychological relief. Renegades could not regain their procreative powers, but they could change their habits of speech.

Survival meant adaptation. The Skoptsy responded, both defensively and creatively, to the practical circumstances in which they lived. But change also resulted from internal pressures. Over the course of the century between Selivanov's heyday and the fall of the tsarist regime, the Skoptsy pursued the inner logic of their own beliefs, struggling over the meaning and purposes of castration, dividing over the legitimacy of individual prophets, reassessing the relationship between their activities in the world and their spiritual existence. It was the world, however, that both sustained and constrained them.

Decrees and Definitions

The law, as we have seen, is what the Skoptsy encountered at the very first moment of collective self-awareness. That inquest confirmed Selivanov in his divine role and baptized the community in the fire of persecution. It obliged the converts to provide personal accounts, which consolidated their sense of distinction. But despite the state's dedication to protecting Orthodoxy and policing the boundaries of true belief, it nevertheless did not confront this outburst of popular zealotry with excessive zeal. Extreme as the founder's fate was made to seem in the retelling, his followers hardly suffered at all. The days of heretic-burning were over. Catherine was hard on the ringleaders but spared the flock. Her policy, however, failed on two counts. Flogging the ecstatic wanderer until he bled real blood made good his transcendent claims. The misguided were meanwhile left to their own devices, free to worship the martyr who had suffered in their stead.

Catherine's successors reversed her approach. Selivanov was allowed to return to the capital. This surprising outcome must have seemed a miracle in itself. Only in its wake did the misery from which it released him take mythic shape. In what the Skoptsy termed their Golden Age, between 1802 and 1820, Selivanov lived in the homes of wealthy devotees, an object of regard in polite society fascinated with his aura of holiness and the naive folk spirit he seemed to exude. Whoever it was who impersonated the interrupted character of Kondratii Nikiforov-Trifonov-Selivanov, called in this period simply "the old man," he seems to have radiated authority and conviction. Whether or not he actually met with the emperors Paul and Alexander, the stories suggest that he was the kind of man to have done so. Only in 1820 did Alexander decide to have him put away, but his monastic hosts were instructed to treat him well, "out of compassion for his advanced age and pity for his errors."[1]

Officials apparently counted on using the patriarch's charisma to influence the flock, by convincing him first to abandon his convictions. It was the practice not the beliefs that the state was after, explained the minister of internal affairs in 1806. It was a mistake, but not a crime, to confuse saintliness with purity of the flesh. Castration was a different matter, though what to do about it was unclear. "Experience shows," the minister wrote, "that errors of this kind are not prevented but only encouraged by formal prosecution and public discipline; gentle methods of persuasion are of greater use."[2] The strategy was attempted. Alexander himself seems to have commissioned a tract designed to refute Skoptsy dogma on doctrinal grounds. Published in 1819, it was written by a member of Mme. Tatarinova's spiritual gathering, the civil servant and former major Martyn Urbanovich-Piletskii (1780–1859).[3] In taking Christ's regard for sexual chastity as a charge to remove the organs of sin, Piletskii warns the Skoptsy, they fail to realize that evil inhabits not the body but the soul. Castration turns causality on its head; worse, it impairs the believer's moral potential. Unable physically to enact his wicked desires, he holds himself superior to his fellows, succumbing to spiritual pride. In fact, the psychological roots of desire survive the loss of the genitals; frustration only magnifies lust. In the struggle against carnal temptation, by contrast, the ordinary Christian achieves the humility essential to virtue. Deprived of the capacity to love, Piletskii warns, the castrated cannot direct this potentially dangerous impulse toward divine ends and therefore cannot achieve salvation.

Some of these arguments resurface, in different guise, later in the century. There is no evidence, however, of the pamphlet's having any immediate effect. Too sophisticated to influence the Skoptsy core, it would not have impressed Selivanov, who was in any case unable to read. The church's most authoritative hierarch, Metropolitan Filaret of Moscow (1782–1867), complained that the composition showed too much sympathy for the notions it tried to refute. Piletskii himself felt the brunt of repression once Nicholas I came to the throne and treated Tatarinova and her associates to the kind of penance formerly reserved for folk heretics: a term of monastic confinement, in Piletskii's case within the very walls Selivanov had inhabited not long before.[4]

Selivanov's incarceration was a measure of official exasperation with his stubborn ways and continuing influence. In 1801, at the start of his reign, Alexander himself had opposed the use of punitive measures: "By their ignorant and harmful behavior," he remarked, "[the Skoptsy] have harmed themselves enough already."[5] Attempting to get Selivanov to cooperate, he sent Prince Aleksandr Golitsyn, the procurator of the Holy Synod, to speak with the old man. Golitsyn emerged from the interview with what he described as a promise to discourage castration, but these were surely empty words.[6] The superior of the monastery to which Selivanov was later confined claimed that the leader had returned to Orthodoxy, though without actually repenting of his former beliefs.[7] In short, it seems, Selivanov managed to remain in the good graces of church and state, without compromising his image in the eyes of the flock. No great surprise: dissembling had from the start been used to protect the enclosed terrain of true belief from intrusion, hostility, and repression. Even in appearing to renounce the faith, Selivanov would have sustained the larger purpose of deceiving and eluding the spiritual foe.

Alexander, like Catherine, seemed reluctant to hold the credulous simple folk accountable for the error of their ways. But the consideration he showed the prophet was not in fact extended to his flock. The decrees issued during Alexander's reign conform, rather, to the harsh views of the minister of justice. In a memorandum composed in 1807, intended as confidential but soon widely known, he described the Skoptsy as "enemies of humankind, moral perverts, and violators of religious and civil law."[8] The enthusiasts left behind when Selivanov was removed to Siberia continued to preach the faith. For promoting or performing castration on others, offenders were sentenced to military service in Georgia, the Caucasus, or Siberia. As of 1816, self-castration became an offense as well, but the law was not retroactive. Women who castrated themselves or others could be sent to work in Siberian textile mills. It was not in principle a crime to have been castrated by someone else. Yet boys castrated before the age of consent, thus not responsible for what they had undergone, could be dispatched to the army (as drummers and pipers). The cases brought against local leaders after 1820 were not numerous, but they uncovered centers of Skoptsy activity in various provinces around Moscow, as well as in St. Petersburg.[9]

While Selivanov was being treated with kid gloves in the capital, his followers navigated the byways of this confused legal maze, not infrequently to their own advantage. They learned to tell the right kind of tales. Knowing that they were exempt from prosecution for castrations effected before the 1816 decree and also when it could not be proved that they had performed the operation on their own (or, in some interpretations, consented to its performance), the Skoptsy answered questions accordingly. Excuses were circumstantial and bold: one retired soldier said he had been wounded in the scrotum while fighting Napoleon in 1812; another claimed to have been walking through beseiged Moscow, also in 1812, when he encountered two men in uniform, who castrated him on the spot; a third blamed an old man who got him drunk.[10] Despite the government's increasingly vigorous approach and the severity of the laws, most Skoptsy, in the course of actual trials, were returned to their customary lives, on the notion that they were misguided rather than fanatic.

Officials were aware that knowledge of the law prepared the accused to defend themselves. The antisectarian decrees were issued on an ad hoc basis, intended for bureaucrats alone. Even after statutes penalizing heresy were included in the Code of Laws, first published in 1832, the regulations governing administrative repression of false belief remained confidential. But in 1825 the Ministry of Internal Affairs complained that the tactic wasn't working. "Under questioning, many recently discovered Skoptsy pretend to have been castrated by strangers. From this one can conclude that they have in some way discovered the limits of the law and therefore either hide the names and whereabouts of those who castrated them or, having performed castration on themselves, blame it on others, usually deceased, knowing that they themselves cannot be prosecuted if they are victims. For the same reason, some do not even bother to pretend that their castration predates the law." As of 1826, therefore, tall tales that blamed damaged genitals on the intervention of unknown persons, accident, or illness or on being subject to force or rendered unconscious were considered the equivalent of intentional self-castration and penalized as such.[11]

Thus it no longer served a purpose to pretend that one had fallen victim to a stranger's designs. Since 1812 the law had treated dissemblers as "miscreants" but exonerated defendants who "honestly confessed."[12] Even before this date, some people chose to save themselves by naming others. In 1806, for example, a landowner sent one of his serfs to the army as punishment for ordinary misconduct. When the man's testicles were found to be missing, he was charged with self-mutilation to avoid the draft. In defense, he offered the name of a man he claimed had castrated him for religious reasons. His confession included a melodramatic account of his subjection to the knife, blindfolded and gagged. The story earned him freedom not only from military service but from serfdom as well. In reward for full disclosure and repentence, he was allowed to register in Moscow as a merchant of the third guild.[13] In general, however, the enticement to bear witness must have failed, since it was repeated in an 1847 ruling, which insisted that those who named their castrators "will be considered innocent and freed from prosecution. The identified seducers and castrators will be penalized under the law."[14]

During the first fifty years of its existence, in sum, the community had constantly to defend itself against discovery and repression. The stakes were high and the rules confusing. Alexander, like Catherine, had wished to avoid penalizing false belief as such. Officials were instructed to tolerate "heresy" (raskol) and focus on "disturbances of the peace" and the nefarious act of castration.[15] The policing of thought as well as action presented less of a problem for the aggressively conservative Nicholas I, who succeeded Alexander in 1825, in the wake of the Decembrist revolt. In this abortive confrontation with authority, members of the military and cultural elite had challenged the principle of autocratic rule. Nicholas reaffirmed it. His was the age of "Orthodoxy, Autocracy, and Nationality" (Pravoslavie-Samoderzhavie-Narodnost'). The coupling of state and religion was, of course, nothing new. Religion had served as a bulwark of political legitimacy since the Muscovite princes had consolidated the Russian lands and established themselves as sovereigns of the Orthodox domain. Peter the Great, in continuing this tradition, had insisted on the predominance of the political over the ecclesiastical arm, incorporating the Holy Synod into the secular apparatus. Catherine and Alexander, in privileging the social over the doctrinal element in persecuting the Skoptsy, had followed this pattern. The slogan adopted by Nicholas I was simply more emphatic.[16]

Nicholas, however, did indeed pay more attention to disciplining the boundaries of true belief. As the defender of absolute values in a world of revolutionary change (the 1830s and 1848 occurred on his watch), Nicholas treated religious dissent as insubordination. Despite the traditionalist rhetoric in which it was cloaked, intensified interest in the radical sects was not a throwback to some golden age of intolerance. It belonged, rather, to the project of administrative modernization.[17] These were the decades in which statutory law achieved its first systematic appearance in print, in which the criminal code was reorganized and revised. In this spirit, the law now classified objectionable creeds on the basis of what they preached and correlated sanctions to the level of the offense. The type designated as "especially harmful" included the

Dukhobors, Ikonobors, Molokans, Judaizers, Khlysty, and Skoptsy. The last two were reproached with the mistake of "worshiping man" (chelovekoobozhanie), for believing that their leaders were divinity incarnate.[18] They were described, in the most virulent terms, as "heresies associated with savage zealotry and fanatical attempts on their own or other's lives, or with vile and unnatural acts."[19] Harsh penalties were imposed for these offenses even after corporal punishment was eliminated from the Criminal Code in 1863. The "vile act" of self-castration incurred loss of civil rights and exile in perpetuity to remote areas of Siberia inhabited mainly by peoples of non-Christian faiths. A term at hard labor was added for performing the operation on someone else or allowing it to be performed on oneself.[20] Even to preach the faith was to risk a life of exile.[21]

While denouncing the sects for doctrinal errors, the decrees concerning the Skoptsy defined the essential danger not in religious but in social terms: undermining marriage, deforming the human body, and destroying the basis of procreation. These consequences stemmed as much from the physical act as from any dogmatic justification with which it was connected. The Skoptsy were objectionable, in the words of a later Senate ruling, as "a thorough perversion not only of Orthodoxy but of Christianity as such." Yet, even so, repression was motivated primarily by other concerns: "In the Skoptsy heresy the antisocial element predominates." Prosecution was justified because "the state cannot tolerate associations that achieve their goals by immoral methods incompatible with the social order, even if these associations assume a religious guise."[22]

For all the talk of social harm and doctrinal deviation, the regime struggled throughout the nineteenth century to define what precisely it was about this self-evidently objectionable act that offended legal norms. The confusion prompted numerous interventions by the Criminal Cassation Department of the State Senate, which heard cases on appeal.[23] On the one hand, the Senate ruled in the 1870s that removing the genitals did not itself constitute an illegal act except in the context of the fanaticism promoted by Skoptsy teaching.[24] On the other, the harm inflicted continued to be described not in religious but practical terms, as "the physical and moral disfigurement" of members of society, as well as damage to the family, construed as the "basic foundation of social life."[25] The prohibition covered not only the removal of organs involved in procreation, however, but mutilations that did not have directly social consequences because they did not inhibit intercourse or conception.[26] If castration did not have to be successful—anatomically (a botched job) or physiologically (the case of women)—to qualify as a crime when connected with unwelcome religious convictions, and if successful castration (amputation) was conversely not an offense in and of itself, then, critics observed, the target of legal intervention was not, in fact, the act, or even its effects, but its intended meaning.[27] The distinction between belief and practice invoked in Alexander's reign had worn thin. Membership in a sect promoting "savage zealotry" and "vile and unnatural acts" became grounds for conviction in and of itself. An uncastrated believer who had never castrated anyone else committed a criminal offense simply by advocating the practice.

The regime seemed to have something of a guilty conscience on this score, however, perpetuating the contradictions it could not resolve. In the face of repressive decrees and statutes, the Senate continued to deny that religious teaching should be the object of repression. The law, it reaffirmed in 1893, could target only actions "incompatible with the most important interests of private persons, which are protected by the state, and with the basic demands of social morality."[28] The Ministry of Internal Affairs, responsible for policing non-Orthodox confessions, might have been expected to focus precisely on the issue of correct belief. Yet in the 1890s it defended the prosecution of sectarians not as a means of regulating the spread of religious ideas but in the interests of social welfare.[29] Critics complained of circular thinking. But even critics believed some kind of penalty was in order.[30]

It must be kept in mind that the Skoptsy were not the only group to be targeted on the basis of religious error. Old Believers, the most numerous of all, suffered various legal disabilities and restrictions on the exercise of the cult, although they were not prevented from pursuing their community affairs in the open. Khlysty, Molokans, Dukhobors, and Baptists in their turn were deprived of civil rights and sent into exile. The laws against them were harshest during the reign of Nicholas I, but local circumstances sometimes worked in their favor. The Molokans, for example, enjoyed an almost privileged existence in Transcaucasia, to which they had been transported as exiles but where they were treated with some consideration as ethnic Russians among the local, non-Christian population.[31] The reform of the legal system under Alexander II (reign 1855–81) also benefited the Skoptsy, as they themselves acknowledged. In retelling the history of persecution, Gavriil Men´shenin (1862–1930), the community's self-declared scribe, held Nicholas I responsible for "repressive decrees against heretics in general and Skoptsy in particular. Under Alexander II all these repressive measures were revoked. The judicial statutes [of 1864] subjected all sectarians, including Skoptsy, to the judgment of the general courts, bound by general laws, not secret circulars, instructions, and orders. The interference of administrative authorities in legal cases against the Skoptsy occurred less and less frequently."[32] Alexander III (reign 1881–94), who came to the throne in the wake of Alexander II's assassination, distinguished himself by reversing his father's reforms. On matters of religion he was inconsistent. While civil and cultural restrictions on the Jews increased, the legal rights of Old Believers expanded and penalties for ascribing to heretical beliefs diminished, except in the case of the most extreme groups.[33]

Relaxed vigilance did not extend to communities, such as the Baptists, considered politically or socially objectionable.[34] Least desirable of all, the Skoptsy continued to be prosecuted under their own special statute. Once in exile, they were subject to an especially rigid regime. Siberian authorities exercised strict supervision over their slightest movements.[35] Concessions made by the government in the 1880s and 1890s shortened the duration of exile and made it easier for convicts who had served their time to rejoin the social order. Local bureaucrats, however, did not extend these benefits to the Skoptsy. "Whoever is familiar with the kind of person who, even today, serves as local commissioner in such faraway frontier spots as the Iakutsk region can easily imagine the situation of Skoptsy exiles under their control," commented Men´shenin.[36]

The statutes under which the Skoptsy were convicted deprived them of civil status and sentenced them to Siberian exile as permanent colonists ("ssylka na poselenie"). Beginning in 1883, the regime allowed those who had already served a specified time to register in the peasant estate, thereby recovering formal rights. Local officials, however, often prevented the Skoptsy from doing so. Even those who managed to take advantage of the new rules were not permitted to move from the places to which they had been assigned. Over the years, as the regime continued to modify the general conditions of exile, the Skoptsy submitted countless petitions requesting inclusion in one or another imperial decree, but they usually met with rebuff.[37] A few supplicants obtained permission to relocate, but the authorities insisted that each case be considered on its own; the Skoptsy as such could enjoy no such right.[38] In response to the challenge of the 1905 revolution, the government affirmed the principle of religious toleration and alleviated restrictions on the Old Believers and other non-Orthodox faiths, but the so-called fanatical sects were excluded from these provisions.[39] Only in 1905 did the decree of June 25 finally allow the Skoptsy, along with other exiles, to leave Siberia, and many profited from this change, but the community was hard hit by the surge of repression directed against sectarians across the board, and the Baptists in particular, after 1910.[40]

Extravagant, naive, or folkloric as their faith may seem, in relation to the outside world—its dangers, constraints, and opportunities—the brethren were remarkably down-to-earth. Throughout the community's existence, the members responded adroitly to the terms of the law, providing endless frustration for statesmen trying to influence their behavior. They perfected the art of spinning fanciful yarns to conceal the ritual origin of bodily markings. They denied any knowledge of the sect and its creed. Their strategies did not always work. Many, as we shall see, experienced the full weight of criminal sanctions. From the point of view of the authorities, however, success was also hard to achieve. It was difficult, as Alexander I had realized, to punish souls who had "harmed themselves enough already." Singling out the leaders, especially for corporal sanctions, only enhanced their worth. Selivanov made his name, literally, in exile. Sent to Siberia, believers welcomed the chance to sojourn in the promised land where the Redeemer had spent his sanctifying days. In army units and monasteries, the condemned spread the faith.[41]

Despite these paradoxes, Nicholas I did not abandon legal means. Most Skoptsy trials during his reign involved small groups of active individuals, almost all male. Some culprits were sentenced to punitive military service and monastic confinement.[42] But the strategy did not greatly reduce the number of faithful at large, and it only reinforced their dedication. Officials therefore experimented with less drastic ways to bring the Skoptsy into line. Trying to foil the psychology of martyrdom that made the brethren so hard to curb, they resorted to techniques of so-called moral suasion. The attempt rested less on any sympathy for the misguided common folk than on frustration with their shrewd and stubborn ways. Sentencing them to penal battalions was not enough, the Orel provincial authorities were instructed in 1849. The best way to discourage converts was "to cast the Skoptsy in a ridiculous light," parading them before their neighbors in women's clothing and dunce caps.[43] For having excluded themselves from the male sex, the costumed wretches were described, for benefit of the crowd, as lunatics. They met with laughter and derision. In one village, the women sang sarcastic wedding songs. Children screamed and whistled, pelting the Skoptsy with dirt. Relatives wept from shame. One reproached his nephew for dishonoring the clan, warning that he had sold his soul to the devil. Old-timers said the repulsive crime had disgraced the entire community.

Were the neighbors indignant? Were they putting on a show? Either they managed to convince officials of their sincerity or the latter saw what they wished to see. The report concluded: "the method is capable of achieving its goal, which is to arouse disdain and repulsion toward the Skoptsy among the common people." The Skoptsy themselves were unaffected. "While being led about in this fashion, they may seem bashful. But afterwards they are entirely indifferent to the scorn that has come their way. Having endured the operation that saves their souls, they say, no pain can affect them. Obduracy and bitterness are inevitable, since their physical condition cannot be reversed. The moral approach is designed not for them but for the common folk, on whom . . . it has an obvious impact."[44] Even village audiences sometimes failed to show the proper emotions, however. When Skoptsy were displayed in similar disguise a few years later in Nizhnii Novgorod province, the crowd refused to respond with indignation. The pitiful figures appeared to them as martyrs. Old women wept, some offered coins.[45] If the punishment was meant to teach the public as well as the culprits a lesson, the technique clearly did not work.

Image in the Glass

Despite occasional indiscretions, the Skoptsy were intent on shielding the secrets of their cult to guard against discovery and repression. Their pursuers were no less convinced that knowledge was the key to control. How did they obtain it? Testimony accumulated in the 1820s and 1830s in connection with the trials. Informers sometimes volunteered their services as well. One such source was the Ekaterinburg merchant Vasilii Kliukvin, a reformed Old Believer who gathered information on local sectarian groups, which he passed along to the procurator of the Holy Synod. Asked to establish contact with the Skoptsy, he posed as a true believer and recorded his observations.[46] The authorities also valued the evidence provided by a state peasant who lived with the Skoptsy for ten years before revealing what he had learned—or perhaps what he thought he was expected to reveal.[47]

By the 1840s it was time to make sense of the scattershot data. Knowledge must be systematic to be applied. What was needed in relation to all the dissenting sects, some officials decided, was a more comprehensive view based on solid research. Lev Perovskii, minister of internal affairs from 1841 to 1852, was a technocrat who valued scientific methods and professional expertise.[48] He established a secret commission, which in 1845 issued four volumes of material on the various heretical sects. The third, dedicated to the Skoptsy, explains their practices and recounts their history on the basis of official records and the testimony of followers interrogated by the courts. It reproduces the text of sacred verses and the narrative of Selivanov's earthly and spiritual quest. Intended for the instruction of administrative colleagues, the report mixed supposedly objective information with frankly opinionated views. Despite its bias, it functioned as the standard for later treatments. It was cited by expert witnesses in courts of law. Professor Nikolai Subbotin, when reproached in an 1871 case for relying on the work of a bureaucrat, insisted its author was nevertheless "a remarkable scholar and literary man," whose research met "the highest scholarly standards."[49]

This scholar-bureaucrat was Nikolai Nadezhdin (1804–56). His role

in the production of the report demonstrates its deeply political meaning, on a personal as well as official plane. Nadezhdin began his career as
the editor of a literary-philosophical review, and it is in this capacity that
he is mentioned in general histories of Russia. He was responsible in the
1830s for publishing one of Petr Chaadaev's explosive "Philosophical
Letters," which questioned the value of the Russian cultural tradition
and its ability to hold its own on the world stage. This error of editorial
judgment earned Nadezhdin a rebuke and a term of exile. With the
backing of Perovskii, who liked to foster intellectual careers, Nadezhdin
got the chance to restore his reputation. Appointed to edit the journal of
the Ministry of Internal Affairs, he also directed two secret commissions
on religious dissent. The report on the Skoptsy, which did not bear his
name, appeared in a limited edition. Its purpose was not to turn
Nadezhdin's superiors against the sect (their revulsion could be assumed)
but to influence them in favor of himself.[50] After his work on the secret
commissions, Nadezhdin went on to become a leading figure in the
Imperial Russian Geographical Society. An early exponent of the meaning of Russian folk identity (narodnost'), he is considered one of the
founding fathers of Russian ethnography.[51] The Skoptsy served him well.

But attributing authorship to Nadezhdin does not tell the whole
story. The job was not originally meant for him but was first assigned to
another of Perovskii's protégés, Vladimir Dal´. Of German and Danish
descent, Lutheran by confession, and a physician by training, Dal´ came
to public attention in the 1830s with a collection of Russian fairy tales. In
1845 he convinced Perovskii to support the creation of the Imperial
Geographical Society, in which both he and Nadezhdin were active. In
the 1860s, after Dal´ had left St. Petersburg, the society provided some of
the intellectual clout behind Alexander II's Great Reforms. The folko-
rist's most significant scholarly achievement was the annotated dictio-
nary of the Russian language in use to this day. Like Nadezhdin, in short,
he considered himself a custodian of Russian national identity.

The least attractive example of this defining impulse, and the least
well known (until the appearance of reprints in post-Communist Russia), is Dal´'s 1844 treatise commissioned by the Ministry of Internal
Affairs, in which he demonstrated that Jews murder Christian children
for ritual purposes. As a student of folklore, he might have been expected
to treat the allegations of Jewish wrongdoing common to both Western

and Eastern Christian culture as manifestations of folk simplicity. Instead, he took them literally as illustrations of the pernicious character of the Jews.[52] It was in a similar capacity, as chronicler of moral atrocity, that Dal´ was initially asked by Perovskii to investigate the Skoptsy. The results were printed in a miniscule edition in 1844, similar to the one on the Jews. Nicholas refused, however, to accept as authoritative a work on questions of correct belief composed by someone outside the Orthodox fold. The material was passed along to Nadezhdin, who incorporated the substance of his colleague's labors into the final report.[53]

Dal´ was disappointed: "I have so much fascinating information on the Skoptsy," he wrote, "a shame it's all wasted." Skoptsy teachings, he added, were "so strange and savage; if it weren't for the direct evidence, they would defy belief."[54] The rejection must have been especially painful, since Dal´ had devoted a lifetime to plumbing the Russian spirit, which he considered his own. "You belong to the nation in whose language you think," he declared. "I think in Russian." His Lutheranism did not prevent him from considering Orthodoxy the highest form of Christianity and a pillar of empire. Yet he remained a Lutheran until almost the very end, converting to Orthodoxy only on his deathbed.[55]

Despite the complex authorship of this formally unauthored work, contemporaries considered it of Nadezhdin's making (and I shall continue to refer to it as his). The text reflects the intellectual atmosphere of the 1840s, in which political implications were read into every turn of phrase, whether by gentlemen-philosophers debating the fate of the nation or by bureaucrats trying to inhibit any critique at all. Nicholas saw himself defending traditional values against the threat of modern ideas, but he was no more likely than earlier tsars to think of religion in absolute, rather than instrumental, terms. Adherence to correct belief was a civic not a moral virtue. The decrees condemning the Skoptsy focused on the issue of social harm not doctrinal deviation, as we have seen. It is not surprising, therefore, that Nadezhdin, like Dal´, should emphasize Skoptsy pretensions to political rather than spiritual authority.[56] Having assumed an imperial as well as divine persona, in calling himself Peter III as well as Christ, Selivanov had renamed his congregation the "Tsar's Ship" (Korabl´-Tsarskii), to which the sect's other assemblies were tethered like "dinghies."[57] The assertion of political dominance, which

Nadezhdin saw in Selivanov's imperial title and in the sect's centralized structure of command, he considered to be the group's distinguishing feature and the reason it ought to be repressed.[58]

How much of a threat to the established order were the followers of this self-mortifying peasant? Based on administrative records of the preceding fifty years, Nadezhdin estimated that in 1845 the Skoptsy must have numbered at least 1,700, but he insisted that many more belonged to the sect than were castrated and certainly more than were ever brought to light. The problem was not only that many of the castrated eluded detection but that some believers were not physically marked. No evidence, however, confirms Nadezhdin's view that there were 400 adepts to every 2 that were castrated.[59] By this calculation, the faithful would have numbered 300,000 at midcentury. A professor of theology at Dorpat University writing after 1905 put the total (including the non-castrated) at no more than 100,000.[60] In any case, there was, and is, no way to tell.

Not only were the Skoptsy relatively rare, but they did not cause trouble in the usual sense. Preoccupied with evading not confronting authority, they were exemplary subjects in everyday life. In their home villages as well as in exile, the brethren were known for sobriety, hard work, and economic success, both in agriculture and trade. Unlike Pugachev, whose name he invoked, Selivanov organized no mass movement. He mobilized the cathartic power of violence as an instrument of group solidarity, not as a weapon of the weak against the strong. Yet, according to Nadezhdin, Selivanov and his followers represented a similar, no less ominous, threat. "In the dogma, dreams, and hopes of the Skoptsy," Nadezhdin intoned, "political interests predominate over religious ones. . . . No longer human, but still of Russian blood, the Skoptsy cannot imagine any other way to achieve the Kingdom of Heaven on earth than with the accession of Peter III to the Russian Imperial Throne. . . . And this will occur not in peace and quiet, but with 'fearful and terrible thunder': led by the False-Tsar, the people will arrive by the legion, a mighty force, in military readiness!"[61]

In Nadezhdin's eyes the quaint euphemisms of Skoptsy piety veiled the threat of violence in most literal terms. Behind the images of whiteness and purity lurked the bloody reality of genital mutilation, threatening the nation's biological welfare and turning error into a compellingly active force. This inversion of Skoptsy imagery left some of his readers impressed only with Nadezhdin's own naiveté. But his interpretation reflected the paranoid sensibility of Nicholas I's reign.[62] United by the power of Selivanov's dominant personality, Nadezhdin insisted, the sect formed a nationwide network of mutual support and subversive propaganda, a single "brotherhood" or "association," dedicated to the conversion of souls and the material sustenance of the flock. Operating in secret, under cover of religious conformity, they recognized each other by secret signs, just as the Freemasons did. "The Skoptsy brotherhood," the report affirmed, "is a solid, powerful union, sustained by active mutual support. . . . From Petersburg to Siberia, from Siberia to the depths of Russia, everywhere they exchange letters, advice, instructions, and—money!" All the more dangerous for being unseen, the sect "permeates [the body politic] like an invisible poison that eats away at the common folk like a deeply embedded sore."[63]

"Dangerous for being unseen," the Skoptsy posed an "invisible" threat. The question of how to recognize them was central. Busy demonstrating his own loyalty, Nadezhdin was eager to identify the actual enemies in no uncertain terms and to unmask their strategies of deception. Since the Skoptsy routinely lied in court, distorting the messages inscribed on their flesh, their bodies must be made to speak for them. Familiar with earlier descriptions that suggested the castrated male could be recognized by distinctive habits and a "pale, yellowish cast," Nadezhdin insisted that they constituted "a special type that when fully developed turns them into the walking dead, inspiring repulsion and horror." The best readers of this kind of evidence, he believed, were physicians.[64]

A quarter of a century had to pass before such a guide was forthcoming. It took the form of a treatise published in 1872 by Evgenii Pelikan (1824–84), professor of forensic medicine at the St. Petersburg Military Medical Academy and director of the Medical Department of the Ministry of Internal Affairs. By this time, Russia had suffered defeat in the Crimean War. The reforming tsar, Alexander II, had freed the serfs, established elective organs of local self-administration, and modernized the legal system. Under a relaxed censorship regime, professional associations flourished, the press expanded, and the educated public swelled to include those of more humble rank than the privileged writers and philosophers of an earlier generation. Some intellectuals cooperated with "enlightened" bureaucrats (the unexpected offshoots of Nicholas I's technocratic regime), to improve the political system from within. Others benefited from the possibilities opened by reform to challenge the system's very existence.

In these years science acquired a cultural authority that crossed political lines. Nihilists no less than officials heeded its voice. It is this voice that animates Pelikan's medical inquiry into the causes and consequences of castration. Like Nadezhdin, he was also a bureaucrat and wrote with an institutional purpose and restricted readership in mind: in this case, forensic experts called to testify in trials for ritual castration. But where Nadezhdin justified a policy of administrative repression, Pelikan responded to the context of the reformed criminal courts, newly oriented to proof and procedure.

As early as the 1830s, the authorities had called on medical experts to provide objective evidence to counter the fantastical claims of Skoptsy defendants, who routinely pretended to have achieved castration by accident or illness.[65] Filling this need, Pelikan marshals a mass of detail: unblinking description of organs, techniques, and consequences; the accumulation of case studies. His task was to discern the spiritual motivation behind mute physical signs and to categorize the visible results in clear diagnostic terms. To this end he enumerates the various methods of castration and how they can be read from the scars. Seeking the "special type" mentioned by Nadezhdin, he describes castration's physiological effects. In the case of men, he asserts, only those altered before sexual maturity show signs of physical change: shrunken genitals, high voices, sparse body hair. The rest can be recognized by their listless demeanor and sallow complexion. The expectation that the consequences of castration must "show" was so strong that Pelikan characterizes the affected women in similar terms, knowing that their reproductive systems remained undamaged.[66]

Intending to motivate the switch from relative toleration to more active repression, Nadezhdin had mobilized a rhetoric of anxious hyperbole: the empire is in danger, mankind in peril, the dead walk the earth. Pelikan achieves his authority by opposite means. Designed ostensibly to

Medical illustration: "minor seal." The technique of excising the testicles derived from the practices of animal husbandry.

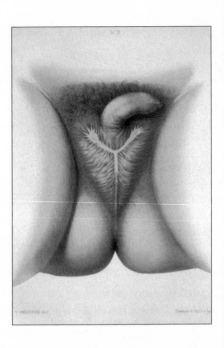

Medical illustration: "major seal." On the extreme version of castration, Pelikan commented in his terse, professional manner: the operation "is accomplished either at the same time as the removal of the testicles, in which case the scrotum is tied together with the penis and both are severed with the same instruments or simply with an ax; or else the penis . . . is removed later" (5).

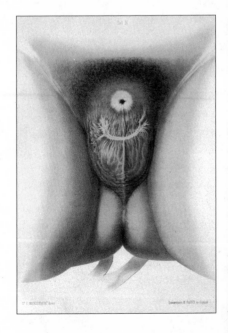

The five medical illustrations on these pages are from E.V. Pelikan, *Sudebno-meditsinskie issledovaniia skopchestva i istoricheskie svedeniia o nem* (St. Petersburg: Golovin, 1872). Engravings by V. O. Merzheevskii.

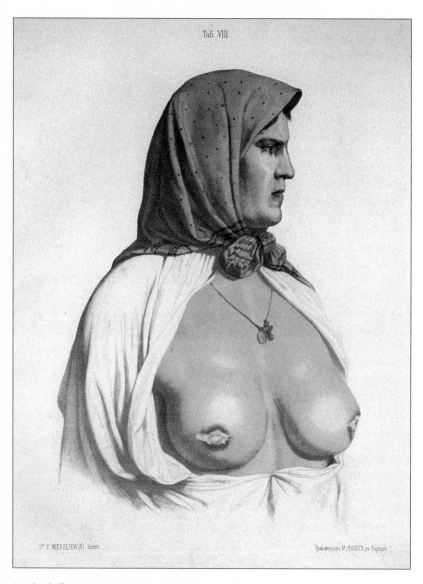

Medical illustration: excised nipples. An example of the "excision, removal, or cauterizing of the nipples" (60).

Medical illustration: female genital mutilation. This operation did not affect the woman's ability to have sexual intercourse or conceive. Some left the faith to marry and bore children. Whether or not the Skoptsy demanded the so-called castration of women is unclear. Some sources say Selivanov opposed the practice; some claim Lisin put a stop to it. Data from the later trials show, however, that castration of women continued into the twentieth century but that it was less frequent than the castration of boys and men.

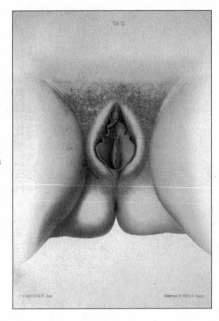

inform not shock, the text aims for scientific detachment. So do the color-washed medical illustrations showing abbreviated genitals, male and female, and female torsos with excised nipples and breasts. Pelikan's intricate concern with clinical detail has the paradoxical effect, however, of echoing the sect's own obsession with genitalia, especially the male. We learn how much these "simple folk" knew about the testicles, the scrotum, the relation between urinary tract and seminal vesicles, the sensations created by clitoris and nipples; how carefully they patrolled the sites of pleasure and desire. We know from Nadezhdin and other sources that the Skoptsy considered the penis an instrument of the devil, the "key to hell" or to the "abyss" that was the vagina. Yet the attention lavished on the deadly organs appears almost loving in its excess. Pelikan, too, seems caught in the dialectic of presence and absence, love and hate, awe and repugnance.

Recycling much of Nadezhdin's material and swept into the vortex of emotion even as he struggles for scientific remove, Pelikan nevertheless reflects the different political context of Alexander II's reign. The contrast between the Nicholaevan official and the medical professional is nowhere clearer than in their understanding of how castration affected

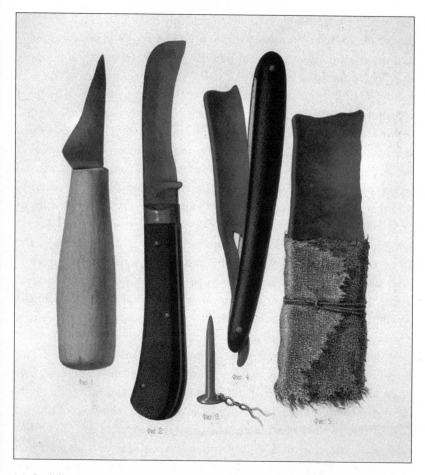

Medical illustration: tools of the trade. The nail was used after full castration to keep the urethra open and permit urination.

sexual desire. Nadezhdin in fact does not have a coherent position on this subject. At times he insists that castration destroys the sexual urge, depriving the Skoptsy of human feeling. More often he emphasizes the paradox that physical incapacity might not hinder, but even enhance, the thirst for physical satisfaction, magnifying desire "to the point of savage, frenzied, even bestial rage."[67]

The bureaucrat of Nicholas's day perceived raging passion that demanded the imposition of external controls. In a later period, when society was given more (though still restricted) responsibility for its fate, the medical officer preferred self-regulation to police. He stresses the danger posed by loss, not excess, of desire. Pelikan thus echoes, in a secular vein, the argument advanced by Piletskii from a theological perspective. Where the latter extolled the moral value of sexual desire as a precondition of spiritual achievement, the physician defends sexual desire as a cornerstone of social existence: "Once he embarks on sexual life, the normal man starts to find the opposite sex attractive: the first instinctive call of love also inspires him with the urge to noble action and great deeds and with devotion to the fatherland. The young man castrated before puberty knows none of this: he remains indifferent to his environment, lacking the smallest germ of noble aspiration, sense of duty, or civic obligation. . . . The onset of puberty does not bring family happiness; manly courage and lofty dreams are alien; rather, he acquires the vices of persons with limited vision and crude morality: egoism, cunning, perfidy, and greed."[68] Secular virtue, in Pelikan's view, consists not in the absence of desire or in submission to external controls but in the ability to channel the impulse toward socially constructive ends. Desire is a precondition of strong character and civic welfare.

This welfare was threatened not by the accident of a few aberrant cases but by the possibility that castration might spread. Changing views on how the Skoptsy attracted and retained converts also reflect the shifting discourse of Russian public life. In an age when religious enthusiasm swayed the cultural elite, Piletskii considered believers misguided but sincere and therefore took seriously their spiritual claims. In an era when conformity ruled, even in matters of the soul, Nadezhdin projected the regime's instrumentalist assumptions onto the enemy's designs. He envisioned a core of desperate fanatics preying on luckless victims, the objects of trickery and compulsion. He preferred to discount the possibility that converts were truly inspired by the faith or even susceptible to persuasion. Yet he credited some of the sectarians' popular appeal to their mystical ardor, folkloric rites, and naive spiritual idiom. The semblance of virtue among the Skoptsy, even if misleading, might arouse the peasants' respect. Once recruited, however, converts had no choice but to remain. The physical effect of the Skoptsy prayer meetings, with their repetitious movements and recitations, "exerted a powerful force on body and soul," Nadezhdin asserts, "like a magnetic enchantment, or, more simply, an intoxication that creates dependency, which among crude natures, easily becomes an overpowering passion, like an incurable 'addiction to drink.'"[69] In short, dependency in one form or another.

If those who joined voluntarily were demonstrating only weakness of character, not strength of conviction, in Nadezhdin's view, others were forced or bullied into the fold. Material need, he believed, was a strong inducement to join the sect and stay involved. The wealthy sectarian community provided shelter for vagrants and runaway criminals, he affirmed, whom they supplied with false papers and new names. To the poor peasant they offered relief from the military draft, escape from serf-dom, economic support, and the hope of equality and fellowship. They adopted the children of their own needy relatives, sheltered orphans, and took as apprentices the offspring of impoverished villagers. Explaining the sect's appeal in material terms made the community seem sinister and mercenary, while relieving converts of responsibility for their choice.[70]

Pelikan, like Nadezhdin, is loath to credit Skoptsy believers with true belief. Bringing the wisdom of science to bear on the question of motives, Pelikan concludes that "mental blindness (or extremely one-sided mental development)" was the precondition for susceptibility to fanatical religious faith. But like Nadezhdin, who contrasts the calculated evil at work among the hard core with the naive vulnerability of the mass, Pelikan also tries to have it both ways. As a forensic expert he insists that the Skoptsy are responsible for their actions and therefore compe-tent to stand trial. Mentally limited, perhaps, but not insane, the Skoptsy reveal no organic abnormalities, do not behave strangely in everyday life, hallucinate, or rave. The sectarians' creed was systematically propagated and comprehensible to others, whereas the ideas of the insane were meaningful only to themselves. Skoptsy conversions, Pelikan maintains, might be the result of emotional contagion akin to mass hysteria, or sim-ply the consequence of ignorance, but they do not indicate mental dis-ease.[71]

Pelikan does not consider the exaltation resulting from Skoptsy wor-ship a sign of mental imbalance, but he nevertheless denies that it is a genuine spiritual state. He describes it rather as a form of temporary instability that can be explained in physiological terms. As participants

swirled and waved their arms, their bodies experienced an almost nar-
cotic intoxication derived from pressure on the nerves and brain. Both
the Khlysty and the Skoptsy used the expression "to get drunk without
drinking" (chelovek plotskimi ustami ne p'et, a p'ian zhivet). Some
physicians believed that the flow of blood to the extremities produced a
pleasurable light-headedness, "resembling a faint." The physical pressure
weakened the rational faculties, stimulated the imagination, and loosened
the inhibitions: "lubricious, selfish, and other, mostly base, inclinations
come to the surface and struggle for satisfaction." The experts all emphasized the enhancement of erotic desire as a consequence of these exer-
tions.[72] Thus, if believers joined the sect in their right—if simple—
minds, they might emerge functionally deprived of reason.

Excited Indignation

Skoptsy rituals may perhaps have induced states of exaltation and
unreason in their participants; their contemplation certainly induced
states of unreason in learned men. Not only Nadezhdin (echoing Dal'),
but also Pelikan, the man of science, indulged extravagant fantasies on
the subject of Skoptsy ritual. These inventions bore a close resemblance
to the myths that circulated about the Jews, and not only in Russia.[73]
Pelikan repeats accusations that Skoptsy ingested the excised testicles or
breasts of castrated believers. He also echoes the claim that young girls
were impregnated during sexual orgies. Their infant boys, he asserts,
were pierced to the heart and drained of blood, which was imbibed during communion. The infants' desiccated corpses were ground to powder
for use in preparing communion bread. Although Pelikan refuses to
believe that the Skoptsy fed on severed breasts, he remains convinced
that "mortification of infants and communion with their blood is a reli-
gious-historical fact."[74]

If science could thus descend to folklore, it should be remembered
that folklore was simultaneously making scientific claims. Perovskii considered himself a modern administrator and engaged Dal' and
Nadezhdin to raise the professional level of his staff. Yet the difference
between fantasy and observation seems to have escaped these educated
men no less than it evaded the spiritually inclined Skoptsy—and with

less excuse. The Skoptsy, after all, expressed their faith precisely in the convergence of other- and this-worldly truths. The bearers of secular discourse, however devout they personally may have been, supposedly respected this distinction. But rhetorical imperatives sometimes gained the upper hand.

It is perhaps a reflection of Dal´'s concurrent preoccupation with the Jews as well as the Skoptsy that Nadezhdin harps on Skoptsy clannishness. Like the Jews, he insists, they constituted a "conspiracy [zagovor: a classic term of anti-Semitic rhetoric] against the rest of humankind."[75] Both groups marked their relation to God by stamping the penis with the holy seal. Both supposedly possessed great wealth, wrung from the labor of hapless employees, peasants, and subordinates. These analogies, in which the Skoptsy suffered from comparison with the Jews, not the reverse, became standard rhetorical turns.[76] The existence of affluent Skoptsy entrepreneurs was brought to public attention in the late nineteenth century during various high-profile trials, and researchers often stressed the division between the wealthy and the poor, wage-earning members.[77] It is the language used to describe these social facts, however, which reveals the underlying mythic structures. Portraying the Skoptsy as ferociously money-loving became a cliché of antisectarian writing. Having deprived themselves of human love and renounced all familial ties, it was said, they devoted their energies to acquiring wealth. Like the Jews, some did, in fact, deal in precious metals and lend money at interest. For this reason, as well as their entrepreneurial success, both groups were said to profit at the common people's expense. Many Skoptsy had become millionaires, Nadezhdin asserts, partly as the result of commercial crimes. "Only the Yids," he remarks, "equal them in their wholehearted devotion to the Golden Calf."[78]

Such rhetoric colored most "respectable" references to the Skoptsy in this period. The salacious details of alleged atrocities—sexual orgies and ritual cannibalism—surfaced in Baron August von Haxthausen's influential account of the Russian village, written in the 1840s.[79] Similar flights of fancy added spice to the reflections of the pseudo-ethnographer Pavel Mel´nikov (1818–83), another employee of the Ministry of Internal Affairs, whose voluminous publication of archival documents and extensive commentaries in the 1870s offered later writers a supposedly authoritative supplement to Nadezhdin's report. Such myths were echoed in populist interpretations, as well.[80] The accounts of defectors and renegades also offered detailed descriptions of Skoptsy ritual practices, in a tone of morally saturated excitement, to which readers or courtroom audiences might respond with sympathy and prurient fascination.

The theatrical element was particularly effective in the new courtrooms created by the Judicial Reforms of 1864, which introduced open trials and a novel concern for due process. It is in the 1870s that cases involving entire communities first come to public attention.[81] Some of the proceedings appeared in print. The castrated Kudrin brothers, Nikita (age sixty-two), Andrei (age fifty-nine), and Dmitrii (age forty), were tried in Moscow Circuit Court in 1871 along with twenty-four women and one old man, described as thin, jaundiced, wrinkled, hairless, deaf, and barely able to walk. The women wore white kerchiefs on their heads. The accused were interrogated before a jury of fourteen men, including five from the urban lower classes. The courtroom filled with a largely female audience, eager to feast their eyes on the strange creatures and hear discussion of issues and organs not usually mentioned in public. The stenographic record of six days' testimony was published in book form, no doubt on the assumption that many would find it a lively read.[82]

The Kudrin family had begun as serfs on a Tula estate. Dmitrii had been castrated at the age of ten, Andrei at seventeen, after their own father had converted. In the dock, Dmitrii appeared hairless, effeminate, and youthful. Andrei had a small beard. The latter had first come to Moscow as a servant to his master. There he displayed an entrepreneurial flair. By now a wealthy merchant, he had earlier been tried for castration but released and granted permission to continue living in Moscow.[83] His businesses, run with his brothers, included money changing, ribbon manufacture, horse breeding, and a photography shop. One of the arrested women was his original business partner. Many of the others worked in the ribbon factory. Nineteen women had some kind of scars suggesting ritual castration. All denied belonging to the Skoptsy. In the end, Nikita Kudrin, his daughter Anna, and eleven women were acquitted. Andrei, Dmitrii, the frail old man, and thirteen women were sentenced to exile.

Before the verdict was pronounced, the ladies in the audience would have been able to hear the secretary read from the report of Nikita Kudrin's medical exam: "His member is moderately developed, the scrotum extremely small, the surface deeply wrinkled. Across the front, on either side of the seam there is a wide scar, which forks toward the root of the genitals. . . . When palpated, the scrotum appears entirely empty, the testicles absent." Andrei was missing his penis as well. Nikita's daughter Anna, aged twenty-nine, was described as possessing a bust in proportion to her build, "correctly formed, with nipples of normal shape but pale. . . . The large and small labia, the clitoris, and surrounding tissue are normal, and there is no scarring. The hymen surrounds the entire entry to the uterus but shows slight tears along the edge, not of recent origin. . . . There are no signs of damage to the breast or genitals; the hymen is intact."[84]

The same ladies would have heard the full catalogue of such descriptions. They would have listened to the accused deny that any operation had occurred or claim not to remember how the lips of their vulvas had vanished. The president of the court would have announced: "Gentlemen of the jury! Here is Akulina Petrova, missing her clitoris and labia minora. Here is Matrena Afanasieva, with hollow nipples. Here is Mariia Danilova, with fissures around her nipples. Here is Avdot′ia Ivanova, missing the labia minora. . . . Here is Avdot′ia Vikulova, whose nipples are split."[85] What the damage indicated was harder to tell. The audience would have had their emotions swayed, as attorneys invoked poverty and ignorance to argue that the women were innocent of error and even of guile. These were not "fanatical sectarians but simple, uneducated women," they told the jury, "for whom the mystical ravings of the Skoptsy were incomprehensible, for whom the basic question of life was obtaining the next crust of bread." Poverty did not make them cunning or dangerous. It made them suffer. "Women raised on feather cushions might easily explain every mark on their bodies. The incidents causing the marks would be so rare as to remain forever fixed in their minds. But the defendants were raised in the village and have spent their entire lives in deprivation, at the hardest physical labor. Their bodies have endured bruises, scratches, scars, and perhaps even blows. No wonder they fail to remember the exact reason for every little scar."[86]

Populist Revulsion

Despite the principled objections of some jurists to the terms of prosecution and the arguments of defense attorneys before the bench, few outsiders showed any sympathy for Skoptsy teaching in its own terms, and none excused the form of ritual expression. The negative consensus can be illustrated by the failure of Nadezhdin's harsh vision to provoke an adequate response, even from the social radicals of the 1860s. These populist democrats hoped to arouse peasant rebellion against the possessing classes and the regime. Though secular themselves, and influenced by Western socialist thinking, they would have welcomed any sign of popular self-assertion, even in religious guise. They embraced the very prospect that filled Nadezhdin with alarm: that sectarians, already at odds with the traditional conformity of the peasant mass, might turn to other forms of opposition.

From the safety of London, the populist Vasilii Kel´siev (1835–72) reissued the four volumes of material assembled by Perovskii's secret commissions, of which the third concerned the Skoptsy.[87] The London reprint, which appeared between 1860 and 1862, made its way back to the homeland, spreading information originally intended only for trusted servants of the state. By disseminating the confidential reports, Kel´siev may have wished to arouse public concern for the very communities the state wanted to suppress. He may have wished to equip radical activists with insight into a force they might try to mobilize for their own ends. But if radicals imagined religious nonconformists as heroic victims of oppression and standard-bearers of an enlightened dawn, the Skoptsy frustrated their dreams.

Curious to see how Nadezhdin's version squared with real life, in 1867 Kel´siev went to visit a Skoptsy community in Romania, where some had sought refuge from the law. He published his observations in a journal oriented toward the progressive-minded educated public.[88] The expatriot Skoptsy congregated in the cities of Galati and Jassy, where the Romanian authorities left them free to develop a comfortable way of life and to retain contact with their brethren at home. In the 1860s there were about six hundred in seven different colonies, where many worked as cabdrivers.[89] Those Kel´siev encountered were well-to-do, well-informed, and willing to talk to strangers. Some had read Nadezhdin's report—in the London edition!—which they denounced as nothing but slander and lies. Kel´siev was ready to believe that they were not the deluded fanatics Nadezhdin had described, but comparable to religious eccentrics in other lands: "In the West," he writes, "people naturally drawn to the mysterious join the Masons, Jansenists, Mormons, Shakers, or Perfectionists. Here they become Dukhobors, Jumpers, Khlysty, and Skoptsy. . . . Mystical faith is unavoidable in our completely cynical age."[90]

Kel´siev's attempt to normalize the Skoptsy does not, however, succeed. Opposed to everything Nadezhdin stood for and partisan of all he feared, Kel´siev nevertheless reveals what he and the bureaucrat had in common: a visceral repulsion for the object at hand. As servants of the state, Nadezhdin and Pelikan shared an interest in unmasking hidden threats to the national welfare in order to counteract them. They insisted on the particular look by which the Skoptsy could always be known, no matter what disguise they assumed in daily life. The radical Kel´siev sought out the Skoptsy not to denounce or betray them, but to contradict the voice of authority that used description as a repressive tool. In the end, however, his own descriptions amount to the same thing: a language of moral indictment.

Kel´siev, no less than the official outsider-experts, uses the coin of cultural stereotype. Locating the Skoptsy between the Jews ("that scourge of Moldavia") and the "Negroes" of Turkey, Kel´siev is struck by their unmistakable demeanor and their divergence from the human norm. "Their faces are completely bloodless," he writes, "pale and dead. This is not the pallor of an old man or invalid, not even that of a corpse—this is the absence of something under the skin. Their skin is somehow differently attached to the muscles, not as firmly as ours: it is thinner and more mobile, as if wanting to crawl away. . . . When you shake their hands, the skin feels soft, flaccid, and cold. . . . Nothing about them shines: not their skin, nor their eyes; even their hair lacks sheen—everything is lifeless."[91]

Committed, as a revolutionary populist, to the notion that peasants could be inspired through the influence of propaganda and education to abandon their traditional submissive ways and reject what they had been taught to revere, Kel'siev was not inclined to neglect the role of custom and learning in folk piety. After describing the effects of physiological change in producing the characteristic Skoptsy look, he pursued cultural explanations as well. All sects, after all, had their peculiar manners: "Pupils always imitate their teachers in the smallest details. Joining a sect means assuming its habits and rejecting one's past." In the case of the Skoptsy, Kel'siev observed, "speckled shirts, waistcoats, and kerchiefs do not reflect their dogma; they are not a sign of their faith. This is their fashion."[92] They were obvious even when fully clothed.

In the end, Kel'siev concludes, the appearance of nonconformity was deceptive. The Skoptsy might offend the laws of nature and deviate from the religious norm, but they were all too ready to submit to social convention. They were also, alas, politically loyal. Historical fables to the contrary notwithstanding, "they would be happy," Kel'siev writes, "to shed their blood for both tsars: the invisible and the ostensible. One guards the other's throne; one reigns in heaven, the other on earth. There can be no enmity between them. Moreover," he adds, wistfully, "there are too few Skoptsy to stage a political revolt."[93]

The Skoptsy are difficult to love. The populist can only share the bureaucrat's disgust at castration and its physical results. But even when he manages to dispute official views, he finds nothing to encourage his own hopes. Contrary to Nadezhdin's claims, the Skoptsy, Kel'siev finds, show no sign of political disaffection. Nadezhdin makes much of the sect's hostility to marriage and family ties and its suppression of sexual difference. Kel'siev is dismayed to recognize among the sexless brethren the same patriarchal regime that dominated ordinary village life. Sexual egalitarianism was part of the program of social reconstruction espoused by 1860s Russian radicals. Their romantic attachment to the alleged virtues of simple, agrarian ways often came to grief on the issue of how peasant men treated their wives. The Skoptsy, it seemed, were no better than their neighbors in this regard. Skoptsy women, though often unmarried, were subject to the same verbal abuse and male domination that ordinary woman encountered in conventional peasant households.[94] In the end, Kel'siev is forced to conclude that Nadezhdin, though wrong

"Siberian Skoptsy." Photo G. Bogdanovich, Irkutsk. GMIR, f. 2, op. 29, d. 120. (Copyright © GMIR.) This studio portrait conforms to the genre of "individual types" (tipichnye lichnosti), which nineteenth-century photographers used to illustrate the social landscape. The Skoptsy produced many such images of themselves. Gavriil Men´-shenin sent a good number to Bonch-Bruevich for the archives. On the question of whether the Skoptsy were identifiable by their appearance (anatomical or sartorial), this photo offers evidence to the contrary. The telltale overcoat and white neckerchiefs are missing. The man on the left has a healthy beard and the others might very well be shaven.

"Romanian Skoptsy." Photo M. Margulies, Jassy. GMIR, f. 2, op. 29, d. 120. (Copyright © GMIR.) This pair, by contrast, has the puffy, smooth-cheeked look of the "obvious" Skoptsy. They appear to be wealthy city-dwellers and, like the rustic Siberian types, are clearly well-to-do. The overcoats conform to the typical Skoptsy style, but the men do not wear white neckerchiefs or hold white cloths.

to think the Skoptsy were likely to lead a peasant revolt, was correct to describe them as repulsive, unmanly, and hopelessly patriarchal.

In the same year that Kel'siev's observations appeared in print, Afanasii Shchapov (1830–76), a fellow populist, published his own reflections on the subject in another progressive journal.[95] Shchapov, in other circumstances, had been willing to humor the naive elements of peasant thought (in particular, a stubborn loyalty to the throne) to further his own political goals. But the misguided elements of Skoptsy belief exhausted his patience. No sharper indictment of the Skoptsy emerged from any conservative pen.[96] Shchapov denounced castration as a vestige of Oriental primitivism, a "savage, barbarian, antiphysiological idea" imported from Turkey and imposed on the "poor benighted" Russian folk. Transmitted by Finnish tribes, this Eastern tradition combined with the Finns' "crude shaman psychology," "pagan fetishism," and "mystical pantheism," to emerge "thinly veiled in church-Byzantine spiritualism" as the Skoptsy creed.[97]

Some of the contradictions of Russian populism are evident in the vehemence of Shchapov's response. Dedicated to loving the people, radicals deplored not only the people's oppression by outside forces—the upper classes and the state—but also their subjection to ignorance and tradition. Ready to subordinate themselves to the victims of injustice, young people who enjoyed the benefits of modern culture felt that they must raise the moral level of the masses, even as they struggled on their behalf. In this spirit, socially conscious physicians decried the poor sanitary conditions in peasant huts, would-be revolutionaries influenced by John Stuart Mill as well as Charles Fourier regretted the subordination of peasant wives, and Shchapov found the peasants' intimate behavior "distorted, unnatural, antihygienic, and immoral." The "savage, antiphysiological" castration sect showed "how far the errors of the benighted masses can lead them from nature."[98]

To the 1860s "enlightener," committed to bridging the culture gap between elite and common folk, the solution seemed clear: the folk must learn to "love the light of Western science." "The populace needs to know the laws of nature," Shchapov declared. Without this knowledge, it was bound to develop the nervous pathologies embodied in "mystical-idealistic doctrines" such as those of the Skoptsy—a clear example of mental derangement.[99] Better than flogging or Siberian exile, or dunce caps and women's skirts, sex education was the answer: Western wisdom to counteract the obscurantism of the licentious East.

The convergence between conservative and radical responses to the Skoptsy reflects ideological patterns deeper than political conviction. Shchapov, the populist, and Pelikan, the medical official, shared respect for scientific truths. Yet neither resisted the lure of the lurid detail, taking stories of Skoptsy cannibalism at face value.[100] The anticommercialism evident in Nadezhdin's hostility to the Jews as well as the Skoptsy was echoed in the 1890s, for opposite ideological reasons, by Vladimir Iokhel´son (1855–1937), an ethnographer of radical views who specialized in the native peoples of Siberia. Observing Skoptsy exiles in the Olekminsk region, he denounced them as "peasant moneybags [bogachi i kulaki], whose coldheartedness, hypocrisy, and insatiable greed were absolutely harmful." The attempt to lead a purely spiritual life, he observed, led the Skoptsy to the other extreme: "the crudest materialism"—"passion for profit, love of money, and boundless greed." Blending arguments from Nadezhdin and Pelikan, Iokhel´son agreed that castration did not stop desire but only deformed it: the urges experienced by castrated men were "unhealthy and incomplete, . . . not the passion that sustains an awareness of duty and social responsibility, proud valor [muzhestvo], and high-minded fantasy, but purely animal lust." The faithful were not merely indifferent to the outside world but actively hostile—a result of their "ungrounded social organization, which lacks the animating principle of family life."[101]

It would have been hard for Iokhel´son, writing after Nadezhdin, Kel´siev, and Pelikan, to observe the Skoptsy with a fresh eye. His descriptions of Skoptsy appearance confirm what earlier texts would have prepared him to see: a distinctively repulsive physicality. The "yellow, beardless figures with lackluster, lifeless eyes and straight, greasy hair" move with "an uncertain shamble, like the side-to-side roll of a becalmed ship." The women are "old, obese, and faded," he writes, with "puffy faces, dark circles under dull eyes, and flattened manly chests." When you reach for the "extended hand, yellow, cold, and damp, a protest rises from the depths of your soul."[102]

Renegade Realism

The literature of disparagement had its own conventions. Affirming his loyalty to Nicholas I's repressive regime, Nadezhdin conjured visions of political networks and subversive plots that resonated with the conservative idiom of the day. Other writers associated in some capacity with the state employed a similar rhetoric of excited alarm: Pelikan and Mel´nikov repeated Nadezhdin's descriptions of murder and cannibalism. But realism, as much as reckless fantasy, could signal a writer's revulsion and hostile intent. This was an approach favored by those Skoptsy who wished to repudiate the faith and reposition themselves in the social landscape as trustworthy citizens of the world. By providing information, they helped the guardians of Orthodoxy do their job. By revealing secrets, they sealed their apostasy.

The vivid character of such accounts is demonstrated by the sample that Pelikan weaves into the fabric of his own, clinically detached prose. It is the purportedly authentic description of castration as rendered by the man on whom the operation was supposed to have been performed. The voice is identified as that of Matvei Biriukov, a Skopets who had specialized in castrating others but now claimed to repent of his role. The narrative is taken from records of court testimony dating from 1865. Pelikan's purpose in borrowing the insider's voice is to confirm his own and the reader's horrified distance from the scandalous detail.[103] Biriukov's purpose, in the context of a criminal trial, is to recast himself as victim, not perpetrator, and mobilize the court's outrage on his own behalf.

The tale is compelling. As the first step in ritual purification, Biriukov explains, the "teacher" ties a string around the scrotum above the candidate's testicles. "Then seizing a rusty razor, he said: 'Christ is risen!' And with these words my testicles were no longer mine. Though stunned, I did not lose all feeling but watched as blood poured from my veins in two great streams on either side, forming a wide angle. 'All my blood will drain away,' I said. No, he said, 'it knows how much to flow.' But the blood kept gushing, collecting in pools. Finally I grew faint, but the teacher stopped my fall. He laid me on the bed, where the pools of blood clotted. . . . After this operation I suffered for a long time."

In the second, more dramatic procedure, the teacher uses the same rusty razor, which in this case severs the penis only at the second try. The blood takes longer to gush from the wound, but Biriukov falls immediately into a state of shock. Later, he reports, "the pain was awful and remained intolerable for several weeks. I suffered horribly. When I reclined the blood would begin to pound as though someone were hammering a nail where the severed penis had been, hammering so hard that blood spurted from my body and I would rise from bed drenched. How many blood-soaked rags piled up! The suffering made me think that death was inevitable, but the application of candle wax and hempseed oil began little by little to heal the wound, and I felt some improvement." Six weeks later he was back on his feet.

This is a story of stoic endurance in the face of excruciating pain embraced as the key to salvation. Yet rhetorically the stoicism now works to opposite effect. Biriukov lingers over each frightful detail not to glory in his exaltation but to demonstrate his agreement that what he suffered (and then practiced on others) is gruesome, cruel, and wrong. To describe the act in literal terms is to deprive it of transcendence. The "horror story" reverses the original meaning. The physical suffering that once earned him spiritual redemption now, in narrative form, as an act of apostasy, earns him redemption in a secular mode. By exposing the mere physicality of the sacred act, he achieves "innocence" before the law. Betrayal becomes repentance, which exempts him from the status of incurable fanatic, an enemy of true faith and of the national welfare. Biriukov did not, however, control the context in which his story reached the page and he provides no reason for the reversal. In uncovering the secrets of his trade, had he lost his faith, or was the blood-curdling description an act of manipulation? Did he hedge full disclosure by refusing to name names and implicate fellow believers? Did the performance work—was he acquitted? Did he abandon the sect or return to the brethren in the wake of the possibly successful ruse? We do not know.

Whether opportunistic or sincere, courtroom confessions could have practical results: defying the discipline exercised by the Skoptsy community over its members; winning clemency from the court. Another example of the narrative of repudiation from roughly the same period was designed not simply as a form of betrayal or to achieve an immediate practical aim. This renegade's story was made public not by an outsider but by the subject himself, who thus controlled the circumstances of revelation. Gerasim Prudkovskii (1830s?-1909) intended by telling his own tale to enact his separation from the community of his fellows and expose it to persecution and contempt. Recounting his experience in the faith was a gesture not only of treason but of revenge. Telling tales also endowed Prudkovskii with the new identity of a writing self: no longer the willing slave to formula or chanter of holy verse, but the author of a personal script. The revelation comes in the form of memoirs published in a literary journal in the early 1880s, under the title "Voice from the Grave of the Living Dead."[104] Disclosing community secrets, rejecting allegory and evasion for the psychological specifics of a single life, the faceless sectarian pledged to sacred silence becomes a man of letters dedicated to telling secular tales. Yet, the disavowal of what now seemed false belief takes the form of still another spiritual journey through suffering to the Light. Moral archetypes are not easily abandoned.

Whatever the story's formal attachment to the structures Prudkovskii wishes to leave behind, the very act of narration performs a separation. The story's content itself emphasizes the theme of breaking away, focusing on two moments of spiritual migration: his family's original conversion and the reverse coming-to-consciousness that prompted him to take up the pen. The saga begins with the generation of Prudkovskii's parents, who relinquish the relative comfort of wealthy peasant life for the hard road of salvation. Castrated at the age of ten, Prudkovskii does not leave the closed world of the brethren until, turning thirty, he takes a job on the outside.[105] Work on a riverboat opens him to an unknown range of human emotion, including attraction for the opposite sex. Accused by vigilant believers of forbidden intercourse with "the world" (1:51–53, 61, 69), Prudkovskii begins, in anger and sorrow, to question his faith. Eventually he decides not only to abandon the community but to unmask its moral failings and describe its criminal practices with an insider's knowing eye.

The central figure in the first part of the tale is that of Prudkovskii's aunt (never named in his account). The apple of her father's eye, she was one of two daughters and three sons of a prosperous village elder in the Sevsk district of Orel province, the heart of Skoptsy country (Selivanov's point of origin) and still rife with prophets in all the neighboring towns (3:127–28). Setting their sights on the author's father, about to marry, the Skoptsy tried unsuccessfully to save him from his fate. They did not prevent the wedding, but it had unexpected results. Following local custom, someone was supposed to hurl a jug against the wall in token of the bride's expected defloration.[106] This time a drunken guest took unsteady aim and the jug shattered against the head of the old man's favorite daughter. Covered in blood, she sank to the ground, apparently lifeless. The blow was not fatal, but it boded ill. Drawing their own lesson from the event, local Skoptsy women urged the victim to adopt the faith, evading the physical abuse and reproductive dangers of family life symbolized so conveniently by the misguided jug (3:142). Indeed, it must have seemed to the injured girl the perfect emblem of her own fate, no doubt also at the hands of a drunken man, on her eventual wedding day.

In the wake of this misfortune, the anxious patriarch tried to keep his daughter from falling under the sectarians' spell, but to no avail. Despite her defiance, Prudkovskii tells us, the father loved her too well to beat her into submission, as was his paternal right. Instead, he reads to her from Scripture. Rather than weakening in her resolve, she impresses him by her skill in interpreting the sacred texts (3:142–43). The scene, which Prudkovskii could not have witnessed since it must have occurred, if it occurred at all, either slightly before or at the time of his birth, sometime in the 1830s, presents a touching portrait of the powerful old man shaken in his authority by the force of love and frustrated by the equally powerful character of his female child. It is a scene in which two peasants, both able to read, struggle over the meaning of a text.

The old man, who is the tragic figure in his grandson's tale, "pleaded, threatened, and cried bitter tears," saying the daughter was dishonoring his name and depriving him of the joy of seeing his "beloved beauty" safely wed. But her new faith has only strengthened the daughter's already formidable will. "Do what you want, old dad," she says, "like St. Barbara's father tormented her!" She then sings him a holy song about St. Barbara's spiritual engagement to the Lord and her readiness to die in the name of the Holy Spirit.[107] This aunt played a central, not to say fatal, role in Prudkovskii's life, and he clearly takes the father's part in the struggle over her spiritual fate. Yet he is not without sympathy for her plight. Indeed, he comments, the faith appealed strongly to peasant women seeking escape from the hardships of married life. In contrast to the unremitting toil, abusive female in-laws, frequent blows at her husband's hand, and endless pregnancies that awaited a prospective bride, the Skoptsy offered fellowship and the pleasures of holy worship (3:143–44).

This interpretation of the sect's appeal to peasant women reflects the perspective of many educated Russians of the period, who deplored the hard lot of women in peasant households.[108] In adopting such a view, Prudkovskii speaks in the voice of his new persona, the culturally distanced observer. His remarks should not be understood as a reflection of insider status but as an element in the posture of repudiation. The aunt's own version of her choice, as the analogue to St. Barbara's submission to pain for the sake of the true faith, gives her a place in the acknowledged narrative of holy suffering. Her nephew's telling, by contrast, presents her in flight from the pain and travails of human existence; it depicts her alleged spiritual calling as the recoil from physical and material hardship.

It is the patriarch's suffering, in Prudkovskii's view, that constitutes the greater spiritual valor, because it is not of his own making. Mourning the loss of his "beloved daughter, the joy of [his] life," the old man fears his sons will follow her example and reluctantly asks her to leave home. Overcome by longing, he soon invites her back: "Let her pray as she wishes," Prudkovskii imagines him to have said, "if only I can have her before my eyes" (3:145–46). The contagion cannot, however, be contained, and the two elder sons now follow their sister's example. They even try to bring the old man into the fold, but he is unmoved. This indeed was the peasant householder's nightmare: instead of helping him in old age, his adult children were dissipating the fruits of his lifelong labor. Taking his hard-earned property in payment to the sect, "for the Lord's sake," the sons argue that "sooner or later one must leave one's visible dwelling places' and depart for 'the granaries of heaven'" (3:147–50).

The sons are finally arrested, the old man deprived of the office of village elder and sent to prison as well. There he dies, the grandson tells us, of a broken heart, grieving over his devastated fortunes (3:151–53).

Sergei, the youngest son, who has not yet joined the sect but has nevertheless been confined along with the others, is released on the promise to marry. In his nephew's telling, he is trapped by the voracious prophets intent on ensuring the spiritual purity of the clan by making a clean sweep of its members. Somehow induced to have himself castrated, Sergei loses his chance of marriage. Exiled to the Caucasus, he leaves the author and a little sister, along with their mother, without male support, in a state of dire poverty. After a harrowing escape from exile, the uncle returns to die of the horrible wounds inflicted by corporal punishment, bitter over the sectarians' fatal impact on his life, a martyr, in his nephew's eyes, to their unscrupulous zeal (3:160–64). Uncle Sergei thus achieves moral transcendence, in Prudkovskii's tale, through the double experience of castration and corporal punishment. The nephew frames him as the victim of religious fanaticism, yet consecrates his heroic stature in the same terms the faithful would have used.

Prudkovskii's own fate depends on the authority of the headstrong aunt, who survives the first round of imprisonment to return to her dominant position in the family and in the congregation to which she belonged. Until she gives the word, the boy remains untouched, though the threat of castration hangs over his head (3:167–68). The description of the act, when it finally occurs, is the dramatic centerpiece of Prudkovskii's story, and he relates it in unrelenting detail. The specificity marks the narrative as one of betrayal, but its form reflects the persistent structures of meaning that continued to organize his spiritual life. No less than the Skoptsy founding tale and the story of Uncle Sergei, the depiction of his own fate depends for its moral impact on the model of the sufferings of Christ—powerless, childlike (the Son of God), innocent, and raised to distinction the moment he is destroyed.

The agony unfolds in stages. Bound and blindfolded in the larder used for the ritual event, the boy awaits the first blow: "They tied a string around 'the first part,'" Prudkovskii recalls. "One of the Skoptsy stood behind my back, threw a kerchief over my head, and took a strong hold of my arms, which were crossed over my chest, while another came at me with a knife. I felt a sharp pain in the seminal vesicles, cried out and gasped for breath. Afterwards they put me in a tub and applied some sort of salve. A month later I had recovered" (3:171–72). The boy anticipates the second operation with dread, knowing it to be more awful still. The reader's alarm grows, too.

For the second stage, he is led into the special room, where the stove is already burning. Trembling in his undershirt, wracked by sobs, he implores the Lord to help him. In the adjoining room, his aunt waits and his mother weeps, while the brethren sing to the Lord Jesus Christ and the Holy Mother. When the men start to bind his arms, the boy struggles and delays, Prudkovskii remembers, asking for yet another prayer. "Through the thin wall of the larder, one could hear my aunt cough. 'What's going on in there?' she asked in a low voice. One of the Skoptsy stepped through the door and began to whisper. I heard only, 'it's no use, he's not cooperating!' Peering into the room, my aunt started to berate me, but seeing my terror and dismay, she burst into tears. Recovering her composure, she said: 'If you do not want *this* then you are not one of us and we will have no pity on you. Wherever you may go you will be called a half-goat.' The door of the larder closed shut" (3:173–74).

Purified and white as doves, the Skoptsy anticipated their place among the chosen. As the Gospel said (Matthew 25:32–34): "And before him shall be gathered all nations: and he shall separate them one from another, as a shepherd divideth his sheep from the goats: And he shall set the sheep on his right hand, but the goats on the left. Then shall the King say unto them on his right hand, Come, ye blessed of my Father, inherit the kingdom prepared for you from the foundation of the world."[109] This was the threat his aunt invoked: to be neither sheep nor goat, stuck between worlds, suitable for neither. Apparently cowed, the boy suffers the genital violence his aunt once experienced so traumatically in purely symbolic form. His, he makes sure to impress upon us, was literal and unredeemed.

In the second operation, Prudkovskii describes having felt as though "a beast had grabbed me with its teeth and torn out half my belly." Choking with the intensity of pain, the boy screamed with all his might, echoing the protracted ritual cry, "Chri-st is risen!" "Behind the wall," Prudkovskii writes, "there was first sobbing, then quiet. The castrator went out and announced that we had 'flown across the burning river' and then tossed a part of my body into the hot stove" (3:174). Prudkovskii ends by evoking the excruciating pain that followed the operation. "I lay in the tub, afloat in hot blood. Nausea came and went." He bled profusely. "Some excitation deep in the wound caused it suddenly to swell, and I felt strong pressure on the bandage. Then, with a shudder, the swelling shrank and the backed-up blood (you could hear the gurgling) spilled from under the bandage in warm streams. Feeling the symptom approach and trying to prevent the painful shudder, each time I curled up into a ball, but it was useless: it happened over and over. For an entire week I was lifted each morning from a puddle of blood. The dried spots stuck to my shirt and shook against me like jelly" (3:174–75).

Blood was not incidental to the purpose of this rite: "without shedding of blood is no remission," as Paul had said (Hebrews 9:22) and the faithful repeated.[110] Young and healthy, the boy survives, as did a surprising number of children and adults.[111] But soon, having tired of the authorities' continual pursuit, Prudkovskii's aunt and mother turn themselves in. Upon questioning, the boy answers with the prescribed phrase, explaining he had been castrated "for the kingdom of heaven's sake" by Uncle Sergei, now dead and safe from danger (3:177). Like most Skoptsy children, he lied about the circumstances of his initiation, to shield the real perpetrator from the law and protect the faithful.[112]

The insistence on realism in the depiction of these ritual events is a strategy designed to puncture the mystique of figurative language, to dispel the aura of sacred euphemism with which the Skoptsy enticed new converts into the fold and invested the brutal experience of pain with transcendent meaning. Readers are supposed to relive the hemorrhaging, nausea, terror, and despair. The stylistic impact of this narrative is the opposite of the one produced by Selivanov's tale, in which magical images and improbable events intertwine with the recognizable details of common experience (the floorboards in a peasant hut, the bending of rye in a field trampled by human feet, the refreshment of milk warm from the cow) to burnish the circumstances of everyday life with a mystical sheen and testify to the living presence of a messiah. Expressions are formulaic, as if recited in prayer. Personalities are larger than life, devoted either to goodness or evil.

Prudkovskii, for all his psychologizing, however, indulges in caricature as well. The bit players in his tale, various unscrupulous prophets, in particular, are incarnations of malice. On the other side of the ledger, the patriarch embodies nobility and good sense, although he is also shown in the web of tangled feelings. Uncle Sergei is heroic in suffering, though unable to resist the pressure to conform. His mother is an innocent soul, who submits to the faith without truly believing—or so the adult Prudkovskii would like to think: a victim no less than he (2:79). It is the nameless aunt who is most thoroughly developed as a dramatic character. We witness her painfully mixed emotions as she imposes her convictions on the little boy, whom she no doubt believes she is saving from damnation. For all the venom Prudkovskii spews at the Skoptsy and at particularly sinister figures, and despite the prosaic gloss on the origin of his aunt's faith, which reduces her to a sociological item, he never doubts that she is sincere. When reporting the cruel threat with which she cows him into yielding to the knife, he does not establish an ironic distance.

The aunt who compels his fascination, and even empathy, is the mirror image of himself; or rather, he is her opposite number. Resisting her father's authority, she frees herself from family claims and joins a community in which women could be prophets and moral leaders. He, by contrast, eventually finds a voice in repudiating the community she has chosen. He gets into trouble as a young adult, just as the aunt had done in approaching adulthood, when he comes into contact with a cultural system different from the one he has known. The sense of lost alternatives now casts his youth in the shadow of tragedy rather than fate. "I involuntarily recalled my childhood," he notes, "that horrible moment when, bleeding profusely, I heard my mother's sobs. The memory made me regret every drop of blood shed for such a vile destiny" (1:62). Learning to read and write (1:1–2), he equips himself for passage out of confinement. Yet it takes him a while to break away. His aunt's sinister threat—"you will not be one of ours," you will be "a half-goat," neither fish nor fowl, woman nor man, saint nor sinner, mutilated but not saved—must have echoed across the years. Once his mother dies, he finally resolves to enter the world in which asserting one's selfhood is the mark of belonging, not treason.

The former peasant breaks with the ethos of subservience and asserts his independence on the printed page in an act of social transcendence. Yet the old structures of meaning, the traditional terms in which the story could be told, retained the power to invest this secular autobiography with its narrative force. For all the worldliness of the cultural instruments he adopts for the task, Prudkovskii models the figure of his vulnerable self on the original figure of Christ. But he has abandoned the context in which this pathos will do him any good. He is left in double solitude, bereft of fellowship and alone in the world.

It would have been difficult for Prudkovskii to have found a place in that world. Losing the stigma of castration was impossible, in formal as well as physical terms, even if one managed to detach oneself from the fold. Castrated persons charged with belonging to the sect could be exonerated if they persuaded the court that they had renounced the sect's teachings. Even when sentenced, believers might still escape the full impact of the law. Skoptsy in Siberia sometimes petitioned for permission to return to European Russia and occasionally obtained it.[113] In 1905 many took advantage of the imperial decree shortening their terms of exile. But even when shielded from the threat of punishment, because they had been acquitted of charges or already served their time, people who had been castrated were obliged by law to mention this fact in their passports.[114] With elegant self-contradiction, the state penalized not only the act of castration but also the attempt to conceal it. The brethren, for their part, applied pressure on those who tried to break away, subjecting them to various forms of harassment.

One of Prudkovskii's motives in renouncing the world he came from was the desire to find a medium of self-expression. For the next generation of believers, the conflict between loyalty and personal expression was less acute. But the claustrophobia of marginality had not diminished. Whether fervent or disillusioned, cynical or sincere, the Skoptsy were hemmed in by a hostile world, vulnerable to dispossession and displacement, confronted by the outsider's horrified regard. And yet, they did not succumb to repression but persisted as a community for almost a century after Nadezhdin issued his devastating report. How did they manage? What strategies of evasion, camouflage, and adaptation permitted them to survive and even flourish? To answer these questions, we turn to issues of community and accommodation.

3 ❧ BOUNDARIES AND BETRAYALS

I N the 1870s, just as Prudkovskii was pulling away from the faith, the Skoptsy themselves were splitting asunder. Exactly one hundred years after Selivanov had declared himself the Savior reincarnate, another inspired peasant announced himself as Selivanov's successor. Near the town of Melitopol in Tauride province, above the Azov Sea, the tailor Kuz'ma Lisin challenged believers who had grown complacent in their faith. Some, enjoying a prosperous life, assumed that physical sacrifice was enough to guarantee salvation. Some avoided castration altogether. Under the banner of renewal, Lisin promoted both virtue and castration.[1]

Local prophets had competed for authority in the past, but the rivalry had always subsided. This time, revelation led to rupture, and the flock broke apart. Nikifor Latyshev's father was among Lisin's fervent disciples, but not everyone accepted the call. Just as Christ had met with hostility and disbelief, Latyshev explained in later years, so the newest Redeemer was also distrusted. "Christ . . . came from the heavens not always as we would like, in a burst of thunder and lightning, but quietly, meekly, and also powerless and weak as a human being. This diminished him quite a bit in the eyes of those who love power and domination on earth. For this reason . . . faith foundered, and hopes in Him were dashed." When Lisin announced his divine mission, the people "had not expected such a Christ, they did not love Him, and not loving Him, they did not love those who believed in Him."[2] The born-again proclaimed themselves the "victors over nature," but the skeptics denounced them to the police.[3]

Years after the traumatic events, Latyshev recalled the moment of arrest in 1873. His father had laid his worldly goods, two daughters, and three sons on the altar of salvation. Two of the brothers—Nikifor, then

Petr Latyshev with his sons, Fedor, Andrei, and Nikifor. The inscription, in what looks like Men´shenin's hand, reads: "The Latyshevs were sent to Siberia in 1876. They lived in the Iakutsk district, in the village of Charan, 450 versts from the city by the high road to the Sea of Okhotsk." GMIR, f. 2, op. 29, d. 104. (Copyright © GMIR). The photo appears to have been taken in the early 1870s, before the adults were sent into exile, when Nikifor (at center, hand on his father's shoulder) was about 12 years old, Andrei (standing behind) about 15, and Fedor (seated left front) about 20. Their father (seated right) would have been about 50. The white neckerchiefs and white cloth held by the older two were a symbol of purity. The family also included two daughters, Irina (at this time 23) and Pelageia (18); both were fervent believers, as was their mother, Irina Fe-

dorova (about 47). Lisin chose the older daughter as a prophet, and the mother, "when shown a photo of the Redeemer, said she was happy to see him and believes he is on earth." Nikifor, however, rarely mentions the women of the family, despite their intense devotion to the cause. Petr's brother, together with his wife and two children, also joined Lisin's camp. See "Sudebnoe sledstvie po delu o krest´ianakh Lisine i dr., obviniaemykh v rasprostranenii skopchestva. Obvinitel´nyi akt" (Tavricheskaia gubernskaia tipografiia, 1875). GMIR, f. 2, op. 5, d. 223, l. 25–28 (pp. 63–68).

Petr Ivanovich Latyshev and his son Andrei Petrovich. In pencil on the reverse: "This is my father Petr Ivan[ovich] Latyshev and my brother Andrei Petr[ovich], three years older than myself. My father spent 23 years in exile in the Iakutsk region and died at the age of 103 in Aleksandrovsk, Ekaterinoslav province, working in the machine-building factory 'Communard.'" The inscription is signed: "N. P. Latyshev, minor writer, amateur of writing." GMIR, f. 2, op. 29, d. 388. (Copyright © GMIR.) Elsewhere Latyshev says his parents died in 1919, which would have made Petr, born in 1825, 94 at the time of his death. Andrei was born in 1862, and appears to be about 40 in this photo. If so, the photo would date from about 1904, when the family was still in Siberia, and Petr would have been about 80 years old. Both father and son wear the predictable overcoats and clasp pieces of white cloth in their hands. Andrei was murdered in 1924; Fedor starved to death in 1933. Latyshev does not mention the fate of his sisters.

twelve, and Andrei, fifteen—were set astride the "white horse" of castration.[4] Indeed, as Latyshev described the scene, they had been "lying with warm and bleeding wounds, sweetly and deeply sleeping, when as many as one hundred peasant men, with staves and pitchforks, led by the elders and clerk of the village and district, battered down the locked door. At first glance I did not grasp what this meant. I asked myself where these fierce and malicious people had come from. What did they want from us? Why did they want to beat us with pitchforks and staves? How had we harmed them? I remember, there were acquaintances and neighbors who had always respected us as models of sobriety and the hard-working life. Now they appeared as our executioners. We had not, as far as I remember, made a secret of our convictions. Then why these staves and pitchforks, these ferocious peasant mugs contorted with rage? But the ritual of malice and hatred was enacted. We were put under arrest like bandits. After such a delicate cleansing-ablution I could scarcely move my legs and was led or carried, I don't remember which, and together with my brother Andrei driven off to the police."[5]

In 1875, 136 of Lisin's followers (85 women, 46 men, and 5 boys) were tried in criminal court on charges of belonging to the Skoptsy sect. The proceedings of the "monster trial" were held in a specially constructed wooden structure resembling a fair booth, which was designed to hold the numerous participants (including 150 witnesses) and a curious public. "What a spectacle!" Latyshev recalled. Of the adults, 76 were found guilty by a jury of peasants. Some observers were impressed, however, by the dignity and seriousness of the accused: "Not merely in the eyes of their followers, but even in the eyes of Orthodox people, the Skoptsy on trial appeared as martyrs for their ideas, worthy of sympathy and respect."[6]

The trial and his parents' conviction dramatically changed Latyshev's life. But the most important change—castration—had occurred already. Unlike Prudkovskii, Nikifor Latyshev eventually accepted the benefit incurred by the amendment to his physical being. The violence he rejected came from outside. His personal story, however, like Prudkovskii's, was part of a saga larger than himself. And Latyshev, like the vengeful renegade, shaped an identity through its telling, not, in his case, to condemn the world from which he came, but to protect it from the slings of misapprehension. As part of that attempt he later sent his copy of the original bill of indictment, along with the personal manuscripts of which this painful story is part, to the keeping of Bonch-Bruevich. Latyshev was no doubt encouraged to think the tale worth telling by seeing his name in print: in his early forties, not yet having begun to write, he went through the court transcript. "When they tried me I was small, now I am big," he scribbled in the margin, and signed his name, sounding very much still a child.[7]

The Melitopol case was not the only Skoptsy trial that came to public attention in the decades following Nadezhdin's report.[8] Even after the revolution of 1905, with its promise of religious toleration, the repression of sectarians persisted. An official survey of prosecutions under way in the year 1912 shows a total of six hundred Skoptsy being tried in nine provinces.[9] Each time, the police carefully assembled the evidence. Entire communities were interrogated, bodies inspected, households inventoried, neighbors and kin called in witness. Personal testimonies were recorded; collective portraits emerged. The material gathered in some of the trials held between 1910 and 1915, involving together almost 350 defendants,[10] along with the testimony in the Melitopol case, permits us to draw a cross-section of community life across four decades. The ordinary folk who imported death into their own biographies can be caught red-handed in the act of living. With considerable help from one of their own, we get to peer through the looking glass, into the curtained rooms of the believers' "ostensible" dwellings. It is what Nikifor Latyshev, for one, wanted those of us in a different age and of impartial spirit to see.

Sheep in Goats' Clothing

Castration separated the sheep from the goats, as Prudkovskii's aunt had boasted. A form of corrective surgery, it returned males and females to the prelapsarian asexuality disrupted when Eve and Adam entered the cruel flux of time, with its cycles of conception, birth, and death. But the Skoptsy were also a living community, *in* time as well as beyond. White as snow and pure as doves, the sheep grazed the same worldly pastures as the "stinky" goats.[11] They did not flee the Orthodox village but observed local customs and attended church, "po iavnosti," as they expressed it: for the sake of appearances. Contact posed a risk, to be sure. Prudkovskii had been tempted away. But interaction with the outside world was necessary for economic survival. Respect for social norms may also have helped the faithful blend into the landscape of everyday existence. The Skoptsy went to market, hired workers, engaged the services of lawyers, built and furnished houses, divided the household tasks between women and men in the usual manner, and wore respectable clothing when venturing out.

Having one foot in the world did not contradict the basic premises of Skoptsy belief. The miracle at the center of their faith was the return of Jesus Christ in the person of Kondratii Selivanov. This reembodiment echoed and underscored the original meaning of Christ as the human incarnation of the divine. Castration enacted the principle of embodied salvation for each individual soul. In pursuing a double life of inner spirituality and outward conformity, the Skoptsy obeyed the same principle on a communal scale: all-too-human in practical affairs, they were heavenly angels behind closed doors. But how, in fact, did the community manage to survive for over one hundred years, in the face of suspicious neighbors and hostile laws? What held the faithful together, even when spiritual renewal tore them apart? What structures resisted the pressures of time and of cultural contact?

The Skoptsy were accused of undermining family life, destroying the difference between the sexes, and repudiating the love and affection that sustain kinship ties. In fact, the family was the backbone of Skoptsy community existence. The congregations were not composed of isolated individuals, lonely nonconformists unmoored from the harbor of extended kin. The vast majority of adherents were related by blood or marriage to at least one other believer. Relatives who remained outside the fold might appear as witnesses for the prosecution or, more ominously, initiate proceedings on the heels of family feuds. The Skoptsy world encompassed loyalty as well as rivalry and betrayal. It was a transposition, not a negation, of ordinary family life.

Indeed, one could argue that castration reinforced the power of family and kin. Shared stigma held them together, marked bodies made defection unlikely, and children were prevented from becoming adults. The larger structures survived the shift into the realm of transcendence: entire

clans sometimes migrated intact; extended households, including servants and other hired hands, found themselves under a single, heretical
roof.[12] With the exception of their leaders, the first converts in the 1770s
did not, as we have seen, represent the marginal elements in village life.
Nor, despite the example of Prudkovskii's aunt, did the flight from sexuality express a peculiarly female need. Some congregations included
more women than men, but the discrepancy is not overwhelming. Since
men no doubt more easily escaped arrest, we can assume that the actual
communities were probably well balanced. In the Ufa households arrested in 1911, men even outnumbered women. There, two sibling
groups and one couple with children included sixteen males and eight
females. Nor was there a contrast in the generational profile of the sexes:
each ranged from youth to old age, underscoring the familial rather than
personal character of their spiritual migration.[13]

Did women, as the subordinate sex, tend to follow the initiative of
their menfolk in taking up the new life? The trial records show that both
men and women were more likely—and in equal measure—to join the
community in the company of relatives than on their own.[14] Who took
the lead is harder to determine. Some stories were clearly designed to
win the favor of the courts. The wife of Kuz´ma Lisin, the Melitopol
prophet, claimed to have rejected the Skoptsy faith and to have joined
the community only under pressure from her husband and her brother.[15]
The wife of a convert in the Perm case was disappointed when her husband renounced all sexual relations. She herself, she testified, had refused
to convert and enticed him back to their marriage bed.[16] Other women,
by contrast, resisted pressure not to heed the Skoptsy call. Prudkovskii
depicted his aunt pitting her will against her father's and drawing her
brothers along in her wake. Latyshev mentioned an enthusiastic aunt
who tried to join her sister's family in their new convictions. She was
stopped by her husband, who not only beat her into submission but
helped turn his in-laws over to the police.[17]

Female converts often achieved considerable prestige within the
community,[18] and some women elected castration, in the form of scarring or the excision of tissue from their genitals and breasts. Stories were
also told of operations performed on little girls by older women, such as
the case of Anna Shipova, whose genitals were "snipped" by smithy's

shears when she was twelve.[19] Yet the pattern of castration underscores
the central importance of men in the holy brotherhood. Male defendants
in court cases were almost twice as likely as females to bear ritual scars.[20]
In the two largest communities brought to trial, castration was practiced
most intensively on boys and young men. In the Melitopol case, 12 of the
46 male defendants were under twenty-one; 10 of the 12 (83 percent)
were castrated, compared with only 60 percent of the older men.[21] The
1911 Kharkov case involved 142 defendants, among whom 8 of the males
(11 percent) were under twenty-one and all castrated, compared with 85
percent of the older males. In both communities, almost all the boys had
been inducted by fathers or other relatives, who thus ensured that the
children would never start families of their own. Many of the adult males
had, of course, been castrated in adolescence or childhood themselves.
Like Christ, they were fated forever to be sons, never fathers.

The pattern is but an extreme variation on a common theme: all
peasant families subordinated young to older men. The Skoptsy were no
different in perpetuating the authority of adult males over entire households and communities. Some congregations seem to have coalesced
around a nucleus of male leaders. As we have seen, the three Kudrin
brothers, together with an unrelated old man, gathered a following of
twenty-four women, ranging in age from fifteen to eighty. The males
were all castrated, and the majority of females displayed ritual bodily
marks. The senior women served as the spiritual heads of individual
workshops and households. The Kudrin congregation was unusual, however, for its lopsided structure. Most of the women had been recruited to
labor in the Kudrins' various enterprises and were then drawn into the
faith.[22]

Men also took the prophetic lead in the Melitopol and Kharkov
communities. Three initiated the new inspiration that split the Melitopol
Skoptsy: the married, thirty-three-year-old Kuz´ma Lisin recruited two
unattached, middle-aged males as his associates. A younger unmarried
woman accompanied him in a lesser role. Nikifor's father, Petr Latyshev
(aged fifty) was the patriarch of the largest single household to follow the
call. In the Kharkov case, one of the clans replicated the skewed construction of the Kudrin congregation. The Rakov cousins, sixty-year-old
Feofan and fifty-year-old Stepan, ran a farmstead housing eleven women

related to them in various degrees, from sisters and mothers to cousins and nieces. Until her recent death, Feofan's elderly aunt, the "Granny Mitrofanova," had lived there too.[23] Women like Granny and Ekaterina Bozhkova were considered prophets, but they did not rank on a par with the men. Castration, for all that it was intended to clear the anatomical decks, left the patriarchal order unshaken.

How the community constructed its internal hierarchy is not entirely certain, however. Women were treated with disdain and distaste, yet some were respected for their prophetic gifts. As recounted in the passion tale, Selivanov himself had been invested with the mantle of Godhood by Akulina Ivanova and Anna Romanova. It is obvious that men loved their mothers—and probably also their wives, with whom they lived until the end of their days. Castration itself, the sect's distinguishing mark, seems to have functioned ambiguously among the believers. Some who had made the sacrifice disparaged the others as inferior and unenlightened.[24] However, not all the prophets had taken the ultimate step.[25] Their abstention was explained as a way to protect the leadership against repression. Perhaps the power of their spiritual calling made castration seem a redundant means to salvation, already accomplished through divine grace.

Trial depositions indicate that some brethren ceased to view castration as the ultimate goal, and some communities seem to have reverted to a form of spiritual dedication that avoided the ritual altogether.[26] Latyshev describes the "New Skoptsy" who followed Kuz′ma Lisin in 1872 as accepting a more rigorous form of commitment, including the crucible of self-mutilation. Yet Lisin's followers were sometimes referred to as "spiritual Skoptsy" because they emphasized self-discipline and virtue over the physical ordeal. Latyshev himself explained that castration was "good, pure, and worthy of a godly man, but alone it will not save or justify." While he advocated the procedure as the best way to "remove the body polluted with sin," Latyshev denied "that physical castration alone makes a man pure and having attained Holiness; no! God forbid. Those who think this would be making a big mistake. Spiritual purification, spiritual sanctification, that is the real sanctification. That is the real resurrection, the real gift of God."[27]

Then why was castration necessary at all? It was more than an obstacle to sexual misconduct. The experience of suffering and pain was itself a means of purification. Yet boys of ten or twelve were too young to understand the ordeal in any but the simplest terms, as a condition of belonging to the community their parents had already joined. When performed on the young, castration was a form of baptism, designed to ensure the passage to salvation. Nor did the trauma always produce the expected results in adults who accepted its purpose. As Latyshev lamented, the sign could be empty of meaning. Not all converts, moreover, volunteered. Although considered an obligation, the ritual was sometimes described as an honor.[28] It was not something everyone expected to achieve before reaching the next kingdom, for many of the elderly were uncastrated at their deaths. Yet those who had not attained salvation in the flesh, or had abandoned it as a goal, defended the practice with fierce pride when interrogated in court.

In daily life, of course, the faithful showed their loyalty not by confessing their dedication but by shielding the community from prying eyes. The arts of camouflage and denial, as we have seen, were critical to survival. At least in the Orel case, however, some believers seem to have revealed their castration to friends or neighbors, who were attracted by the opportunity for spiritual heroism and undertook the ordeal themselves. But castration was certainly not a condition for joining the faith, and converts may not always have been informed of what lay ahead on the road to perfection. A newcomer might be shocked and turn away or get the evangelists into trouble. The Orel inquest was possibly set in motion by just such misplaced trust, when Trifon's two neighbors exposed themselves in the stream, hoping perhaps to convince him to follow their example.

Perhaps Trifon only invented the tale, for the Skoptsy did not care to advertise their distinction. In addition to circumspection, the appearance of conformity was another important defense. Although they repudiated the sacraments and pledged to avoid weddings and other common rites, the Skoptsy made a point of attending church. In addition, the conventional family structure of their communities worked as a kind of demographic camouflage. On one level, its persistence reflected the pattern of spiritual influence that drew new disciples into the fold and the networks of dependence arising from kinship ties. On another level, the persis-

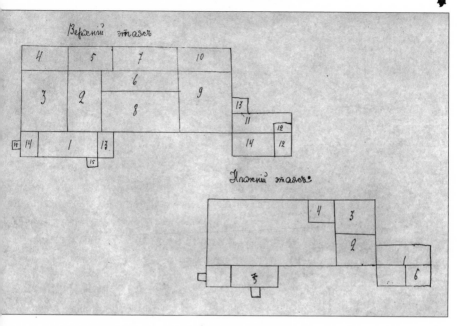

Floor plan of the Ivanovs' house in Ufa. "Protokol obyska v dome Ivanovykh" (February 7, 1911). GMIR, f. 2, op. 5, d. 208. (Copyright © GMIR.) Rooms on the upper floor (top left) include an entry (2), a ceremonial space (3), a living room (4), Andrian Ivanov's bedroom (5), his sister Anis'ia's bedroom (7), the male lodger's bedroom (10), a kitchen (9), dining room (8), and watercloset (13). The lower floor (bottom right) comprises a kitchen (2), storeroom (4), and bedroom for two female lodgers (3).

tence of familial arrangements served a practical goal. It was easy to argue, when asked by outsiders or the police, that residents and visitors had assembled as members of extended households or clans.

Ironically, however, camouflage sometimes had the opposite effect of attracting attention. As part of their deliberately marginal relation to the outside world, the Skoptsy positioned themselves either on boundaries or with their backs to the crowd. Sometimes they erected their dwellings on separate farmsteads or on the fringe of villages. They also lived in townhouses on city streets, among a variety of neighbors. The buildings had one thing in common, however: entryways faced a courtyard closed off from the street or road and guarded by dogs. The dwellings accommodated individual living space as well as common rooms for ceremonial pursuits. The brother and sister Andrian and Anis´ia Ivanov, for example, made a good living as merchants in the city of Ufa. Along with their shop, they owned a large masonry house, which they shared with a close associate and two old women. Its floor plan shows the location of the various bedrooms, as well as kitchens, pantries, storerooms, and a large assembly space, presumably intended for worship. A sign of the Ivanovs' standing as members of the urban middle class, the house boasted a water closet off the kitchen.[29] At the Ivanovs', as in other Skoptsy homes, the exterior windows were shuttered or curtained.

Although designed to foil the curious, Skoptsy dwellings were curious enough to attract attention. They were distinctive in their secretive way. Their inhabitants, too, stood out by virtue of their discretion. A resident of Ufa had wondered at his neighbors' reclusive habits. The next-door household, he had noticed, consisted of several men, two women,

and a girl—nothing in itself remarkable. But they avoided conversation and kept to themselves. He observed that the doors were always locked and was struck by the thickness of the newly erected fence around the courtyard. At night the shutters were always closed.[30]

Like secrecy, personal appearance was also a form both of concealment and of marking. Outsiders, as we have seen, noted the smooth, puffy faces of men castrated at an early age. Iakov Shein's neighbors in Riazan declared that he "look[ed] like a Skopets."[31] Newspapers described the Kharkov defendants as "men with yellow, hairless faces; pale, thin women, horribly wrinkled old crones with low voices."[32] Even Latyshev used similar language, when he recalled how "the pale yellow faces of the purified caught the attention of the curious."[33] It wasn't only their skin that gave them away. When dressed for the photographer's studio or a business affair, well-to-do Skoptsy donned proper attire that was

Harvest of grain on the fields of the Skopets Prokopii Ioakimovich Men'shenin (right corner). GMIR, f. 2, op. 29, d. 122. (Copyright © GMIR.) On the reverse in G. P. Men'shenin's hand: "The harvesting machine belongs to the Skopets A. D. Kir'ianov on the field of the Skopets Prokopii Ioakimov Men'shenin. . . . Workers are standing around the machine. In front of the horse is a nonobservant Skopets (Orthodox); on the front horse sits a Tatar boy; holding the reins is a secular exile; sitting on the machine is a Skopets and the one standing alongside it is, like the first man, also a young, nonobservant Skopets."

Prokopii Men'shenin (1837–1911?) left Siberia in 1906. The photo was probably taken a few years earlier, when he was in his sixties. Aleksandr Kir'ianov (b. 1828) had arrived together with his parents and two sisters and settled in Spasskoe. The information comes from the colonists' own census lists: "Imennye spiski skoptsov i skopcheskikh selenii Iakutskoi oblasti, Olekminskogo okruga" (1902; notes as late as 1909). GMIR, f. 2, op. 5, d. 250, l. 4, 40b., 31. In regard to "nonobservant" brethren, Latyshev commented in 1910: "There are some Skoptsy, especially the young, who regret being Skoptsy and do everything, including cosmetics and massage, to change their appearance not to resemble Skoptsy." N. P. Latyshev, "Nachalo moego povestvovaniia." GMIR, f. 2, op. 5, d. 261, l. 55.

as odd as it was supposed to be unobtrusive. Kel′siev noted the "speckled shirts and waistcoats" of the Romanian brethren, a combination as characteristic in its way as any other folk costume.

Of course, it was not always possible to tell. Gavriil Men′shenin's father had been castrated as an adult. Photographed at work in the fields, he can be mistaken for an ordinary peasant. Kuz′ma Lisin and Petr Latyshev, Nikifor's father, appear no softer than other men of their age and station. But there was often something not quite right about these reticent folk. Knowing that they were different, yet often not sure how, neighbors called them Masons, "fasters" (postniki), or Khlysty; sometimes also Shtundisty (the Russian term for Baptists) or Molokans.[34]

Accusations of religious misbehavior were common in the Russian countryside, even in the late nineteenth century. It was simply the worst thing you could say about your neighbor, to get him into trouble and out of the way. Your enemies might not be sectarians at all.[35] If you knew they were, it was knowledge you could use to keep them in line, and ill will there certainly was in abundance. As Latyshev complained, "The world does not want to have such witnesses to its enslavement to sin, enslavement to the dark, unenlightened life."[36] "Sometimes, there you go, a decent person from the outside world seems well disposed to you. No sooner does he find you are one of the Skoptsy than all of a sudden there's that contempt. For what? The Skoptsy are after all always purer in the flesh, more sober and more pious. Why then hate and despise them? Nevertheless they are despised and belittled. This is their lot on earth, among sinners."[37] But, though Orthodox folk may have rejected the Skoptsy method of salvation and looked with distaste upon those whom it marked, the evidence suggests that ordinary people were capable of considerable indulgence toward the odd sheep in their midst. As one observer of local mores in the southern town of Nikolaev observed, "The neighbors knew [the Skoptsy], but except for pity and revulsion, mixed with contempt, they felt no other emotions."[38] When used with reference to the Skoptsy, the sectarian label acknowledged that some sort of nonconformity was at issue. Local peasants or townsfolk often seemed reluctant, however, to cause real anguish by accusing the Skoptsy of being what they obviously were and inviting persecution.

Tales of disclosure provide a clue to the way the Skoptsy were perceived in the periods of calm between the moments of crisis. The betrayals followed no typical pattern. Sometimes, having repented, believers turned themselves in. Other times the local police received anonymous complaints.[39] Once in a while, as in Orel province in 1772, neighbors alerted the authorities to suspicious goings-on. In Latyshev's community, one part turned against the other. Once the believers' unity fractured, villagers rushed into the breach, brandishing pitchforks and staves, enacting the "ritual of malice and hatred," as the boy Nikifor remembered in later years.[40] On occasion outsiders disturbed the unspoken terms of forbearance that allowed the heretics to survive amongst the Orthodox folk. Such was the case, for example, in a village near Ekaterinburg, where, in December 1912, a newly installed police inspector went for an evening walk in the company of a local peasant. Passing the only house in which light still glimmered, the inspector asked his companion whose it was. The peasant had no difficulty explaining: mother and daughter, recently returned Skoptsy exiles, were no doubt holding prayer services at that very hour. A raid, hastily mounted, confirmed what he said. Had the policeman not been new to the job and alert to signs of odd behavior, the villagers would no doubt have continued to let rumors fly and left mother and daughter safe behind drawn curtains.

The denunciations almost always note that rumors had long abounded. In certain cases the Skoptsy relaxed their guard and their existence became common knowledge.[41] Describing the Skoptsy of Tauride province in the 1860s, Latyshev says "almost all lived in the villages as wealthy peasants and the priest visits them once a year with greetings on the big holidays."[42] Clearly people chose to let sleeping dogs lie until something interfered with the habit of neglect. A wonderful example of such knowing without knowing emerges from the testimony of a local clergyman in connection with the 1910 Kharkov case. In 1909, when he spoke to the police, Ioann Dobronitskii had served as deacon of the village church for ten years. Soon upon arriving he had made the acquaintance of the capacious Rakov clan, known locally as Molokans, because they refused to eat meat. As he now told it, Dobronitskii received a friendly visit from Feofan Rakov's sister Anastasiia and his cousin Ekaterina Bozhkova. Dobronitskii reciprocated the goodwill by deciding to get to know them. He also learned that his own housekeeper, the peasant Ul´iana Galushkina, and her daughter Zinaida belonged to the sect. Ul´iana informed him that prayer meetings occurred in the homes of three families: the Rakovs, the Guzhvas (an elderly father and three grown but unmarried daughters), and the Beletskiis (another patriarch, his middle-aged son, and a male relative). Ul´iana herself had been introduced to the sect by a sister.[43]

If Dobronitskii had reason to doubt Ul´iana's words, he soon had the testimony of his own eyes to go on. Shortly after his arrival in the village, he and his wife paid a daytime visit to the Rakovs. As they entered the building (undefended by the usual dogs), they noticed a pile of shoes and boots stacked in the entrance hall. Greeted by the sour smell of sweaty feet, they heard the stomp of bare soles on the floorboards and spied a group of people through a crack in the door. Disturbed at their appearance, Stepan's sister Marfa stopped them in the hall. The deacon's wife nevertheless made her way into a large room filled with barefoot women in white kerchiefs, who fled at her approach. In the midst of the general alarm, the other Rakovs emerged, wearing ordinary clothing, and politely greeted the clerical pair as though nothing untoward had happened.

It is not clear on what grounds the Skoptsy and Dobronitskii agreed to coexist, but they had certainly done so. When it later came to testifying, the deacon offered a number of details about the personnel and habits of the congregation, but nothing the villagers themselves failed to report, nothing that could not have been common knowledge: the timing of prayer services, who was castrated and by whom, who exercised special authority. Among the women, Feofan's sixty-year-old cousin Ekaterina Bozhkova, known as "Beloved Mother" (matushka), had until recently shared the deference due her own late mother. This "Granny Mitrofanova," one defendant maintained, had practiced "snipping" the genitals of little girls to make them pure for the Heavenly Kingdom.[44] The witnesses' statements demonstrate that villagers were not in the dark about the Skoptsy and their ways. Everyone, including the clergyman, had known about them for a long time. Once told, the stories testify to the silence that went before. While finally discharging his duty as defender of the faith, Dobronitskii also acknowledged his own transgres-

sion: he ought presumably to have alerted the authorities at the first suspicion of what was going on.

Indeed, Dobronitskii's relationship to the group was sufficiently ambiguous to open him to suspicion of more than complacency. Denunciation was a two-way street, and at least one defendant set out in the opposite direction. Matvei Isaev, a peasant in his mid-thirties, claimed that
he had agreed to castration on the urging of the deacon himself, who
had, moreover, been present at the event. The operation had occurred,
according to Isaev, in his own apiary, performed by a man Isaev was no
longer able to name, who had severed Isaev's scrotum with an axe. Dobronitskii had then plied him with a salve. A medical exam verified that
Isaev's testicles were indeed missing, but the rest of the tale could not be
confirmed.[45] The very particulars that made the story ring true also cast
its authenticity into doubt, for these were generic details: the apiary, the
axe, the Jerusalem balsam, the castrator's forgotten identity (contrasting
with the clear memory of Dobronitskii's action), the two weeks to get
back on one's feet. All predictable, plausible, familiar, and for that reason
dubious. What is certain, in Dobronitskii's own telling, is that for over a
decade he turned a blind eye to the practice of the most egregious form
of heresy in his own backyard.

He was not the only clergyman to have done so. The Kharkov priest
Mikhail Nikolaevskii waited four years before investigating a parishioner's complaint that eager Skoptsy were intent on adding her to the
fold. The ease with which he finally breached the inner sanctum, despite
the menace of barking dogs, reinforces the impression that Skoptsy secrecy was a cooperative endeavor. Apprised one day in November 1908
that worship was in progress at the Zolochevskii place, the priest finally
went to see for himself. The father, it seems, had recently died, leaving
three sons and their grandmother. The faithful had gathered to honor the
dead. In the courtyard Nikolaevskii encountered the youngest brother,
Petr, still in his teens, who entreated him tearfully to withdraw. Unde-
terred, Nikolaevskii peered through a window to find a circle of figures
clad in white. Once inside, he was met at the kitchen door by Zakharii,
the eldest brother, pale, agitated and drenched in sweat, wearing a long
white ceremonial shirt, tied at the waist by a blue belt. The twenty or so

guests were similarly breathless and perspiring. One accused the priest of being a "false prophet." After what he described as futile attempts at discussion, Nikolaevskii finally left.[46]

Aside from the ease with which the clergyman managed to penetrate the Skoptsy stronghold, the other notable feature of this tale concerns the origin of Nikolaevskii's information: a close relative who betrayed the community's open secrets. The parishioner who complained that she was the object of zealous pursuit was Zakharii Zolochevskii's sister, Agaf'ia Popova. She had worked for twelve years as the housekeeper for Iakov Kuznetsov, a wealthy grain merchant of peasant origin who was a leader of the Kharkov Skoptsy. She seems willingly to have participated in sect activities until her brother Zakharii tried to pressure her into castration by the time-tested tactic of beating her up. At least that is what she told the priest. Medical exams ascertained that all three Zolochevskii brothers, as well as their grandmother and Iakov Kuznetsov, had signs of genital alteration. Popova had none. But some Skoptsy in the Kharkov congregation claimed that she had served as Kuznetsov's assistant and was called "Mother of God," the designation reserved for female prophets. Despite her protests, Popova's involvement with the sect does not seem in doubt; nor does the falling out that led her to denounce her brother. What she believed in her heart is another thing. Kuznetsov himself had complicated relations with his brothers, one of whom joined the sect, while the other testified against him.

A sibling feud also led the peasant Ivan Razinkov, from a village near Kharkov, to denounce his own sister, Aleksandra Razinkova, as the principal female figure, the "Mother of God," among a group of local sectarians. On the occasion of a visit to their thriving farmstead he noticed suspicious gatherings and observed the participants' pale and sickly hue. Again substituting one pernicious heresy for another, the locals told him that the "Shtundisty" had moved to town. When Razinkov seemed too inquisitive, Aleksandra warned him that his time too would come. Perhaps the brother heard her warning as a threat. Razinkova, who denied belonging to the sect, claimed that Ivan had accused her falsely in order to get his hands on her wealth. Among the visitors to her farmstead were various members of the Pakhomov clan, also riven by bitter conflicts. They included the brothers Nikolai, Kuz'ma, and Iosif, as well as Iosif's two daughters and Nikolai's wife and small son, taught to wave a spindle and cry "Holy Ghost, Holy Ghost, Holy Ghost!"[47] Only the matriarch, Evdokiia Pakhomova, stood apart—proud, defiant, and hostile, testifying against them in court. Nikolai retorted that as long as she refused to join the faith, she would cease to be their mother.

Another parent left out in the cold was Pavel Khodakov, father of five sons, who spoke as a witness for the prosecution in the 1915 Riazan case.[48] As he told it, a classic strategy of child rearing had ended in spiritual catastrophe—or was it an ugly contest over family wealth? Pavel had sent his oldest son Kuz′ma to Moscow, when he turned twelve in 1894, to work in a money-changing shop owned by the Allenov family. Five years later, following the normal apprenticeship route, Kuz′ma brought his younger brother Semen, then thirteen, to join him. Two other brothers, Mikhail and Sergei, came in their turn. They, as well as their brother Iakov, who remained at home, had joined the Skoptsy, though only Kuz′ma had been castrated. When the Allenovs died, they willed their shop to Kuz′ma and Semen, who in this manner improved their social standing greatly. The father, Pavel, framed the story as one of betrayal— by the Allenovs, in the first place, in recruiting Kuz′ma; then by the other brothers, as they set off a chain reaction of conversion. But surely it had been no secret, if only by virtue of their distinctive trade, that the Allenovs were Skoptsy. The old man's indignation seems forced, especially in light of the sons' story.

This was a family in which traditional loyalties failed to hold. Faith was not the issue. Semen testified that his father was often drunk and did not like him. Sergei and Mikhail believed that the old man was trying to squeeze them for cash. The father, for his part, claimed he had lent Kuz′ma and Semen a considerable sum when they took over the Allenovs' shop, which they had never repaid. Now, in old age, just as they owed him deference and support, the sons threatened to leave him in the lurch. Traditional expectations were now empowered by modern means: Pavel hired a lawyer.

But that was not all. Kuz′ma and Semen were the focus of hostility from other quarters. Once the two were arrested in June 1913, their brother Sergei complained to the Moscow police that one of the witnesses for the prosecution, Stepan Abashin, was trying to extort payment

in exchange for the promise to testify in their favor. With the knowledge
of the police, Sergei invited Abashin to the Khodakovs' shop to pick up
the money. Caught red-handed, Abashin denied taking the bribe. When
a packet of money was found in his jacket pocket, he accused the Khodakovs of planting it there. Trying to enlist the forces of order on his own
behalf, Abashin testified that Iakov Khodakov had recruited a number of
his, Abashin's, relatives to the Skoptsy sect. Fearing that his nephews were
next in line, he had helped get the Khodakovs arrested. Behind the cloak
and dagger of modern melodrama—the phone calls, the planted money,
the sting—lie the entanglements of old-style family feuds: Stepan
Abashin defending a clan divided against itself from the influence of the
Khodakovs, equally divided. And the use of the authorities to fight one's
own fights was also far from new: in 1772 the two bathing companions
had mustered the power of the military recruiter to bring their opponent
to bay, and the injured party had retaliated by calling in the church.

Such examples of internecine strife, motivated in some cases by
hope of material gain, supported the stereotype of Skoptsy life as a heart-
less affair, devoid of human affection, devoted to the accumulation of
wealth. As the professor of theology Timofei Butkevich testified in court,
the Skoptsy were supposed to demonstrate "extreme hostility to blood
relatives, not excluding parents and children."[49] In fact, the Skoptsy seem
to have conducted themselves with the same mixture of conflict and loyalty as people outside the fold. At least that is the impression gleaned
from the personal letters seized by the police. Several of these, sent in
1910 and 1911 between Skoptsy in the Romanian outpost of Jassy and
relatives at home, show that private affections survived and business and
family did not conflict.

In December 1910, Il´ia Popov received two such letters from his son
in Tomsk, in which charity, money-grubbing, and piety mingled in unequal parts. "Dear Father," the younger Popov wrote, "I got your letter
and telegram, from which it's clear the die did not fall in your favor, but
what can we do? We must keep up the fight and realize we aren't working to make ourselves rich but for the common good and for the less
materially unfortunate [sic] brethren. Later they will thank the Lord God
for inspiring you and the others, and so thanks to your energy and dili-
gence a free shelter has been established where impoverished older

brethren who can no longer work live secure. God cannot but hear their prayers. . . . The spirit rejoices at the awareness that I haven't spent many years vainly trampling our damp mother earth but have left some little something for my brethren to remember me by. This, papa, is the goal for which we should patiently and consciously strive." After this high-minded prelude, the son turned to more concrete affairs: one Aleksei Nikulin, "God grant him eternal salvation, has agreed to donate 5,000 rubles; M. I. Neverov 1,000, P. V. Efremov 100, S. M. Afanas'ev 100, N. T. Neverov 500, Petr Pavlovich Zverev 50. Vik. G. has not yet said how much but promises to give. . . . By the way, I beg you, send thank-you letters right away, if possible with a gold stamp for such as A. B."[50]

In line, no doubt, with the usual Skoptsy circumspection, the nature of the great undertaking is never disclosed. The son makes clear, however, that his goal was to enlist the wealthier brethren in community projects, which they supported while pursuing interests of their own. Among those solicited by the younger Popov were two business partners, who in 1916 founded the grain-trading firm of "Neverov and Zverev," which boasted the latest in billboards and stationery. Petr Zverev was a success story. In 1896, at the age of twenty-one, he had been exiled to Iakutsk with his father, sister, and older brother Iakov. Even then, in the settlement of Petropavlovsk, the Zverevs were wealthier than the rest. In 1906, after the general exodus of amnestied exiles, Petr settled in Tomsk.[51] Iakov Zverev was also a prosperous grain merchant, who complained in 1911 that passport regulations interfered with his ability to trade and were causing him serious losses.[52] The documents show that family bonds and commercial solidarity intertwined. But the community also felt the effects of disrupted reproductive life. The problem of supporting the elderly was exacerbated by the discontinuity of generations. The Romanian Skoptsy financed an old-age home, and Siberian colonists provided refuge and subsidies for those who could no longer work and had no children to support them.[53]

Nadezhdin was not mistaken in thinking the Skoptsy were united by a network of shared information and economic interest. He was wrong, however, to suppose that love and loyalty were overcome. Indeed, news, money, and personal ties followed the same intricate lifelines. In January 1911, Iakov Labutin, a peasant living in Ufa, received a letter from his son in Jassy, replying to one of his own and commenting on tensions among the brethren connected with the same affair that preoccupied the Popovs.[54] "Dear papa," the younger Labutin wrote, "I waited a long time for your letter and instinctively guessed something was wrong and instead of joy today's letter brings unpleasantness but I still believe we must finish what we've started or it will be a real shame, I believe you, it's hard to resist people who have their own faith, mind, and conceptions. Let's recall the immortal Lev Tolstoi, who described how [Prince] Nekhliudov [in the novel *Resurrection*] gives away his land to the peasants and they complain he is cheating them. No, father. Champions of an idea don't lay down arms halfway. I earnestly entreat you, father dear, do not relent, all the more so as your comrade-in-arms is the respected Iv. A. and with such a man you can take Port Arthur by storm. . . . Now that the business is going well . . . why pay attention to those like Zubkov, who screams like a Pharisee about himself, we need people with property and God has provided enough of them, like Nikulin, who's giving 5,000 rub. . . . No, father, I earnestly entreat you and Iv. A. don't abandon the almost completed affair. The fellows in Petersburg are ready to give. . . . May God grant you wisdom in this generous affair."

At this point Iakov Labutin was being interrogated in connection with the Ufa trial. His son let him know the grapevine was working. The source of the news was one Platon Kiriukhin, who served his fellows as unofficial information-broker.[55] "Today I got a telegram from Kiriukhin," Labutin junior wrote, "saying the Senate has overturned the Kharkov decision: the 127 will be tried again, there's nothing new with us," he added without drawing breath. "The Zasetskiis lost their mama, poor things, now they're distressed, Lazar and Iak. Serg. are coming to celebrate name-days. Papa, don't scold me, I'm having my foot treated by Professor Muratov and Doctor Karelin and a student is massaging me, but the nasty thing still refuses to walk. For God's sake write."

Telling Tales

Courtyards were entered, thresholds crossed, unspoken compacts broken. Strangers and enemies made their way into the inner, timeless space of communal salvation. The faithful then found themselves exposed to public view in the court of law. Because the statutes focused not only on acts or appearances but also on meanings, the defendants were asked to interpret the evidence brought against them. When arrested for belonging to the Skoptsy sect, the unlucky victims naturally denied the charge. They also invented improbable tales to explain incriminating facts. Such ploys can be found in the testimony from 1772, and they multiplied in the legally ambiguous 1820s and 1830s. In the 1875 Melitopol case, the faithful stubbornly refused to implicate their leaders, until some of the followers broke rank and confessed, opening the door to further admissions. Nikifor Latyshev, along with his brother Andrei and three other boys, initially claimed they had performed castration on themselves. Andrei said he had cut himself with a folding knife, which he passed to Nikifor, who did the same. They claimed to have bound the wounds with rags and spread the balsam they had bought in town with money their mother gave them. Nikifor said his cousin Fedor had described how to cut and bind the scrotum. Once the castrator admitted his guilt, the brothers confirmed his story.[56] Like Prudkovskii and other boys, they had remained loyal.

The adults, it seems, were less reliable. As Latyshev later put it, some "abandoned their faith for fear of being convicted of it."[57] When charged with numerous acts of castration, Grigorii Kartamyshev—the prophet Kuz'ma Lisin's right-hand man—repented his errors in court, sobbing wildly, and denounced his friends. As a result, the court punished him less severely than the others. When the sentences were read, the audience was astounded to see Kartamyshev fall to his knees and bow to the ground in front of Lisin, crossing himself with both hands in the Skoptsy manner, and crying out loud: "Forgive me, Lord: I have sinned, sinner that I am." Then quoting from the Gospel according to Luke, he spoke the words of the thief crucified next to Jesus: "Lord, remember me when thou comest into thy kingdom." Listeners would have supplied the following verse, in which Jesus assures him: "Today shalt thou be with me in paradise."[58]

Four years earlier, defendants in the Kudrin trial, even those with suspicious scars, had denied the charges.[59] When the Melitopol defendants were questioned, their answers seemed to indicate a new openness.[60] Indeed, some believers boldly proclaimed their faith in the new prophet. Some could not contain themselves. Filled with "the joy that swept into his heart and . . . the inexplicable ecstasy in his soul," one of the born-again "cried to those around him: open the doors, open the windows! I'm not afraid of anyone or anything! God is on our side! The force of heaven is on our side!"[61] Lisin's followers declared him to be "the Redeemer descended from heaven to earth for the sake of our souls. . . . Our words are not ours but come from on high, from the Holy Spirit." The interrogator was Nikolai Reutskii, author of a recent study of the sect, who listened so intently to their explanations that the faithful dared to hope they had won him to their cause! The Redeemer himself had encouraged them to "speak the truth," Latyshev recalled: "Therefore, having openly acknowledged our Savior as the Deliverer, we more boldly began to tell the investigator, that we are like the Apostles and Prophets of Lord Jesus Christ once were. Therefore it is almost the same to us, whether we live for the Lord or die for the same Lord. You can judge us as you like, do with our bodies as you will, but we will not renounce our calling for the salvation of souls. . . . We gave full rein to our revelation, our acceptance of the Truth as the Truth, of Man as God." These beliefs were enough, Latyshev comments ironically, "for those clever guys in their own terms to establish our abnormality! But the resurrected did not care whether they were normal or not. They believed they had lived to see their Deliverer, their Savior! What could frighten them now!"[62]

Despite the unusual attitude of Lisin's followers, evidence from the post-1905 cases reveals that the ground rules had not changed for ordinary Skoptsy. Defendants usually denied any connection with the faith, even if they were themselves castrated.[63] Testimony recorded during the 1911 investigation in Ufa shows that even the uneducated were schooled in the art of evasion. Some flatly denied any connection with the group: Evdokiia Driamova, an illiterate peasant of forty-one, claimed to be a regular churchgoer, though admitted neither she nor her parents ate meat. "I heard that our lodgers . . . were Skoptsy," she testified, "but I don't know what that is, it never interested me and doesn't interest me now. Are there Skoptsy in the city of Ufa? I don't know."[64] Nikolai Rabeev, an unmarried forty-seven-year-old peasant who could barely read and had worked for the primary suspects for eighteen years, answered in similar terms: "I have no idea what the Skoptsy teach," he announced. "I have never been interested in the Skoptsy sect and have no interest in them to this day." Rabeev claimed to "have sexual relations with women, for which purpose I visit brothels, but I cannot name even a single brothel I have visited. I recall being in one brothel on Bogorodskaia Street, which has since burned down. In addition I use streetwalkers."[65]

Despite Dr. Pelikan's efforts to identify the marks of ritual castration, courts could not rely on physical signs to tell the whole story. The spoken word continued to play a central role in criminal proceedings. The peasants Agaf´ia Sycheva and Grigorii Koloskov, both illiterate, could not deny that her nipples were gone and his testicles were missing. "Twelve years ago," the forty-five-year-old woman declared, "I went to the field in a cart. Along the way my horse smashed into me and injured my breasts and I decided to cut them off. I myself took a knife and cut off my nipples, smearing the wound with the 'balsam' grass that grows in our field. I don't remember how long it took the wounds to heal."[66] Koloskov, a bachelor of sixty-two, took the same tack: "Twelve years ago I knocked my testicles against the pommel of my saddle, after which they became swollen. The testicles interfered with my movements and I decided to cut them off. With this in mind, I went to my apiary in the woods and severed them with an axe. I tied the testicles with a cord, placed them on a stump and hit the axe handle with the handle of another axe. Then I made a bandage out of canvas soaked in butter. I lay in the apiary for an entire day, then got up and walked around and left the apiary on foot a week later. When I was at the apiary no one else was there. I do not belong to the Skoptsy sect."[67]

These accounts are particularly interesting, since the faithful usually avoided describing their techniques to the outside world. Yet here the circumstantiality is mobilized on behalf of denial. Some defendants, by contrast, were proud to admit the faith. "I have heard the charges," proclaimed forty-seven-year-old Nikifor Daletskii, "and admit being a member of the Skoptsy heresy, for which reason I am castrated. . . . It is my deep conviction that not being castrated I cannot be saved and this conviction I have kept to the present time." Castrated only seven years before, his devotion was intense. The confession was not a betrayal. This literate, unmarried peasant, a landowner also active in trade, refused to bring evidence against the others.[68] Grigorii Koloskov's younger brother, Larion, presented a curious contrast with his sibling. Where the castrated Grigorii denied belonging to the faith and blamed his condition on his horse, fifty-five-year-old Larion, unmarried but with organs intact, said he'd heard the charges and pleaded "guilty to belonging to the Skoptsy sect, although I am not myself castrated, because I consider myself capable of fighting carnal desires by fasting and prayer, but for a young man, whose flesh is stronger, I believe it is necessary to take the 'minor seal' and then the 'major,' that is, to be castrated. I have never had sexual relations with women and, like all Skoptsy, I reject marriage."[69]

Those not only castrated but also previously convicted admitted the obvious but took all responsibility on themselves. The sixty-two-year-old peasant Stepan Kornoukhov, convicted in 1875 and pardoned after 1905, spoke eloquently on behalf of Skoptsy truth but insisted that he had acted on his own: "No one induced me to undergo castration. I came to that conviction myself after reading the Gospels with special attention to Matthew 19:12. I castrated myself with no help from anyone else."[70] Arkhip Kulikov, a peasant bachelor of thirty-seven who had taught himself to read, had also previously been convicted and pardoned: "No one induced me to undergo castration," he affirmed, repeating the familiar phrases. "I came to the conviction to be castrated on my own, after reading the Gospels. I experienced castration at the age of fourteen. . . . I recognize the Skoptsy teachings as correct and will never renounce them."[71]

Defendants in the Kharkov case were masters of the self-contradictory confession. In the Beliaev family, the father, Ivan, admitted to having his testicles severed by a certain Vasilii Bludov, since deceased, who had performed the operation at Ivan's behest with a shoemaker's knife. Ivan said he had been convinced by reading Matthew 19:12 and did not regret the choice, but he denied belonging to the Skoptsy sect. His wife, Fekla, said she had been born with the injuries the medical examiner described. She denied having any contact with the Skoptsy and professed not to know whether her husband or son was castrated. To achieve salvation, she admitted, no one in their family had eaten meat, smoked, or taken a drink for the past ten years, and they often went to monasteries to pray. Their daughter Ekaterina said she had never married because she could not find the right man and denied knowing whether her parents or brother were castrated. Her sister Evdokiia also claimed to be unaware of her parents' condition and said no one in the family belonged to the Skoptsy. Their brother Fedor professed to having been castrated against his will. While he was guarding a melon field near the village, Fedor said, he had been approached by a certain Iakov Trofimov, who had urged him to accept castration. Fedor refused but did not object to showing Trofimov his penis. With the trophy in sight, the latter whipped out his knife and severed the testicles, washed and bandaged the wound, and left Fedor to recover. Three hours later, so Fedor recalled, he was up and walking, convinced to this day that castration was the key to the good life. He too denied knowing any Skoptsy.[72]

Timofei Kritsyn and his son denied being Skoptsy, although they were both castrated. The Guslev brothers, Kuz'ma and Il'ia, had been castrated by their father in their teens. Kuz'ma denied knowing any Skoptsy. Il'ia conceded that he didn't eat meat or drink, but said he didn't know whether he belonged to the Skoptsy sect or not. Feodosiia Pakhomova said her genitals had been injured in childbirth five years before. At about that time, she and her husband had contracted typhus, after which they had stopped eating meat, drinking, and having sex. She had no idea whether her husband or his brother was castrated (they both acknowledged they were but denied being Skoptsy). Iakov Trofimov said he himself belonged to the Skoptsy but claimed not to know any other members.[73]

Circumstantial details peppered accounts that were clearly defensive. In the Naboka family, Aleksei denied that the letters addressed to Romanian Skoptsy which had been found in his house had anything to do with him. His wife, Fekla, pleaded ignorance of everything. Their son Roman said he had severed his testicles with a chisel after reading Matthew 19:12 but knew no Skoptsy. His brother Moisei also confessed to severing his own testicles, in his case with an axe, also under the influence of Matthew, but knew nothing about the Skoptsy. Their family avoided meat, tobacco, and drink, but he didn't know why. Anisim Nemashkalov said he had been wounded in the abdomen in 1877 during the Russo-Turkish war and had also injured his penis. The medics at the field station did not notice, because he covered his genitals with his hands and bandaged the wound himself. On returning home, he told no one. Even his wife failed to notice the change. For some reason, he is called a Skopets, but he has no acquaintances among them. He doesn't eat meat, drink, or smoke, because he "feels like it" and perhaps also "for the salvation of his soul."[74]

Families stuck together. In the Guzhva clan, Fedor, the father, admitted being castrated but denied belonging to the sect. His daughter Marina had vowed not to marry as a way to please God and save her soul. She had heard that all the saints were castrated and that Christ had been castrated at the Last Supper and was crucified as a result. Convinced there was nothing better than the Skoptsy sect, she said she would never leave it, having pledged her oath. She claimed not to know whether she herself was castrated but thought maybe someone had done it to her when she was a child. Her sister Elena had no idea why her own genitals were injured and pleaded ignorance of the Skoptsy and of whether other members of the family were castrated. Another sister, Ekaterina, who had never heard of the Skoptsy, thought her genitals might have been altered while she was still a girl by her late grandmother.[75]

Inventing semiplausible details and denying the obvious characterized most of the testimonies elicited by the court. Also ignorant of the Skoptsy, Mikhail Ledovskii had been innocently pasturing his bulls one night in 1907, so he professed, when two strange men attacked him, beat him, severed his scrotum, and then stole his bulls. Dionisii Sementsov had been driving home one summer over a decade ago, when his horse went off the road and collided with some scythes left by a peasant, which injured him in the leg and the scrotum. When his wound became inflamed, he went to the Kupiansk hospital, where a nurse, since deceased, said that to heal the wound he would have to sever the scrotum and testicles. He agreed to have her perform the operation. Before the accident he was already living as a single man, and now he led a monastic life, avoiding meat, tobacco, and drink. Luk'ian Tin'kov testified that his genitals were singed when his house caught fire twenty-five years before. A local doctor had advised him to have the penis and scrotum removed, but he could not remember where he had had the operation. He denied belonging to the sect, but said he followed his parents' example in refusing to smoke, drink, and eat meat.[76]

As officials had long been aware, defendants who did not confess were usually lying. Iakov Labutin's behavior is a case in point. It is clear from the correspondence with his son that Labutin was an active member of the Ufa community. When questioned in court Iakov said his testicles had been severed when he was only ten, at which time he "understood nothing." "I do not belong to the Skoptsy sect," he declared, "and do not observe its teachings. In my soul I am an Orthodox Christian and live by the teachings of Christ."[77] It was this very Labutin, however, who soon contacted Bonch-Bruevich, asking him, for a fee, to appear as an expert witness on the defendants' behalf, an offer Bonch-Bruevich accepted.[78] After some difficulty in having his credentials approved, Bonch-Bruevich appeared before the Ufa Circuit Court.[79] On grounds of insufficient evidence, the accused were acquitted.[80]

Deceptive tactics worked. The law, though in principle severe, was not always an effective means of repression. Happy endings concluded other post-1905 trials. The Ekaterinburg defendants prosecuted in 1915 had almost all returned from Siberia in connection with the imperial decree of June 25, 1905, releasing the Skoptsy exiles from the terms of settlement in perpetuity. Criminal proceedings against the group were dismissed on the grounds that no new castrations had occurred since the original convictions.[81] Charges were also dropped in the 1915 Perm case because no signs of castration were discovered.[82]

The Kharkov situation was more complex. As Iakov Labutin's son had informed him, the verdict of acquittal rendered in October 1910 was overturned by the Senate in January 1911 and the defendants were rearrested. The evidence here was solid. The procurator blamed the outcome on the "jurors' principled attitude to the subject of the crime,"[83] though it is not clear what he meant by that phrase. The Senate agreed that the jury had been misled by the testimony of a medical expert. Instructed to consider the defendants one by one, the physician had pronounced them personally of right mind. He had then exceeded his mandate and his competence (he was not a psychiatrist) by contending that as a group they suffered from mass sexual psychosis caused by "sexual perversion." The central issue, he had argued, was not religion but pathology. Although the jury was told to disregard his remarks, doubts about the defendants' competence to stand trial persisted.[84] Some journalists were less kind: "The case of the Kharkov Skoptsy," one wrote in November 1910, "throws light on the bold, provocative situation of this sect of man-slashers, as it has developed since the laws on religious toleration allowed the Skoptsy to return from exile. . . . Giving these maniacs freedom has not brought them to their senses but only inflicted unhappiness on them and on other people, who might not otherwise have given a thought to the Skoptsy."[85] The retrial began in late 1911 and dragged on into 1913. In the end, most of the acquittals stood, though some defendants were this time convicted.[86] The procurator himself believed that the central issue was neither sexual nor religious but political and argued that cases against the Skoptsy should be tried, under the statute against subversive organizations, without the participation of juries. Elenskii's notorious memorandum, composed one hundred years before, on Skoptsy plans to take over the imperial throne was cited yet again as the basis for the po-litical interpretation.[87]

In casting the matter in political terms, the prosecution was no doubt influenced by the regime's current mood of retrenchment. The push to translate into effective legislation the promise of religious tolera-tion granted during 1905 had by now met with defeat. The crackdown on independent religious expression after 1910 coincided with the resur-gence of conservative political forces and the increased self-assertion of the Orthodox church.[88] Despite this trend, juries in the Skoptsy trials continued to respect the letter of the law on matters of evidence and due process. It is impossible to tell whether their decisions reflected anything other than concern for the integrity of the task at hand. Perhaps they shared the attitude of ordinary villagers who preferred to leave their peculiar neighbors in peace. Jurors may also have been influenced by the feeling expressed in some legal circles that Siberian exile was not the best response to religious or psychological deviation, however disturbing its form.[89]

Voice in the Wilderness

Nikifor Latyshev gives a vivid account of the consequences of losing in court or on appeal. After sitting in prisons for over three years, from their arrest in 1873 until the verdicts were pronounced in 1876, the Melitopol Skoptsy found themselves on the road to Siberia. Kuz´ma Lisin, the new Redeemer, was to serve six years at hard labor, and the fathers of the castrated boys, including Latyshev's own, were to serve four, after which they and the others could expect to spend the rest of their lives on the remote Aldan, Lena, and Olekma rivers.[90] The journey to Siberia was accomplished on foot, in the company of a motley band of ordinary convicts. The condemned Skoptsy tramped the endless roads, "in foot irons, with all that remained of their wealth in packs on their backs." The rest had been taken from them.[91] "What a contrast!" Latyshev bitterly recalled, still indignant at his own kind being mixed with common criminals. These miscreants "had been fettered for the evil committed among the people," while the brethren were shackled "for their love of goodness, love for God and for all that is Holy."[92]

Exile to Siberia was nothing new in 1876. A hundred years earlier, Selivanov had been marched off to Irkutsk, "by land and by water," as the "Passion" said. In the first half of the nineteenth century, the Caucasus had served as another place of settlement for convicted Skoptsy, as well as Molokans and Dukhobors. Content to leave the Molokans in the southern regions to which they were largely confined, the authorities feared that dispersing the Skoptsy to the four winds only helped spread the faith. In the 1850s the exiled brethren were therefore concentrated in a few designated areas, as distant as possible from Orthodox populations.[93] As of 1849, over 900 Skoptsy exiles were distributed across six Siberian regions, almost two-thirds in Enisei province alone. Others were confined to settlements in outlying parts of European Russia. In 1861 the Ministry of Internal Affairs decided to narrow the range to specific spots in the remote Iakutsk region, a northerly territory of harsh climate inhabited mostly by the cattle-grazing Iakut and Tungus peoples. In 1849, there were only 24 Skoptsy in the Iakutsk region; by summer 1861 they numbered almost 600. By 1894 the total had reached almost 1,500 (two-thirds male).[94] They were divided into eleven villages, of which the two largest were Markha, which had grown from a population of 34 in 1860 to 390 in 1894, eight versts (5.3 miles) from the town of Iakutsk; and Spasskoe, in 1894 population 250.

What was the character of the almost mythical Iakutsk region to which they had been consigned, like the Isrealites "sorrowing on the rivers of Babylon," as they liked to think of themselves?[95] The region as a whole, covering 3,500,000 square versts (about 2,320,000 square miles) of land threaded by a network of rivers, icebound for almost half the year, was cold and forbidding. "Dry air, permafrost, thin snow," from September to May, "lumps of ice that never thawed," strong winds, and winter chills of almost minus-50 degrees Celsius—all combined to make the area inhospitable to human life. In 1900, however, Iakutia was inhabited by just over a quarter million people. The vast majority were non-Russian by ethnic origin, primarily Iakut, but almost the entire population was officially Orthodox by religion. In this sea of cattle-herding clans, scattered Cossacks, a few Muslims, and a "shamanite" or two, the exile population constituted a small community of about six thousand. Half were common criminals and their families, a third sectarians, and the rest political prisoners. Of the sectarians, about two-thirds were Skoptsy, the rest mostly Dukhobors. The city of Iakutsk, founded in the seventeenth century on the Lena River below the confluence with the Aldan, was still a frontier town. "In outward appearance," the Russian encyclopedia noted, "Iakutsk looks more like a prosperous village than a city. There is not a single attractive building, not one paved street, no proper lighting. In place of sidewalks, planks have been laid on some streets, but with many gaps. [In spring] the mud is everywhere a veritable quagmire." In 1900, this metropolis had a population of eight thousand, two bazaars, nine masonry houses and almost a thousand wooden ones; six stone churches and eight of wood.[96]

To prevent contact with the urban population, among whom they might find converts, the exiles were forbidden from living within short distances of the towns of Iakutsk and Olekminsk, farther down the Lena River. This regulation made it difficult to earn a living by practicing useful trades that catered to the needs of the townspeople. Agriculture could, of course, succeed only in the right natural setting. Because of poor soil or unfavorable local climate, colonies wrested from the forest in the 1870s and 1880s had to be abandoned, newly erected houses left to rot. Despite prohibitions on movement, many of the first Skoptsy settlers simply fled the areas they were assigned, having lost the bid for survival. In the forbidding Kolyma region, for example, farther to the north and east, in 1874 the snow melted from the fields only in the last week of May. Grain was sown; cabbage, carrots, radish, and turnips were planted. But a late July frost destroyed the crop. The bitter experience was repeated the next year, after which the Kolyma administrator petitioned for the colonists' return to the relatively milder Iakutsk area, to which they were graciously permitted to move at their own expense.[97]

If status in the original Skoptsy communities was determined by spiritual authority, connected—but not always—with one's level of castration, and by membership in certain clans, in Siberia status was a function of seniority. Those who arrived first controlled the best parcels of land and were loath to share with those who came later. The land problem produced internal stratification and internecine conflict. Acreage fit for cultivation was scarce. The local population consisted largely of Iakuts, who needed vast tracts for grazing. Whatever acreage the administration assigned the Skoptsy diminished the cattle herders' share, yet officials wanted agriculture to flourish. The land belonged to the crown and was held in possession by the exiles only during their lifetimes. When newcomers arrived in established Skoptsy colonies, they were often obliged to renounce any claim to plots of their own and to work for the old-timers as hired labor. By 1894, for example, almost a third of the men in Spasskoe had no land at all, while another 15 percent held insignificant parcels. The average amount under cultivation also varied from village to village.[98]

In addition to differences in the amount of land allotted to each individual man for purposes of meeting tax obligations, the obligations themselves were unequal and tied inversely to legal status. The sentence of exile entailed loss of those civil rights, such as the ability to own property, connected to registration in one of the official social estates (sosloviia). Once their terms were over, the Skoptsy were not permitted to leave Siberia, but some were allowed to recover certain rights. In the hierarchy created by these regulations, the two most privileged categories paid the highest taxes: those in exile longer than ten years who remained without civil rights ("poselentsy polnogo oklada") and those who had regained civil rights by registering in the peasant estate and were therefore able to own land ("skoptsy pripisannye v krest'iane").

Taxed at less than half the rate were those with three to ten years' exile under their belts ("poselentsy polovinnogo oklada"). Those in their first three years of exile were tax-exempt.[99]

The breakup of families also meant that households were smaller than the peasant average. Almost half the households in Markha had no males capable of work, and another 40 percent, only one. As a result the Skoptsy hired not only the local Tungus, Iakuts, and exiled Dukhobors, but also their own impoverished brethren. Reporting in 1902 to the Eastern Siberia branch of the Imperial Geographical Society, a sympathetic observer described a typical indigent loner. Exiled as a young man of twenty-four in 1886, the newcomer had been employed by an older spiritual brother, whose house he later purchased. He had also supported himself as a typesetter in a local printshop. The walls of his two-room cabin were lined with sheets of newspaper and photographs clipped from issues of the popular illustrated magazine *Niva* (The Grainfield). His yard contained no sheds or barns. Without the resources to hire help, he sewed his own underwear, did the cooking and laundry, gardened, and tended the horses and dogs, who were his closest companions.[100]

There thus emerged on the exile landscape rich colonies and poor, wealthy peasants (kulaki) and impoverished field hands (batraki). In the 1890s, new arrivals began to resist the dominance of the earlier generation, petitioning for access to the fields, but each succeeding wave tried to exclude those who came later.[101] Such behavior fit the stereotype promoted by radicals and conservatives alike. As we have learned, both socialists and bureaucrats viewed the Skoptsy as a coldhearted money-grubbing lot, torn by rivalry, though also bound by economic ties.[102] Such observations were turned to ideological advantage. But even the Skoptsy conceded that the pursuit of riches sometimes distracted the brethren from higher concerns. Embittered by exile, Latyshev explained, the old-timers had no consolation but memories and their accumulated wealth. Where conditions were hard and resources scarce, the colonists fell out among themselves. "Where there's sorrow and crowding," Latyshev remarked, "there is also the struggle with the spirit of malice."[103] Even in the homeland, divisions had plagued the faithful. Until the appearance of Lisin in 1872, the congregations had quarreled: "The teachers of these ships missed no chance to entice a sheep away from a neigh-

boring Pastor," Latyshev recalled.[104] Then, of course, the new Redeemer
had again split the flock. But conflict in Siberia may also have resulted
from the disruption of clan and family ties. Often relatives were sentenced and relocated together, but exiles arrived in waves, people moved
between villages, and families broke apart.[105]

Despite these fractures and points of contention, the colonists led a
well-organized life. Under the supervision of the local authorities, the
settlers elected elders, clerks, and watchmen. They hired men to oversee
the shepherds and the grain storage. The villages also provided support
for the aged and infirm, in the form of almshouses and pensions. These
structures no doubt provided a framework that counteracted the relative
fragmentation and social inequality that beset the Siberian Skoptsy. Despite the obstacles of climate, poor soil, and the psychological burdens of
their isolated existence, they managed to sustain a successful agricultural
economy. Old Believers, Molokans, and Dukhobors exiled earlier to the
same area had already demonstrated the possibility of harvesting grain
and vegetables even in circumstances as unfavorable as these. In the
1870s, when the greatest number of Skoptsy flowed into the region, the
amount of harvested grain per capita expanded manyfold. The Skoptsy
earned over half their income from selling the grain at market but also,
like the Old Believers, grew vegetables with which they supplied the
local towns, specializing in the hothouse culture of melons and egg-
plants.[106] Men'shenin described their agricultural practices as different
from those of the ordinary village; they were more like farmers than
peasants, he said.[107]

For all the stubbornness with which the Skoptsy held to their beliefs
and customs, even in the face of persecution, they were remarkably adap-
tive. In the case of social structure, they imitated the model from which
they had broken away. Rejecting ties of blood as a matter of dogma, they
in fact preserved the relationships with which they were born. When
these were weakened by exile, the reconstituted households replicated
conventional forms. The most prosperous type were the so-called nests
of males and females, in which each sex performed the customary tasks.
Unlike indigent brethren such as the single male in his newspapered
cabin who depended on his own labor to make ends meet, the larger es-
tablishments often earned twice as much as they spent. The males them-

Female Skoptsy. GMIR, f. 2, op. 29, d. 119. (Copyright © GMIR.) These middle-aged women are both clutching white kerchiefs. They are posing in what seems to be the interior of a well-furnished house. Note the group portrait of brethren hanging above the plant. The photograph shows how these portraits were used in everyday life. It also creates a mirror image of the process of self-recording.

Skoptsy interior: the "red corner." GMIR, f. 2, op. 29, d. 120. (Copyright © GMIR.) This room seems less well-appointed than the one in which the two women pose. The walls are covered with pages from illustrated magazines. Icons hang in the so-called "red corner" (krasnyi ugol). The brethren are dressed in their ceremonial white shirts.

selves did not work but supervised the hired hands. In the 1880s the Skoptsy exiles obtained the right to will their property to younger household members, so that expectations of inheritance bound the generations no less than in ordinary village life.[108]

The prosperous "nest," everyone agreed, was as solid and attractive as the finest city house, with big windows, flowerboxes, and verandas. The rooms contained upholstered furniture, tables were spread with clean cloths, walls hung with oleographs in fancy frames, large clocks, and studio photographs of Skoptsy in groups, dressed in the typical suit jackets with white kerchiefs around the neck and white gloves, as signs of the faith. The thermometer in a typical house might register 22 degrees Celsius, in sharp contrast to the deep frost outside. The bookshelves would be stocked with volumes in impressive bindings. The compound would be cluttered with outbuildings—everything the loner lacked: bathhouse, hut for the hired hands, granary, chicken coop, cow shed, icehouse, cellar, threshing barn, and nearby a horse-driven mill.[109]

The prosperity and taste for luxury testified to the exiles' triumph over hardship. "The wealth of the Markha Skoptsy is particularly striking," noted a Geographical Society report, "in comparison with the half-starved Iakuts and their dispersed yurts smeared with clay, which seem to emerge from the earth." Even in the town of Iakutsk, "it is rare to see such attractive new houses, with big windows, wood and iron decorations on the roofs, carved figurines, glass verandas, and garden plots under the windows." But appearances were misleading; there was something amiss. "Markha makes a strange impression on someone who sees it for the first time," the report observes. "You can cross the entire village from one end to the other, along all six streets, without seeing a single living soul. Behind the solidly bolted high fences you hear the tireless bark of angry dogs on the chain. Sometimes you hear the rumble of horse-driven mills. Occasionally you see the head of a 'Sister' in a white kerchief peering out the window from behind the flowers and curtains. But on the streets nothing moves; there is only a deathly quiet. You hear no songs, no children's chatter, no clever jokes. You imagine that life in this wealthy, cozy corner has only momentarily died down and will revive after an hour or two. But Markha never comes to life, and even when you find yourself among the Skoptsy inhabitants, you always feel the heavy weight of boredom, lifelessness, and the solitude of people who know nothing besides the all-consuming devotion to profit. They work for profit, deceive for profit, take no step and utter no word without profit in mind. The craving for profit does not let them sleep."[110]

Flaccid and sexless as they might have seemed, the Skoptsy were depicted as stern, hard-driving masters. "The Skoptsy are always busy and give their workers no rest. They understand perfectly that only work produces surplus value and do not retain a worker one extra day without work." Making no distinction between Skoptsy and Iakuts, they kept the crew going from before dawn to past dusk. Rising in summer at four in the morning, the hands went to the fields to plow, harrow, cut hay, and gather the harvest; in winter there was threshing, carting, and work on the mill. Workers were fed at six and again at nine, each time with a potato in skins and salted fish or boiled cabbage or something in dough. In the afternoon they stopped for a meal of broth with fish and kasha, and ate twice again in the evenings. Chores kept them awake until ten or eleven at night. "No worker can withstand this harsh regime for very long," commented the report, noting that the wealthy Skoptsy deserved the hatred they earned. "No one loves the Skoptsy. They even hate each other, behaving with complete hypocrisy, calling each other 'brother dear' but ready to tear each other's throats over a brass farthing."[111]

The industry that ought to have won them praise counted as a moral failing. The reporter for the Geographical Society had arrived with the usual prejudices against the "morbidly fanatical," fiercely egotistical Skoptsy, but confessed that "the longer I observed them, the more pity I felt."[112] But he too could not resist the harsh judgments usually rendered against them. It was a commonplace that Skoptsy were particularly ruthless in exploiting their own less fortunate kind, as well as the local population. No less frequent was the reproach that they used the grain market to profit from their customers' needs. The progressive-minded ethnographer Vladimir Iokhel'son, writing in the 1890s, thought the wealthy Skoptsy agriculturalists did the Iakutsk region more harm than good.[113]

It was certainly not the fault of the Skoptsy that they were confined to the Iakutsk area and had to make the best of bad circumstances. The terms of their exile included "strict supervision" by the Siberian authorities, who prevented them from leaving their official places of residence, even for short trips connected with trade or other economic activities. Requests to visit relatives were routinely denied. Until 1905, the Skoptsy were alone among exile-settlers in being excluded by the local administration from enjoying the benefits conferred by various decrees alleviating the conditions of exile or permitting the reestablishment of civil status.[114] A settler-bard turned the tale of suffering and legal frustration into typical Skoptsy rhyme:

> *with us arrested*
> *they did their best to*
> *keep us unfree*
> *with every decree*

for forty years
with our tears
we suffered and grieved
our labors we heaved
the clouds thundered
in our hearts we wondered

. . .

four decrees
sent all around
for us none was found
to our plea, the reply:
to you they don't apply
here you will stay 'til your final hour
declared the evil power.

The four decrees to which the poet referred dated from the 1880s and 1890s.[115] Only on June 25, 1905, as I have mentioned, were the Skoptsy included in the provisions of the manifesto of August 11, 1904, which shortened the period the exiles had to serve before it was possible to register in the peasant estate and permitted them, after nine years in settlement, to return to European Russia (with a five-year exception for the capital cities). By these provisions, Skoptsy who had completed nine years of exile were allowed, upon demonstrating a record of good behavior, to seek permission to leave Siberia.[116] There was still no guarantee that local authorities might not withhold such permission or that later convictions might not send them back again. Old Believers and other sectarians had gained the right to live anywhere in the empire. But even the Skoptsy who had returned to European Russia after 1905 were limited in their ability to move around by passport regulations that remained in force until 1917.[117]

Many Skoptsy settlers benefited from the amnesty, but others remained in exile, and the endless saga of bureaucratic and legal obstruction continued. In 1913, for example, on the occasion of the tercentenary of the Romanov dynasty, a group of Markha exiles pleaded for the sovereign to remove the restrictions that had survived even the manifesto of August 11, 1904, and the decree of June 25, 1905. Their language is quaint and heartfelt and, judging by the grammar, their own.

Settled in the wild taiga of the Iakutsk region the Skoptsy have endured long years our faces drenched in sweat the earth in the blood of our property of honest tireless labor in the wilderness we have created the greatest settlement in the region of Markha we have developed solid grain husbandry such as no other class of exiles until now unknown in the region living a settled life we have endured privation crowding displacement even hunger and only the ray of light and truth the Grace of our Monarch full of love returned in the manifesto of August 11, 1904, healed our sorrow granting the freedom to leave but with some limitations according to art. 43 of the Criminal Code and art. 147 of the Passport Statute. Offering a prayer to the All-Highest so that Grace will be granted by our Monarch full of love and seeing the

Reading the 1905 manifesto freeing the Skoptsy from exile: postcard. GMIR, fototeka, S-32-IV. (Copyright © GMIR.) As Latyshev recalled, the news of amnesty arrived in Troitsk with some delay, when a neighbor returned from town with the surprising information. Some officials may have taken the time to read the decree to the people it concerned, but this scene is clearly staged. The listeners are as grim as the Skoptsy usually appear before the camera. By contrast, when the villagers of Troitsk heard the news, they went wild with joy, throwing their caps in the air and crying out in happy disbelief.

breaking dawn of new Grace with spiritual uneasiness we await the joyful day of the celebration of the 300th anniversary of the Reign of the House of Romanov in February of this year we Skoptsy-peasants enduring exile for some 50 years and settlers who have received peasant rights venture most respectfully to implore setting our hopes on the Grace of Your Imperial Highness we hope that we too peaceful inhabitants of the furthest borders of Russia where we live a settled life busy with honest toil will not be forgotten on the day of the great celebration commemorating the 300th jubilee of the Reign of the House of Romanov and we will receive full rights as inhabitants forever submissive and loyal servants of our Monarch. . . . As the experience of 1905 shows we hope deeply that a ray of light will penetrate even into our unenlightened life and the most gracious manifesto expected in February of this year will give us joy and we will not be forgotten by the mercy of our Monarch full of love.[118]

The petitioners' wish was not granted. The imperial manifesto of February 21, 1913, did not extend the right to travel and relocate to the Siberian Skoptsy. The Ministry of Internal Affairs continued to review requests on an individual basis and occasionally permitted someone to leave, but the right in principle was denied.[119]

Despite its limited effect, the moment of recognition and release in the summer of 1905 nevertheless attained mythic importance, a sign from God, as unlikely in the Siberian wastes as any other form of redemption. The settler-bard of the village of Khatyn-Arynsk celebrated the occasion with a "triumphal" ode: "On the Liberation of the Skoptsy from Siberia."[120] No doubt the poet was familiar with the rhetoric of panegyric, but the blessings he wished on the merciful sovereign include some that any peasant would invoke: full granaries, peace, and prosperity. In an odd gesture of spiritual altruism, however, he also wished Tsar Nicholas II (reign 1894–1917)—called, as was the custom, by his name and patronymic—numerous offspring and a populous land. Perhaps one principled concession deserved another. Absent also from these lines is the chanting rhyme typical of Skoptsy verses. Perhaps for this the occasion was too solemn.

The Lord kept his word
and brought his people out of
Siberian exile
like the ancient Israelites
from Babylonian captivity. . . .
A Song to Tsar Nikolai Aleksandrovich,
our liberator. . . .
He delivered the destitute and oppressed,
and those crying in the wilderness . . .
Bless him O Lord and accept our prayer
shed your mercy on our tsar Nikolai Aleksandrovich
fill his land
with the light of your glory and with all earthly blessings
. . .
May his reign last many long days
and his virtue grow
and his children live long and happily
and his descendants multiply . . .
and may God's blessing
descend on the entire Russian state, like dew
falling on the earth from on high
and all evil and treachery
and bloodshed in the state come to an end
and peace and quiet and calm
in every dwelling joy and peace.
and there be bread aplenty in the Russian imperial land
and people will propagate and
the fruits will stir and life will
flow anew like a river. . . .
The Lord Angel will bare his sword
and save the deliverer from all evil. Amen.

Disbelief, gratitude, and exhilaration affected everyone. When news of the June 1905 ruling reached the exiles in their distant outpost, they received it with joy. One day in August 1905, Grigorii Demiakov returned from the city, where he had gone on trade, with a copy of the decree granting them, too, the long-awaited freedom. "All present sank to their knees," Latyshev remembered, "thanking God and the Tsar for this Mercy. Some ran around the village crying 'Freedom, Freedom for us!' . . . Some threw their caps in the air, greeting everyone with cries of 'Hurrah! Liberty!' The oldsters knelt down sobbing with joy and disbelief that the Prophesy had been fulfilled for them. Work immediately stopped in the fields and houses. The older brethren declared the day a holiday dedicated to praying for the health of His Imperial Majesty, the Empress, and the entire Imperial House. Everyone assumed a festive air. There was joy on all faces." It seemed like a miracle, indeed.[121]

For all the labor they had invested and the beautiful houses they had built in their decades in the wilderness, the colonists took the first opportunity to leave. When it came time to depart, there were thirty house-

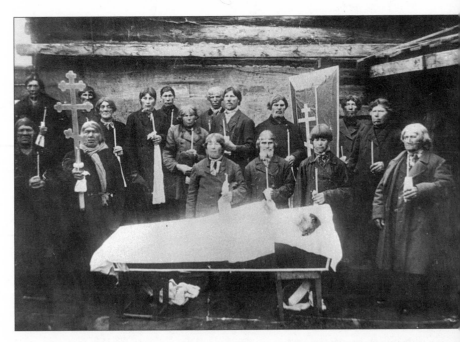

Skoptsy funeral, 1917. GMIR, fototeka, Sm-188. (Copyright © GMIR.) Cf. N. Volkov *Sekta skoptsov,* 2d ed. (Leningrad: Priboi, 1931), 101. The men are holding white handkerchiefs.

holds in Petropavlovsk and thirty-two in Troitsk. Large tracts of forest had been cleared as plow land. "Despite all these material losses," Latyshev wrote, "the Skoptsy who had worked so hard in exile and ruined their health in the forest hurried to leave for some southern place where they could warm their bones. Originally they didn't want to give up their hard-earned property for a song, but finally they sold it for what they could get or just left it behind." Nikifor and his family exchanged their house for a single horse. Kuz´ma Lisin and his domestic companions abandoned everything they owned. The mood was tinged with regret and sorrow. "Not everyone had lived to see freedom." Nevertheless, "the families set out in twos and threes for Iakutsk to await navigation on the Lena River." The elderly men and women trekked almost three hundred miles from the banks of the Aldan to the city of Iakutsk. "Crossing the highest mountains with their string of carts, they could see into the far distance, almost as far as the Chinese city of Peking and the Japanese capital of Tokyo. Looking out over the panorama of forests, peaks, and lakes shining in the sun, the young Petr Zverev cried out: 'Good-bye, you forests and mountains! . . . Where we are going they will hate and despise us even more than your folks do and after a time will perhaps send us packing once again!'" Some released exiles sought refuge in Romania, but most returned to their home villages. Latyshev took a job in a noisy machine-building plant. By 1907, after all their trials and tribulations, the family found themselves back in Fedorovka, which they had abandoned thirty years before.[122]

Inside Stories from the Outer Edge

The portrait thus far constituted of the Siberian Skoptsy has largely reflected the views of outside observers, who demonstrate various degrees of sympathy, always mingled with a certain distaste and disapproval, for the objects of examination. How did the inhabitants of this enclosed world view themselves? In 1900, Gavriil Men´shenin prepared a manuscript titled "Skoptsy Exiles of the Iakutsk Region of Eastern Siberia: Their Way of Life and Economic and Legal Situation."[123] Men´shenin was born in 1862 in Orenburg, later Ufa, province of recently liberated state peasants, Prokopii and Domna, who joined the Skoptsy around 1870. The boy was castrated in 1871. As in the case of Nikifor Latyshev, the critical moment was interrupted by the intrusion of outsiders, this time the police. Gavriil's father was not at home, and he and his mother fled in the cold January night. She and the itinerant old man who had done the job took the ailing boy on horse to Zlatoust, where they met up with Prokopii and Gavriil was able to recover from his wound. By moving from place to place, they managed to evade arrest until Decem-

Gavriil Prokopievich Men'shenin (1862–1930). Photo A. Khaimovich, Tomsk, March 1907. GMIR, f. 2, op. 29, d. 108. (Copyright © GMIR.) As Men'shenin notes on the reverse of this portrait, he was 46 when the picture was taken. He is wearing the characteristic Skoptsy overcoat. A white high-collared shirt shows at the neck. He is robust and not at all effeminate, despite the smooth cheeks. The posture conveys a sense of self-importance. In this same period, Men'shenin wrote of himself: "I have always fought against lies and many did not love me." Letter to V. D. Bonch-Bruevich (May 10, 1909). GMIR, f. 2, op. 5, d. 61, l. 2.

ber 1872, when they were finally apprehended. Along with thirty others
from their hometown, they were transferred under guard to the city of
Cheliabinsk.[124]

Prokopii and Domna were tried in 1874. When questioned, they admitted, in predictable fashion, having been castrated in their own house.
By the clerk's account, they reported that an "itinerant stranger . . . had
stopped for a place to sleep and convinced them of the necessity of castration. They said they had never attended Skoptsy prayer services and
didn't know if any such things occur among the Skoptsy." The clerk
recorded Gavriil's saying that "he shares his parents' faith and follows
their example in external life. If his parents began to eat meat, attend Orthodox church, wear the cross and pray to icons, he would do the same.
He, Gavriil, was castrated by an unidentified old man in the city of Zlatoust, in their own house . . . and does not remember the circumstances."
A medical exam established that the senior Men'shenin was missing his
testicles and most of his penis, his wife her breasts, and the son his testicles. The couple were sentenced to exile, but the court determined that
the boy "understood neither the gruesome and criminal nature of the act
nor its importance in Skoptsy teaching" and ordered him to be raised by
relatives of the Orthodox faith.[125]

Gavriil's parents spent more than two years in prison, awaiting de-
portation to Siberia, while the boy lived with his maternal grandparents
in Ufa. In March 1875, the couple finally set off and, despite the court
ruling, Gavriil was soon obliged to follow in their path. Traveling with
difficulty, his group reached Irkutsk in September 1875. From Irkutsk it
was almost one thousand miles by land to the Lena River, then by boat
in the direction of Olekminsk, where he arrived in March 1876, after a
year's journey. Recalling the reunion with his parents, he later wrote:
"My God, how joyful to see each other once again almost three years
after we'd parted and there was joy and there were tears." He had traveled
nearly five thousand miles. He was now fourteen, his father, thirty-nine,
his mother, thirty-eight. Once prosperous, they now had a pittance to
their name.[126]

The transition was hard. His maternal grandmother soon died, followed by his father's father. His mother's father was murdered by a
daughter-in-law, who killed him with an axe. Between shame and grief,

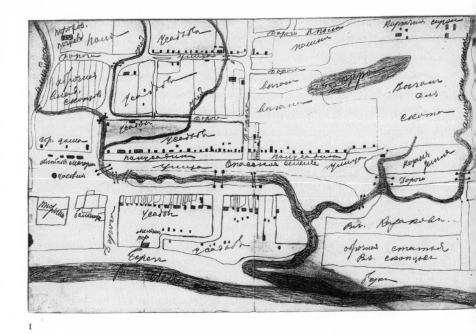

I

G. P. Men´shenin, Plans of three Skoptsy settlements on the Olekma River, 1895. Pencil drawings. GMIR, f. 2, op. 5, d. 274. (Copyright © GMIR.) (1) Spasskoe, on the Lena River, near the town of Olekminsk. Down the center, from left to right, runs the main street, parallel to the small river and to the line of farmsteads and garden plots. In the top right-hand corner, around the lake, are brick barns, plow land, and pasture land. In the top left-hand and bottom right-hand corners are plots under cultivation. In the bottom left-hand corner are grain depots, a chapel, a prison, a hospital, and a mill. (2) Ust-Charinsk, 40 versts from the city of Olekminsk, 25 versts above Troitsk on the Olekma River. More compact, this village consists of a string of farmsteads, a few fields, and a cemetery. (3) Troitsk, 15 versts below the city of Olekminsk. Again a string of farmsteads surrounded by fields. The island is inhabited by Iakuts (whose yurts are shown as black squares), except for the far end, where the Skoptsy cut hay. This was the place where Nikifor Latyshev lived from 1892 to 1906.

Men´shenin explained he had made the drawings in September 1895, while spending three weeks in a town on the Amga River, awaiting a riverboat to take him out of exile and back to western Russia.

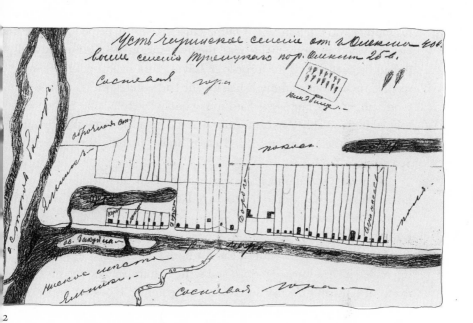

Устъ Чаринское селение отъ г.Олекмо 400...
выше селения Троицкаго пор. Олект. 25 в.

Сосневые   горы

княгинъ

островъ Раздоръ

островъ Блиненъ

обротная от...
Блиненъ

пожня

луга

дер. Закудая

Окра

низкое мѣсто
Блиненъ

Сосневая   горы

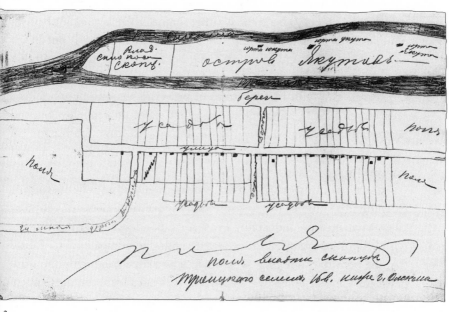

Олекмина

остовъ   Якутявъ

юрта юкута   юрта укута   юрта Якута

спуд повел
скотъ

берегъ

Усадба

Усадба

поле

улица

огородъ

поле

поле

огородъ   усадба

усадба

посл. владенiи скопуа
Троицкаго селенiя 16в. ниже г. Олекма

his mother was often in tears. On the Chara River, he helped his parents clear the land, plant the fields, tend the livestock. In 1881, his mother fell ill and died, at the age of forty-four, leaving him orphaned. Her illness seemed mysterious, as though, he said, she had suffered for "her truth but God only knows, but it was hard to say good-bye to Mama. I cried and sobbed inconsolably for years." After that the men had to cook for themselves, bake their own bread, and clean house. In 1886 they moved to Spasskoe.[127]

By 1892, Gavriil and his father had installed themselves in a solid house. In 1893, they visited the town of Iakutsk, surrounded by cliffs and forests. They toured the nearby Skoptsy settlements, including wealthy Markha. Gavriil was impressed. At thirty, he was a man of some substance in the community. Apprenticed early at both the shoemaking and tailoring trades, he had learned to read and write at fourteen, though his command of Russian grammar was always uncertain.[128] However imperfect, these skills distinguished him from most fellow exiles.[129] They qualified him, while a resident of Spasskoe, to work as a clerk for the local police and as the elected scribe of three Skoptsy villages. He also recorded meteorological observations at the weather station in Olekminsk. At first, he remembered, "knowing nothing, when writing I wrote poorly but all the same got used to it and gave up sewing because I never really liked that work."[130] These occupations not only offered personal satisfaction but acquainted him with the structures of power in the outside world and accustomed him to representing the other exiles. In 1895, he obtained permission from the Ministry of the Interior to leave Siberia for his hometown. Despite his eagerness to be free, he "parted from Papa and my friends, crying and sobbing."[131]

Once back in western Russia, his experience as a go-between prepared him to fashion a role as community spokesman. Between 1897 and 1899, Men'shenin conducted a brief correspondence with Lev Tolstoi, with whom he discussed issues of true faith. He complained to Tolstoi that the brethren were misrepresented: "The Skoptsy, in my opinion, are persecuted and defamed by everyone. I have read a lot about the Skoptsy by various researchers, past and present, which leads me to think there is little truth known about the actual life of Skoptsy and their actual ideals. The Skoptsy in the Iakutsk region live exclusively by backbreaking toil.

They honestly pay all their taxes to the government and community, many attend Orthodox church. They believe unconditionally in the Savior of the world. They obey the government, praying for the sovereign and the imperial house, in their own meetings, it's true, and also for the harvest and for the welfare of the entire world, and so on. They help the poor, in a word, they do everything expected of people who love their brothers. But all the same you hear from all sides that these people are the most immoral, that the sect is the most empty and lacks any ideal Christian feelings."[132]

It was to counter the defamations of "researchers, past and present," that Men´shenin composed his description of exile life. Abandoning the conviction that silence was the best defense and revelation a form of treason, Men´shenin attempted to bring his insider's perspective to public attention. First he sent his Siberia manuscript to *Nedelia* (The Week), a journal associated with the literary review that had published Prudkovskii's hostile memoir twenty years before, but in 1901 it folded. The magazines *Zhivopisnaia Rossiia* (Picturesque Russia) and *Rossiia* claimed that the censor wouldn't pass it, and the boulevard tabloid *Peterburgskii listok* (Petersburg Broadsheet) demanded five hundred rubles. The manuscript remained in the drawer. Had the composition seen the light of day, readers familiar with descriptions of Siberian Skoptsy would have had a feeling of déjà lu. Like other Skoptsy who were able to read, Men´shenin eagerly consumed the literature about them. When responding to misrepresentation, he nevertheless followed the contours of the objectionable texts. Like the reports to the Imperial Geographical Society, which were published as journal articles and pamphlets, his account begins with a review of the various decrees governing the conditions of Skoptsy settlement and cites official statistics on the growth of the exile communities. He repeats the familiar saga of ill-chosen sites, early hardship, colonies that failed, frozen crops, and wasted effort.[133]

Men´shenin's own rendition of the setting he knew at firsthand differed little from the impressions recorded by outsiders. Descriptions of Spasskoe or Markha typically mentioned the Skoptsy houses, so different from anything else around. In contrast to the dark, flimsy huts of their neighbors, Vladimir Iokhel´son remarks, the Skoptsy build their dwellings of solid timber; some were even two stories high. They were

View of Spasskoe settlement. GMIR, f. 2, op. 29, d. 125. (Copyright © GMIR.) At the time this photograph was taken, in the 1890s, Spasskoe had a population of 250. Gavriil Men′shenin moved here with his father in 1886. Not as prosperous as the larger village of Markha, Spasskoe was nevertheless solidly constructed. These houses

notable also for their "large windows with painted shutters and carved decorations."[134] A later account notes the "big windows, wood and iron decorations on the roofs, carved figurines, glass verandas, and garden plots under the windows."[135] Men′shenin too praises the "big, high, attractive houses, with enormous windows, plank roofs, various carved wooden figurines on the windows and gates, flowers on the windowsills, garden plots under the windows, and covered glass verandas. All this can't help but draw the attention of travelers," he says.[136]

have plank roofs and one, at least, seems to have two stories. Judging from the plan, the camera seems to have been positioned at the bottom end of the main street, where the stream takes a turn (note the footbridges).

The travelers whose accounts he may have read usually followed their words of admiration with disparaging remarks. Two Geographical Society reports mentioned, in lugubrious tones, the absence of children's cries, of "family joys and sorrows,"[137] to denote the emptiness at the heart of Skoptsy wealth. Men´shenin, by contrast, notes the absence of another kind of noise. Among the Skoptsy, he writes, "you will not hear the loose drunken songs or see the drunken peasant men, without which you cannot even imagine the ordinary Russian village."[138] Proud of how hard the brethren work and of their mills, workshops, craftsmen, granaries, and livestock, Men´shenin insists that they do not exploit but serve the local population, which can no longer do without them. Relationships described by outsiders in at best ambivalent terms become cause for celebration.

Hard work allowed the Skoptsy to triumph over the harsh climate, as no one could deny. "The Markha Skoptsy," Men´shenin boasted, "became the almost exclusive provisioners of essential products to the city of Iakutsk. It worked out that the local inhabitants each have their own Skoptsy-suppliers, who on schedule deliver all their needs: flour, vegetables, butter, etc. It is to the credit of these suppliers that all their products are of the finest quality, so no one minds the rather high prices. Under

View of Ust-Charinskoe settlement, Olekminsk district, Iakutsk region [190?]. GMIR, f. 2, c 29, d. 122. (Copyright © GMIR.) In this village, as the plan shows, there was only one stre These houses, though snug, are not as imposing as the structures in Spasskoe. In the bac ground are the pine-covered hills. The photo gives a good impression of the winter bleakne

such circumstances, the townspeople live in clover, as they say, and worry about nothing. They are sure the Skoptsy-suppliers will deliver flour, butter, and fresh eggs, and in summertime cucumbers, melons, and other garden produce. And you don't have to remind your supplier that you need such a thing at such a time, he himself remembers what's needed when. No wonder in such circumstances the Skoptsy have become simply indispensable to the people of Iakutsk." In the same way the residents of Olekminsk were dependent on the Skoptsy of Spasskoe for the simplest onion. Sitting in the taverns, mocking the industriousness that so contrasts with their own sloth, the locals forget that their bread comes from grain sown in plow land that has not long ago been wrested from the forest. In fact, Men´shenin affirmed, the inhabitants gained not only from what the Skoptsy produced, but also from observing their agricultural methods.[139] Not surprisingly, Latyshev, too, boasted that Skoptsy villages were distinguished by solid dwellings, barns, and granaries. Some brethren amassed considerable wealth. More productive by far than their peasant neighbors or even the Dukhobor exiles, they supplied the local riverboats with bread, vegetables, and sugar.[140]

Nevertheless, Men´shenin admitted, Skoptsy life in Siberia was not ideal. The vices deplored by outsiders existed, but they resulted from the harsh conditions of exile. "The Skoptsy are accused of avarice, the insatiable love of money. This to a certain degree is true," Men´shenin concedes, "but it is completely understandable. Money is too strong a factor in the struggle with the world from which the Skoptsy expect only insults and oppression for them not to hold it dear."[141] Devoting most of his memoir to tales of administrative abuse, he details the injustice of the laws that governed the exiles' existence: these prevented even those castrated as children, before the age of consent, from leaving the Iakutsk region; they separated non-Skoptsy parents from the offspring who supported them in old age and deprived Skoptsy apostates of the rights associated with the return to Orthodoxy. Writing in the wake of the decree of June 12, 1900, which reformed the exile system, Men´shenin hoped the restrictions on Skoptsy movement would be relaxed. Isolated among themselves, the colonists could not be expected to overcome their "unsympathetic features."[142]

It is surprising, for someone determined to refute the slander of ill-disposed outsiders, that Men′shenin emphasizes not only the distortions induced by the constraints of exile but also problems inherent in the faith itself. "The number of Skoptsy, especially children, who protest against [the faith] . . . is growing with each year," he observes. "Only their confinement in the narrow stifling Skoptsy world explains why there are not even more such protesters. If at least those Skoptsy castrated by their parents' desire or for other reasons not under their control were given the freedom to live anywhere if only within western Siberia, if they were given the freedom to benefit from education and enlightenment, you would soon see the sectarians completely assimilate to the rest of the population." The injustice that most concerned Men′shenin was his own: the case of Skoptsy "castrated at age 10 or 12 and exiled to Siberian settlement."[143]

To a certain extent, Men′shenin, in producing a formal text, distances himself from the community, just as others had done when testifying in court. The tone differs from the more personal and emotional character of two other manuscripts he composed at about the same time, which recount his family's own story.[144] In preparing a statement for publication, Men′shenin's motives were no doubt as instrumental as those of defendants in the dock. Was he not addressing a public prejudiced against the sect and also, in that enlightened age, ready to hear the worst about the tsarist penal administration? Was his goal not to obtain relief for himself personally and for fellow believers? When seeking permission from the local police to return to western Russia, he had sometimes described himself as Orthodox and denied belonging to the faith at all, citing proof that he had been castrated as a boy and brought to Siberia by his parents.[145] Yet, strive as he might for release from legal constraints, mobilizing the tested strategies of narrative evasion and outright lies, Men′shenin found the central pathos of his own life in the Skoptsy faith. Punishment and suffering confirmed this identity, and the story of his Siberian years held him in thrall. His spiritual commitment and role as defender of the faith survived the vicissitudes of two unfriendly legal regimes.

Men′shenin's role was exceptional, as we shall have further occasion to see, but he was not alone among the brethren in wanting to memorialize the saga of collective anguish. The bard of the Iakutsk Skoptsy, whose verse we have already encountered, was one Arkhip Sanin (1849–1929). Born in Kursk province, he arrived in Iakutsk two years before the Men´shenin family. Too poor to get an education, he was possessed of "a passionate desire to learn his ABCs," a goal he accomplished, though not very well, remaining, as he put it correctly, only semiliterate.[146] The triumphal ode to Skoptsy liberation, which we have sampled, was not his first work. In 1902 he finished a manuscript that engages our attention for its curious combination of archaic form and topical content. Selivanov's passion story, a fable of great narrative charm, had often been retold in verse, as we have seen.[147] Sanin used this convention to link the fate of the founding father with the adversity that had more recently beset his flock. The "Skoptsy Passion Sacred Life" (Bytie skopcheskie strady) consists of fourteen sheets in a spidery hand, annotated at the bottom of the page with information about the origins and nature of the faith, the evolution of state policy, the legal terms governing exile, and the experience of exile itself. Echoing the original sacred parable, but without its lyrical appeal, this composition brings the Skoptsy story full circle: affirming the endurance of belief and of a distinctive form of expression, which sanctifies as it transfigures the material of "ostensible" earthly life. Reality was now represented in the form of a scholarly apparatus: in the selection below, a note attached to the line mentioning Article 201 informs the reader that the statute had condemned the Skoptsy to Siberian exile, though this was clearly nothing new at the time.

In eighteen hundred sixty-five
the Second Alexander Tsar
so that his will be done
decreed Article 201
of the imperial penal code
sending the Skoptsy to a harsh abode
in the remotest Siberian outpost
under the strictest guard
the shame was hard
to bear and there
were also formed

◄ Portrait of Arkhip Fedorovich Sanin (1849–1929). GMIR, f. 2, op. 5, d. 352. (Copyright © GMIR.) Typical features include the overcoat, the white cloth, the smooth, puffy face. Born in Kursk province, Sanin arrived in the Iakutsk area at the age of 25. After the 1905 amnesty he returned home. In 1913 he sent Bonch-Bruevich one of his compositions to which he attached this self-portrait, with the inscription, in his own hand: "Portrait of the Author of Skoptsy Passion Sacred Life, Arkhip Fedorov Sanin." He asked Bonch-Bruevich to send a portrait of himself in return. Letter from A. F. Sanin to V. D. Bonch-Bruevich (May 24, 1913). GMIR, f. 2, op. 5, d. 96, l. 2–2ob.

courts of first and second priority
under which police authority
used the force of law
to bring the Skoptsy
even more
misery than before
they tore them from their homes
from the fields and off the roads
to do as they were told.[148]

Even after liberation, the experience of Siberia remained the crucible of spiritual and collective identity. It had confirmed Selivanov's sacred persona, and it provided the narrative pathos for humble scribblers who wished to leave a testament behind. Sanin's curious production introduces secular themes (policy and the law) and discursive mannerisms (the fact-filled footnote) into the distinctive Skoptsy script—quaintly rhymed, crudely rhythmic lines. The mix bears the characteristic mark of representational alchemy, by which the dross of human existence (houses, fields, work, misery, politics) acquires the sheen of allegorical gold. In this case, the content is rather prosaic, and only the attempt to turn it into verse performs the gesture of sacralization. Sanin developed this hybrid genre at exactly the point (1902) when some of his fellows had also begun to appropriate the tools of worldly culture, so as to consolidate communal tradition and at the same time reach a public outside the fold. Sanin himself would have been all too happy to see his compositions in print, as we shall learn. Men´shenin and Latyshev promoted the project of reaching out. The papers they carefully conserved allow us to follow the Skoptsy into the new age.

4 ✎ TESTIMONY OF FAITH

B Y the start of the twentieth century, it was no longer true that loyal Skoptsy defended themselves only by silence and indirection. In the early years of the faith, those who violated the sacred oath had done so for various reasons: to save themselves, to settle scores, to create new identities by negation. When Prudkovskii adopted the language of the mundane world, rather than speaking in riddles or refusing to speak at all, he declared himself a different kind of person. When hauled before the courts of law ordinary believers continued to "twist and turn," evading, denying, inventing.[1] But as they encountered the cultural artifacts of the modernizing world, the Skoptsy embraced new tactics. Some began to see the possibility of opening themselves to the outside as a resource rather than a risk.

Heresy in the Age of Mechanical Reproduction

The new turn was not entirely at odds with old habits. Originating as an oral culture, the Skoptsy used person-to-person transmission to ensure discretion, as an avenue for induction, and as a token of good faith. Outsiders who recorded the sect's beliefs and practices usually did so with hostile intent, to demonstrate its errors and assist persecution. In the early years publication was always the work of the enemy. The reproduction of images, by contrast, had been the work of the faithful from the start. Portraits of the founder and of Peter III functioned as holy icons, alongside the familiar saints. Urban parlors and farmstead common rooms usually featured a table covered in white cloth, bearing artificial flowers, positioned under the icon lamps. Favorites included the Archangel Michael and St. George, both on white horses, St. Barbara, the Savior with the lamb, and John the Baptist. The white horse stood for the purity of castration. Spearing the dragon, symbol of the devil and sexual temptation, also had obvious relevance to Skoptsy belief. St. Barbara, as we have seen in the case of Prudkovskii's aunt, was a useful model. These figures appealed to Orthodox believers as well, but they had special

Iakov Erusalimskii, Skopets, amateur photographer, Romania. GMIR, f. 2, op. 29, d. 120. (Copyright © GMIR.) Posing for another camera, the photographer creates the same mirror effect evident in the portrait of the two spiritual sisters at the parlor table. The Skoptsy were self-conscious about the project of self-representation.

meaning for the Skoptsy, whose repertoire was fairly restricted. Last Suppers, Annunciations, Resurrections of St. Lazarus, Holy Virgins, St. Tikhon and St. Dmitrii (also on white steeds), and St. Panteleimon, the healer, were frequently chosen as well.

At first, the Skoptsy used engraving to reproduce Selivanov's image, but they adopted new technology without any qualms, updating their cultural arsenal in the interests of guarding its resilient core. Photography was a medium they favored. The first Russian art studios opened in the 1840s and achieved an immediate success.[2] The Skoptsy were among those who had their pictures taken. They posed singly or as households and family groups and hung the portraits on their walls. They also went into the business themselves. The three Kudrin brothers, whose case was tried in 1871, had developed a series of enterprises that included, as mentioned earlier, a ribbon factory, horse-breeding stables, a money-changing shop, and a photography studio. Here the Kudrins reproduced the classic portraits of Selivanov and Peter III. They also received a mixed clientele, described by one of their employees as everyone from "Tatars, Armenians, [and] Jews, [to] Princes [and] Counts."[3]

The Skoptsy urge to see themselves mirrored back took other forms as well. The majority of believers had no direct access to the printed word, and the importance of images no doubt reflects this limitation. Yet those who could read savored the literature in which the sect was depicted. As we have seen with reference to Men'shenin, they seemed to crave their own reflection, even in a distorted glass. A visitor to Siberia in the early 1870s noted the exiles' favorable reaction to Kel'siev's Romanian report, despite its squeamish tone, and their irritation with Shchapov.[4] Men'shenin boasted to Tolstoi in the 1890s that he was familiar with all the lies written about the faith and determined to counteract them. In the years after 1905, Skoptsy bookshelves held various learned tomes describing their habits, including the hostile views of Orthodox missionaries.[5]

Literate brethren displayed a homespun curiosity about the spiritual life in general. With the cultural enthusiasm of the semieducated, the more advanced Skoptsy collected a range of printed material designed for a popular readership. Many possessed holy pamphlets. Investigators in the Riazan case discovered such titles as "The Inner Condition of the

ПОЭЗІЯ И ПРОЗА

СИБИРСКИХЪ СКОПЦОВЪ.

АНТИРЕЛИГИОЗНОЕ ОТДЕЛЕНИЕ
ГОС. ПУБЛИЧНОЙ БИБЛИОТЕКИ

Изданіе Г. П. Меньшенина.

ТОМСКъ
Товарищество Скоропечатни А. А. Левенсонъ.
1904 г.

Title page of G. P. Men´shenin, ed., *Poeziia i proza sibirskikh skoptsov* (Tomsk: Levenson, 1904). The stamp, of Soviet vintage, identifies the copy as belonging to the Antireligious Division of the Public Library.

This volume, comprising versions of Selivanov's "Passion" and "Epistle," as well as Skoptsy sacred verses, was used by the community as a way of perpetuating its own traditions. Its publication marked a break with earlier attitudes of secrecy. The book consisted of 314 printed pages, of which the first third concerned the history of the sect and

Human Heart," "On Reason, Faith, and Prayer," "The Voice of True Freedom," "The Truth Is Worth More than Gold," "Conscience Is the Great Tormentor on Earth and beyond the Grave," and a life of the Venerable St. Serafim of Sarov, recently canonized by the Orthodox church. The Kharkov Skoptsy had acquired "How to Know Good and Evil," "Spiritually Useful Reflections," and "The Life and Heroic Feats of the Elder Fedor Kuzmich, God's Great Slave." In addition to the ubiquitous volumes of the New Testament, the relevant passages from Matthew clearly marked, some also collected uncanonical texts from outside the usual range, such as John Bunyan's *Pilgrim's Progress* and Ernest Renan's *Life of Jesus* in Russian translation and Lev Tolstoi's *Thoughts about God.*[6]

Despite this evidence of interest in questions of faith, the Skoptsy were not a people of the book. Truth, as they understood it, could not be found on the printed page, but was a matter of revelation. Accused by guardians of Orthodoxy of taking the language of holy writ too literally, they believed that they in fact penetrated the surface to find the spiritual core: "the letter killeth, but the spirit giveth life." Yet the lettered among them at some point felt the urge to see their own truth recorded in black and white. Knowing that Bonch-Bruevich was preparing a volume about the faith, Nikifor Latyshev remarked in 1913: "Fact is, I'd like to take a look at [your] book on the Skoptsy, being one myself."[7]

Latyshev's comment reflects the turning point in Skoptsy attitudes toward representation which coincided with the new century. For the first time in their history some of the brethren formalized the process of cultural reproduction by using the methods outsiders had mobilized against them or in their stead. In 1904, Gavriil Men'shenin published a collection of verse and holy texts, *The Poetry and Prose of Siberian Skoptsy.*[8]

---

descriptions of the founding prophets (in addition to Selivanov, his disciple Aleksandr Shilov, the founding "mother" Akulina Ivanova, and two lesser prophets, Nastasiia Karpova and Martyn Rodionovich). There were sections on morality, rituals, and verses for various specific occasions (praise, anxiety, sadness, farewell, mealtime). The copy in the State Public Library in St. Petersburg also includes hand-written sheets bound with the rest. The combination of printed and manuscript pages graphically illustrates the continuum of expressive means through which the Skoptsy progressed: from oral, to written, to printed.

By using this volume to guide their ritual life, the faithful codified the process of cultural transmission, while opening it to the outside. The godly, it was now said, included not only those physically castrated but also those "who observed the rules of the Skoptsy sect and its teachings, according to the book *Poetry and Prose of Siberian Skoptsy.*"[9] As Dar´ia Daletskaia from Ufa testified in 1911, the congregation sang from that book.[10] Some of the brethren had personal copies.[11] In Ufa, Andrian Ivanov, who refused to say anything to incriminate himself, told the court that his copy had arrived unexpectedly in the mail. Aleksandra Razinkova, a leader of the Kharkov community, though she pretended to know nothing of its existence, claimed she had found a copy in a railway car.[12] Stepan Kornoukhov of Ufa, by contrast, boasted of the. faith. He explained that "*Poetry and Prose* should have greater significance than the Gospels. In the Gospels the rules of life are expressed allegorically, but in *Poetry and Prose* all the rules of life are explained for people in a manner everyone can understand. . . . In the book *Poetry and Prose* are collected the verses . . . transmitted by the Skoptsy from mouth to mouth and written down by diligent Skoptsy. . . . The Skoptsy consider these verses to be God's wisdom."[13]

The impact of print was, of course, uneven. Dar´ia Daletskaia, born in 1874, sang along with the rest because she could not read. Nor could most other Skoptsy women in Ufa. One-third of the group as a whole were completely illiterate, but almost 90 percent of the men had some level of skill. Twenty years later, a census conducted in the Siberian settlement of Spasskoe recorded under 20 percent of residents as literate; over half had no education at all. Reading enabled the minority to reach beyond their isolation, to follow the news and gather worldly information from the pages of popular journals such as *Niva*.[14] The more pretentious Men´shenin, having left Siberia and returned to Zlatoust, in Ufa province, subscribed to the high-brow *Russkaia mysl'* (Russian Thought). Nikifor Latyshev encountered the Symbolist writer Dmitrii Merezhkovskii in the popular newspaper *Russkoe slovo* (The Russian Word).[15] The data are too sketchy, however, to present a picture of the Skoptsy community as it developed over time and varied from place to place. It is also hard to tell how it compared with the population at large. In one way at least it resembled other groups on the lower rungs of the cultural ladder: among the partially educated Skoptsy males, some developed intellectual ambitions.[16]

In the case of Prudkovskii, such ambition drove him out of the fold. Hostile and aggrieved, he addressed the outside world as a candidate for admission. Men'shenin's purpose, by contrast, was to enhance not diminish the community's worth. Where Prudkovskii used his insider knowledge to escape definition as one of them, Men'shenin did the reverse, adopting the pose of knowing outsider, the scholarly expert, to situate himself as representative of the group. His volume's introduction, which traces the origins of castration in ancient times, the attitudes of the early church, and the early history of the sect, mimics the mode of many an introductory chapter in books written by true outsiders about the Skoptsy. Men'shenin refers to the Skoptsy as "they" and calls the founder a "fanatic." He analyzes the mixture of allegory and historical truth in the founding parable and draws his facts from Nadezhdin's report, despite its hostile tone.[17] If he externalizes his position with regard to what he describes, it is to help the community internalize its lore. Perhaps he also wanted to appease the censor.

Like Prudkovskii, Men'shenin was of peasant background and had also been castrated as a young boy. Nothing in his writing or conduct suggests that he considered his childhood induction an unfortunate event. Nor did contact with the world shake his devotion. Returning, with official permission, to western Russia in 1895, he traveled widely within the empire. After revisiting Siberia, he established himself finally in the province of Ufa around the time of the 1905 revolution.[18] Even before the publication of *Poetry and Prose,* Men'shenin had felt the need to discuss the faith and reach out to the world of letters. In his mid-thirties, as mentioned earlier, he briefly corresponded with Lev Tolstoi, expounding Skoptsy teachings and arguing with the great writer about true Christian belief. Tolstoi was the recipient of hundreds of confessional letters, and often, as in this case, personally replied.[19] In 1900, Men'shenin went to visit Tolstoi at his estate.[20] He was already conscious of his role as community spokesman and intellectual-of-record.

Tolstoi's tendentious novella "The Kreutzer Sonata," published in 1891, depicted the ugly passions that drove a jealous husband to murder his wife. Its explicit evocation of desire, as well as the bleak depiction of conjugal life, had made a great stir among Russian readers. As a would-be intellectual, Men´shenin was familiar with the tale and with the After-word, in which the novelist condemns sexual activity, even within marriage, as intrinsically debasing. He would have noticed the familiar passage from Matthew 19:12, with which Tolstoi begins the story.[21] No doubt anticipating a sympathetic response, Men´shenin asked for Tolstoi's "opinion and true view" of the Skoptsy and "whether they deserve the unflattering judgment of researchers." He also wished to engage doctrinal questions: "I indulge the hope of receiving from you a direct response about the meaning of the chapter in Matthew on which the Skoptsy base their attitude to castration."[22] In reply, Tolstoi took the unexpected tack, given his notorious views, of justifying procreation as necessary for the ultimate perfection of the human race. Faced with the extremity of Skoptsy behavior, others before him, notably Piletskii and Pelikan, had also ended by defending the value of sexual desire. Tolstoi, too, echoed the standard Christian objection that virtue could be achieved only through active resistance to sin; the Skoptsy had misunderstood Matthew 19:12. But Tolstoi was no champion of religious orthodoxy. He had heard the Skoptsy were "moral and hard-working" people, he assured Men´shenin. Whatever virtues they possessed were not, however, the result of castration, an act that disfigured God's creation and violated Christ's injunction against violence. "I have written you as a brother, everything that I think," the writer concluded, "and would be very happy to hear your reaction to my opinion."[23]

Men´shenin was not to be cowed. "I read your letter with deep conviction in the truth of your statements and I rely on your opinion, but forgive me if I burden you again."[24] He pressed Tolstoi for a closer reading of Matthew 19:12. If the Bible did not have castration in mind, why did it refer to eunuchs? He could cite chapter and verse. In Isaiah 56:5, the Lord says he will give the eunuchs "in mine house and within my walls a place and a name better than of sons and of daughters: I will give them an everlasting name, that shall not be cut off." In Luke 20:35–36, Jesus says that "they which shall be accounted worthy to obtain . . . the resurrection from the dead, neither marry, nor are given in marriage: Neither can they die any more: for they are equal unto the angels; and

are the children of God, being the children of the resurrection." In
Matthew 18:8, Jesus says, "Wherefore if thy hand or thy foot offend thee,
cut them off, and cast them from thee." And Revelation 14:4 also had
eunuchs in mind, praising "These . . . which were not defiled with
women; for they are virgins. These are they which follow the Lamb . . .
redeemed from among men."

As for the Skoptsy, they met Tolstoi's own standards. "You say the
Skoptsy violate the spirit of true Christianity. Whom should one consider a true Christian, and what humans have achieved perfection? Jesus
Christ demanded we be chaste but did not demand we reproduce the
human race. He said, from stones I will create a thousand people"—an
approximation of the scriptural, "God is able of these stones to raise up
children" (Matthew 3:9, Luke 3:8). Castration was not the be-all and
end-all, but it was not a hindrance, either. "The Skoptsy do not think the
ideal of salvation consists merely in removing the genitals," Men´shenin
wrote. "At the basis of their teaching is absolute virtue and performing
all the good deeds that Jesus Christ commanded us: that is, be honest,
love your brothers, and be equals. . . . Deeds without faith are dead, and
faith without deeds is also dead. You say that by doing this the Skoptsy
make it impossible to sin, and that's true! They say: Lord, save me, like it
or not! One way or the other the goal is clear: the desire to achieve
chastity, and this opens the way to salvation. . . . One way or another the
Skoptsy can count on God's mercy in life beyond the grave, since they
have condemned themselves body and soul to serving God.

"Excuse me, Count, for burdening you with this, but I am weak in
the literary sense and have no one to rely on, but I completely trust your
dispassion and hope you will say what your inner voice suggests to you,
and I have written all the above not from the fanatical point of view but
to establish the truth."[25] Having begun, in early spring 1898, by addressing Tolstoi as "Most Esteemed Count," Men´shenin was no doubt
delighted to receive a reply in which he was greeted as "Dear Brother in
Christ" (March 11, 1898), a salutation Men´shenin ends by repeating:
"Most Esteemed Our Count, Brother in Christ L. N." (March 31, 1898)
and "Dear Count and Brother in Christ L. N." (May 26, 1899).[26] These
were customary turns of phrase, and love was after all at the center of Tol-

stoi's teachings, as Men´shenin was well aware. But the great writer had responded with interest and respect, which must have gratified the former exile deeply.

The Data Project

Sometime after settling in Ufa province, Men´shenin established a more enduring relationship with another influential, though less exalted, outsider who was busy fathoming the soul of peasant Russia: Vladimir Bonch-Bruevich. Unlike Tolstoi, who looked to the common folk for spiritual wisdom, Bonch-Bruevich had more practical goals in mind. His interest in religious nonconformity dated to the early days of the Social Democratic movement and was inspired by two of its founding fathers. Upon emigrating to Zurich in 1896, the young man was urged by the Menshevik Pavel Axelrod (1850–1928) to study the papers of the late populist Sergei [Stepniak] Kravchinskii (1852–95), who praised the sectarians as "the most intellectual elements of our rural population."[27] Adopting this insight as his own, and encouraged by another Social Democratic elder, Georgii Plekhanov (1856–1918), Bonch-Bruevich decided to write a history of the Russian sects and get to know them. To this end, he established connections with the Tolstoyan exiles and traveled to Canada to visit the relocated Dukhobors. As editor, in 1902, of the emigré Social Democratic journal *Zhizn´* (Life), Bonch-Bruevich argued for the revolutionary potential of the dissenting communities and continued to see them as the progressive element in rural society.[28] To his mind, they possessed three features essential to political mobilization: internal cohesion, awareness of injustice, and experience defending their own unorthodox beliefs.[29]

Lacking any respect for religion but aware of its centrality to peasant life, Bonch-Bruevich hoped to gain a foothold among the marginalized groups by winning their trust. He did this by opposing the views of Orthodox churchmen and soliciting the believers' testimony. In 1908 he published the first in a series of twelve projected volumes based on the material thus gleaned.[30] Decrying the bias of missionaries and scholars, Bonch-Bruevich pretended to objectivity while promoting ideological projects of his own. His tendentiousness offended not only clerics but intellectuals interested in religion.[31] It appealed, however, to the people it concerned. Perfectly positioned in the world of knowledge, affecting a scholarly air but missing the stamp of official approval, Bonch-Bruevich was invited by the Ufa Skoptsy to present their case. He was allowed to appear in Ufa District Court as witness for the defense only, it seems, over the objection of church experts. Not surprisingly, the theologians were unimpressed by Bonch-Bruevich's documentary volumes, his only claim to authority in this domain. His fault, they said, was to "present sectarianism mainly through the compositions and information provided by the sectarians themselves, expressing their point of view. [He] takes everything they say and write about themselves as the truth."[32] It was for this very reason that the Skoptsy had responded to Bonch-Bruevich's advances.

Bonch-Bruevich had obtained copies of Tolstoi's letters to Men'shenin from an intermediary and published them in the first volume of the series on the sects.[33] In 1909 he wrote Men'shenin directly and received a "delighted" reply. Men'shenin had read about the data project in *Russkaia mysl'* and thought of offering his services. He had lots of material on hand, including photographs of "individual types" and sixty-two taken in Iakutsk (useful as illustrations), as well as the rough drafts of his own memoirs. He was too attached, however, to the letters from Count Tolstoi to send them right away.[34] Promising to circulate the call for information, he encouraged Bonch-Bruevich to hurry with the book, which the brethren hoped would present them as they really were. He begged him not to use the material they sent to "write the same abuse and falsehoods as other writers had."[35] After a century of concealment, the need for exposure now seemed urgent. "I am sincerely pleased that you are preparing a volume on the Skoptsy," Men'shenin assured him. "I fully expect the edition will turn out well. I suggest it should be published in a sizable quantity, because the demand will be considerable, if not immediately then once people find out."[36]

Men'shenin not only welcomed the occasion for publicity. Thinking that the mediation of outsiders could work to the community's advantage, he invited Bonch-Bruevich to improve on the supposedly authentic material he was being sent. In *Poetry and Prose*, Men'shenin had published a version of Selivanov's "Passion" that followed the text first printed in Nadezhdin's report. Now he asked if Bonch-Bruevich could not rewrite Selivanov's other text, the so-called Epistle, "in a literary style." Men´shenin did not consider Selivanov "a simple mortal" and was therefore convinced the "Epistle" had been composed not by him but by his followers.[37] The exact wording was not sacrosanct. These Skoptsy intellectuals did not want to seem folkloric or quaint. If someone had suggested that Selivanov's "Passion" had been enhanced by expert editing at the hands of Vladimir Dal´, the possibility might not have distressed them. They had always claimed to live by the spirit, not the letter, of holy writ. Habits of euphemism would only have strengthened their disregard for purity of expression.

The Skoptsy seemed to realize that cultural boundaries were porous. They knew that they were deficient in skills and resources and borrowed useful products for purposes of their own (one thinks of Men´shenin cribbing from Nadezhdin). They did not see the cachet of folk simplicity as something to profit from. They saw themselves not as curiosities but as repositories of a Truth that observed no social location. After the data project was already under way, Bonch-Bruevich took credit for having convinced the Skoptsy to shed their secrecy.[38] But Men´shenin had already violated the oath against disclosure, trying in vain to get his Siberian manuscript published and succeeding finally in seeing *Poetry and Prose* into print. Bonch-Bruevich may have seemed an acceptable collaborator because he rejected the secular and clerical authorities responsible for blackening the Skoptsy name. Men´shenin never indicated, before 1917, that he understood anything about Bolshevik ideas. He valued the connection in his own terms, repeatedly urging Bonch-Bruevich to complete the promised scholarly work and publish the sect's true story.[39] The possibility of publication, moreover, gave Men´shenin himself a reason to write: he was constantly planning his memoirs and explaining why he was distracted by the demands of everyday life.[40] It also allowed him to fulfill his calling as go-between. Known to the brethren as an emissary, he made the rounds of bureaucratic offices to petition on their behalf.[41] Some disagreed with Men´shenin's views; Latyshev once referred to him as a member of the "hostile camp of Old Skopchestvo."[42] Yet the faithful appealed to him as the most educated and informed of their number.[43] Impressed by his accomplishments and connections, the people Men´shenin contacted agreed to donate papers and photographs to Bonch-Bruevich's publication scheme.

The same networking talents that bound the Skoptsy in their commercial dealings facilitated the collection of documents. The case of Arkhip Sanin shows how the process worked. In April 1913, Sanin, by then living in Kursk province, wrote Bonch-Bruevich, explaining he had been contacted by a certain Platon Kiriukhin, who "gave me your address and asked that I send you some information about the life of exiled Iakutsk Skoptsy and their treatment by the Iakutsk administration. Since I've been exiled myself, I have sent my own crude and [illeg.] composition about what I've been able to collect over 34 years of exile in Iakutsk." Sanin also included an autobiographical sketch and a photographic self-portrait.[44] Kiriukhin (1847–1922), a peasant originally from Riazan province, had been released from Siberia in 1900, thanks to the intercession of the critic Vladimir Stasov (1824–1906) and the eminent jurist Anatolii Koni (1844–1924). Tolstoi had mobilized the distinguished pair to pressure the Ministry of Internal Affairs after Men´shenin asked him to intervene on Kiriukhin's behalf.[45] It was the same Kiriukhin who in 1911 had telegrammed the younger Labutin with news about the Kharkov trial.

On receiving Sanin's letter, Bonch-Bruevich immediately wrote back.[46] Sanin then sent him the manuscript of "Skoptsy Passion Sacred Life," composed ten years before, and a more recent treatise titled "What the Skoptsy Believe."[47] All this writing was "hard work," Sanin emphasized, "it doesn't just happen. Each verse or page must be rethought and rewritten twice or three times. This takes quite a bit of mental and physical labor and trouble. I never learned to spell and I am already 65 years old." He suggested raising a subscription among the wealthier Skoptsy to support publication of the book, an idea Bonch-Bruevich rejected.[48]

Sanin wanted recognition, but also a response. The relationship itself gave him a sense of importance. Though he still felt he was breaking the rules of the faith, the enterprise fulfilled a deep personal ambition. "I beg you, Vladimir Dmitrievich, when you get this letter and have read the manuscript I sent let me know in return and describe all your views in detail meanwhile keep this letter a secret from our foolish Skoptsy, better that way, even from Kiriukhin." Despite his poor education, Sanin aspired to authorship: "If you find something suitable for printing, add it to my earlier manuscript, the 'Skoptsy Passion Sacred Life.'"[49] About the "edifying composition," he asked Bonch-Bruevich: "Whatever is false or incorrect, please correct, I wrote fast . . . and cracked my brains, I think it is interesting but it may not suit you. . . . It would be nice if, besides a big general book about the Skoptsy, you would publish separately in a special small booklet the collection of my compositions. . . . Again I beg you to describe for me in detail what is suitable for print and what is not."[50] The connection was a two-way street: "You asked for my portrait," he writes. Would Bonch-Bruevich send a portrait of himself, "so I can get to know you and see you."[51]

Renewal and Rebirth

The desire to express oneself in writing and see oneself in print and to win the approval of a figure of cultural authority characterized all the Skoptsy chroniclers. Bonch-Bruevich did not, however, warm to this particular correspondent. His most fruitful contacts proved to be Men'shenin and his eager recruit, Nikifor Latyshev. Wishing to include as much as possible in the record of Skoptsy life, Men'shenin contacted the latter in 1910, asking for information about Kuz'ma Lisin's breakaway movement.[52] Men'shenin had earlier enlisted Latyshev in another data-collecting venture: a demographic profile of the Siberian colonies. The original link between the two was apparently indirect. When the house-hold registers of Troitsk and Petropavlovsk on the Aldan River had been compiled (sometime between 1902 and 1909), Latyshev asked a friend to forward them to Men'shenin, along with "my respects." "I think his plan is excellent. Let him do his job and enter me, as secretary, in the lists of the truth-seekers. Your humble servant, N."[53] At the same time as he was composing the inventories, and certainly before he received Men'shenin's letter, Latyshev had also begun recording his personal life story, including the saga of his family's travails.[54] Along with Men'shenin's collection of photographs and hand-drawn maps of the Skoptsy settlements around Iakutsk, Latyshev's papers ended up in Bonch-Bruevich's keeping.

The decision to contribute to the historical record was not reached

Skoptsy self-census, recorded by Nikifor Latyshev. "Imennye spiski skoptsov i skopcheskikh selenii Iakutskoi oblasti, Olekminskogo okruga" (1902; notes as late as 1909). GMIR, f. 2, op. 5, d. 250. (Copyright © GMIR.) Residents are listed in alphabetical order by family name, followed by their age, date of arrival, and fate. Some left after the amnesty, some died (l. 24). Latyshev was responsible for compiling the lists. At the end of the list for Petropavlovsk, he wrote: "It seems they're all here. If I've forgotten anyone, may they rest in peace" (l. 25).

without a certain hesitation. Latyshev at first doubted the wisdom of divulging the discord that had arisen among the Skoptsy. Since the coming of the new prophet, he wrote Men'shenin, "the light of truth has still not broken through, although it sparkles like lightning, brightening the vista from horizon to horizon. The [Redeemer's] appearance (what you call the movement) was heard in all the ships and congregations. Everyone listened to the teachers and preachers and learned about it. But not everyone accepted it." If too much were revealed, outsiders might laugh at the "simple, even silly" folk, saying "the Skoptsy await their Savior, the Son of God, according to their faith. But then they squabble: some say he has come, while others don't believe it!" Some brethren indeed condemned the very idea of self-exposure, including Men'shenin's volume, as harmful. But "you and I," Latyshev assured his "dear friend Gavriil Prokopievich, would have no trouble going into print." As men of letters, he inferred, they were more enlightened than the rest.[55]

Latyshev was impressed when Men'shenin informed him of Bonch-Bruevich's proposed study of the Skoptsy. He did not decide to make direct contact, however, until December 1912, after reading a newspaper account of Bonch-Bruevich's role in the acquittal of the Ufa defendants. At that point, he wrote to offer his services as a source of information about the "hidden secrets" of the Skoptsy faith. "I am not mentally ill," he assured his new correspondent, anticipating an unbeliever's fears, "as people who talk about God and the truth are usually considered."[56] He had already given Men'shenin some of his manuscripts, which he intended for Bonch-Bruevich to keep and consider his own.[57] By 1915, Latyshev had completed four notebooks recounting his life, the story of his particular community, and his reflections on higher things, which he sent directly to Bonch-Bruevich.[58] The relationship thus begun lasted until 1939, when silence finally descended.

We have already encountered Latyshev and heard him describe the frightful moment in 1873 when angry neighbors broke down the door and found him and his brother resting in a pool of blood. Like Men'shenin and Sanin, he had a shaky grasp of grammar and spelling. But unlike them, he had a true writer's calling—and a talent that justified his obsession with words. His job, he said, was "to separate the wheat from the chaff, the sheep from the goats, to discover the truth, God's

truth."[59] His letters reveal a man of humor and warmth, of spiritual bold-
ness and personal reticence, eager for intellectual exchange and contact
with the world, yet proud of the fate that had cast him in the painful role
of ultimate outsider. Being a writer allowed him both to reveal his faith
and to transcend his human condition. "If you saw me in person," he
wrote Bonch-Bruevich in 1914, "you would determine that I am proud
of nothing but expressing my thoughts and impressions on paper. Personally speaking, I am not talkative but shy in the extreme, barely know
how to talk, and what I manage to say comes out rather silly and incoherent. . . . I live a quiet, solitary life and moreover have lived all my fifty
years in toil and poverty. That is why I am happy, happy to be good for
something, and not just anything! but as a spiritual writer!"[60]

Latyshev's notebooks promise to convey a message "to the reading
world, less about myself personally than about those few, obedient to the
commandments of Christ, who abandoned all their property and, following their calling, submitted to the judgment of the World." The desire
to talk about himself was, however, irresistible. In the midst of describing
the adventures of his early years, he confesses he "ought not to be telling
these stories at all, since in the very first lines I promised I would talk
about heroes worthier than myself."[61] In fact, the subjects are fatally
intertwined. His own story and that of his family are also the story of salvation.

Nikifor Petrovich Latyshev was born, as we know, in 1863 (the year
after Men'shenin, ten years before Bonch-Bruevich) into a prosperous
peasant family in the village of Fedorovka, north of Melitopol in Tauride
province. The family's fate was tied to Kuz'ma Lisin's momentous transformation from humble tailor into self-styled Second Redeemer. Lisin's
revelation did not, however, materialize out of thin air. The saga began in
1872, when Fedorovka was visited by emissaries from Galati, the Skoptsy
colony in Romania. Safe from legal prosecution, the expatriates had
developed a secure urban existence. Material comfort and spiritual complacency led the wealthy Efim Kuprianov to begin "hungering for the
light." Preaching the renewal of sanctity, he attracted a few dozen others,
including Kuz'ma Lisin, who called themselves the "Society of the Holy
Elect." Expecting at any moment to be revisited by the Son of God, Lisin
and two others left the city of Galati one fine day in June 1872 and

Opening page of Nikifor Latyshev's notebook, called "The Beginning of My Tale" (Nachalo moego povestvovaniia) (1910). GMIR, f. 2, op. 5, d. 261, l. 2. (Copyright © GMIR.) The story begins: "In 1872 in the Romanian city of Galati a religious movement appeared among the Skoptsy! One of the most influential of the Skoptsy, in terms of position and education, was Efim Semenovich Kuprianov. He had had his fill of so-called worldly life. At the same time he noticed the Skoptsy religion was leaning in the direction of worldliness. . . . He truly desired to free himself from the fetters that had begun to block his path . . . and began to seek a way out! How to leave the darkness for the light? And where to find this Light if not from above? Little by little he prepared himself by reading and understood that Light comes only from above—God's True Light!"

climbed a local rise, which they later dubbed Mount Zion, echoing Revelation 14:1, "a Lamb stood on the mount Sion." There Lisin began to prophesy. Calling his two companions John the Divine and Vasilii the Great, he declared himself to be Kondratii Selivanov in his Second Appearance.[62]

In his notebooks, the adult Nikifor returned to these events time and again. The drama of revelation and the trauma of betrayal and expulsion were central to the community's continuing sense of its own destiny. Latyshev renewed his own spiritual commitment by recapitulating the intensity of the particular visitation that had sealed his fate. By telling the story, he conveyed to the world the reasons why he had been content to have left it. At the same time he opened a door to compassion and understanding. Many of the details of his tale were most certainly invented. Latyshev was only twelve years old when the crisis began to unfold. He must have culled the recital from the memories of his elders, from his childhood recollections, and from the resources of his imagination. The result achieves what he hoped it would. It conveys a sense of how it felt to be lifted by the Spirit and rejoice with one's fellows that salvation had come! It is worth retracing our steps to the moment of Lisin's inspiration.

When the faithful next gathered for prayer, Latyshev writes, someone had cried: "'Christ is risen!' Three times so that several, hearing this miraculous, blessed news, fell on their knees in fear and trembling. . . . The rejoicing of souls . . . was at this moment fantastic, noisy and joyful, full of some kind of unearthly ecstasy. The Skoptsy oldsters later would say: 'Where did we get such energy and courage? It was as if we were flying on wings, singing the hymn of Praise to the Almighty Creator with His Son the Redeemer our Dear Father.'" As Latyshev later explained, the faith was in need of renewal. "The merciful Redeemer, our Dear Father, in the person of Kondratii Selivanov, or, more accurately, in the person of Peter III, constantly preached in his teachings that . . . each Coming of the Savior from Heaven to earth demands a resolute struggle of the soul with the flesh. . . . What kind of a ship is it, even with sails that are full of wind, if it has no Leader, no Pilot? Where is it supposed to go, with nobody directing it, and if it is under the direction of everyone, all the passengers at the same time, what will come of that? Disorder. And indeed everyone knows that where there is disorder, everything is unsolid and shaky. . . . With the passage of time . . . the spiritual gradually was arrayed in the natural and carnal and things had gone so far that all that was spiritual and Godly was enveloped in shadow and ritual."[63] The prophets had gotten into the habit of forgiving sins, such as the offense of getting married. Many in the Melitopol district were not castrated. Many were rich and proud. It was necessary "to break the outmoded regime of self-loving habits of Teachers and Prophets who replaced the spiritual and holy with the Flesh and ritual, which was intolerable in both the first and second coming of the Son of the All-Highest."[64]

Lisin, "having lit the lamp in one place, . . . hurried to another." Crossing the border illegally, as the Skoptsy expatriates were wont to do, the new Redeemer and a few selected men had returned to Russia to spread the word. Arriving in the area of Fedorovka, they made contact with key families among the local Skoptsy. Nikifor's father, Petr, happened in the neighborhood as the faithful were gathering for nighttime prayer and participated in the animation. Evfrosiniia Iarkina, their prophet and teacher, said "the Golden Time was upon them." Members of the congregations "heard the sermon with the thrill of a certain ecstasy. According to the stories and memory of the witnesses, the sermon flowed smoothly, sometimes soft, sometimes as loud as thunder from the Heavens, inspiring fear and trembling in those unsure of their intentions." Just as Akulia Ivanova had once annointed Selivanov in his sacred role and convinced her followers to treat him as divine, so Iarkina recognized Lisin as the Savior. "You are a pillar reaching from earth to heaven, and on this pillar are golden rings, and all believers and those who love God must grab onto these rings, then their souls will not remain in death, and moreover you are a Great Soul, a tree reaching from earth to the heavens and on this tree many birds will build their nests." "Reborn as new creatures," the godly, upon hearing such words, "cooed like white doves until the break of dawn."[65]

Lisin would ask: "Is the Holy Spirit with you, brother?" If the listener wavered, he would warn: "My sweet little words do mark, take them to your sweet little hearts. The time is approaching, the door to heaven is open, the day of Salvation has come."[66] With ecstasy came the challenge to new commitment. "Christ bore the burden of suffering," Latyshev remembers the prophet to have said, "and we must must drag nature with its acquired habits across the thorns and prickles, otherwise what kind of followers of Him and His teachings are we!"[67] Over a hundred Skoptsy from the surrounding families responded to the call. Thirty or forty, among them Petr Latyshev, took the holy seal. "Burning with the desire as soon as possible to wash our feet, according to the commandment of Jesus Christ, hurrying toward the kingdom of the living God, turning away from darkness toward life, we had ourselves castrated," Latyshev recalled.[68] "Blessed by the Dear Father Redeemer, the surgeons labored, removing the bodily parts no longer needed in the new life, one after the other, so in one fell stroke blood flowed, the soul rejoiced, the body was purified!"[69]

As we know from the story of Lisin's betrayal by those of the brethren who refused to heed his call, not everyone rejoiced. Latyshev compared their resistance to the reception of the original Jesus, when not all had recognized him as the Son of God. So it was now, that some Skoptsy from the born-again families rejected the new revelation. Skeptics among the brethren considered Lisin "entirely uncelestial, no different from ordinary Skoptsy." Thinking a new Messiah would be accompanied by "sound and thunder, from which the earth would shake under our feet and the arch of the heavens tremble, and the mountains move from place to place," they were disappointed that no such events accompanied the arrival of the Skoptsy Redeemer, just as they had not when Jesus first arrived. The wiser among them "do not care whether his name is Kondratii, Petr, or Kuz'ma. Only the message and Mission of Christ are important, because Christ comes from Almighty God Himself."[70] Those with the power of spiritual perception did, in fact, recognize the "sound and thunder" and were not disappointed: "the believers saw the Glory in what he spake and his Great Power and the Angels surrounding the Word of God, and the thunder in the words of the Prophets, waking the souls from sleep—everything that others could not see, because their eyes were bound and ears stopped."[71]

These last, as we know, feared that the revival would expose them all to persecution.[72] Lisin seemed not to care, as he made the rounds of the villages, proudly wearing the ceremonial costume usually confined to sacred space, that peasants might take notice of his long white shirt and report on his "overly free manner of speech," as he delivered his message in the broad light of day. Wealth had earned the local Skoptsy the respect of priests and village notables, who "visited them with greetings once a year at the big holidays." Lulled by the comforts of the world, Latyshev complained, these lazy believers had wanted to have their cake and eat it too (in Russian, the hayloft full and the goats fed). They had strayed far from the path of virtue.[73]

Some greeted Lisin therefore "with stony hearts." Prayers were rudely interrupted as angry brethren attacked their fellows with sticks. Spiritual discord and internal strife shattered the community's peaceful existence. Some "saw in this Coming power and glory, suspended as on the clouds of prophesy. . . . Some turned away from this novelty, others were attracted like flies to the honey. Some had faith, others greeted their faith with malice. Some saw in this joy, others poison."[74] The newly redeemed, in Latyshev's words, "dreaded neither Fear nor Death but defeated in themselves the animal-cerebral existence [zhizn′ zhivotnaia, dushevnaia] and accepted the Spiritual-Godly life [zhizn′ Dukhovnaia-Bozhiia], life in Christ and with Christ, with their Savior-Redeemer. We to this day live in Hope of the Radiant future, leading an earthly existence in purity and Sanctity." Others, however, renounced the Savior and the faith, returning "like washed pigs back to the mud," to escape the threat of arrest and expulsion.[75]

Betrayed by the devotees of the easy life, the dedicated were arrested and tried. But though the court had listened to the converts pour out their hearts, its views were not altered. The Skoptsy, of course, were unfazed by persecution. As always, they experienced the mundane in mythic or scriptural terms. "Strange," wrote Latyshev, "what was visible to the blind and deaf and those unenlightened in the secret of God's people, however educated they might be. Pontius Pilate understood a lot of what Jesus Christ said, though it amounted to nothing at all! Afterwards, of course, he was astonished that the Son of God in the person of the Carpenter from Nazareth said something about God's Truth, but at the time he didn't get it, any more than the Gentlemen Experts and Officials defending their dominant religion from other religions, even if true ones." With the passage of time, Latyshev reflected on the proceedings and tried to decipher the terms in which he and his fellows were viewed. Just as the experts who testified in the case wished to explain the psychology of the Skoptsy, so Latyshev made an effort at interpretation in the other direction. "The expert took from his interrogation [of the prophet Lisin] only one thing," Latyshev explained: "that a person, though not deprived of reason, as evident from his answers, but alien to our understanding and in addition harmful by his invocation of another God who does not want to live with our God . . . [w]hen such an undesirable manifestation comes before the court it must be removed and destroyed. . . . The interrogator summoned from Petersburg departed reassured, with a report on how this Manifestation was not a real one, lacking Power or Glory."[76]

Because of the blindness of the unenlightened, many, including Latyshev's parents, were sentenced to Siberian exile in the area of Iakutsk. Five boys, including Nikifor and Andrei, along with a group of girls, all judged innocent by virtue of their age, were released: the girls to various convents, the boys "into the hands of poverty and bitterness." The brothers supported themselves at various jobs: "we had to forget about Saving our Souls and save our bodies first." Nikifor worked in Simferopol as lackey to a member of the circuit court, followed by a stint behind a store counter. A few years in a carriage-painting workshop taught him the skills, which he used to open his own shop together with Andrei. Ten years after the arrest, Nikifor had wearied of these mundane pursuits. It was then that he encountered Terentii Rosliakov, another of the boys freed after the trial, who had returned to the area on business. Terentii described the life he had found in the Holy St. Vladimir Monastery in Kherson, at the mouth of the Dnepr River, where his sister had been sent by the court. "Carried away" by his friend's stories, Nikifor accompanied him by railroad back to Kherson.[77]

Thus began Nikifor's experience with the worldly aspect of the Orthodox religion. The monastery's superior inscribed the young men as lay brothers when he learned from their passports that they were Skoptsy. In this wealthy sanctuary, where the cream of Russian high society came to see St. Vladimir's holy remains and view the archeological relics from the ancient city of Kherson, Nikifor served as the superior's factotum. In this role, he managed to glimpse Alexander III and the imperial family, on the occasion of the tsarevich's birthday in 1886. With the appointment of a new head not to his liking, however, Nikifor lost his taste for serving the clerical elite and left for the city of Yalta. Reduced again to painter's work, in 1890 he resolved to join his exiled kin.[78]

Having gathered their belongings, Latyshev and his brother Andrei arrived by post horses in the city of Irkutsk on September 1, 1890. By then the Lena River had frozen over, and they spent the winter at various odd jobs. In May they found a ride on the boat of a wealthy Iakutsk merchant, arriving in that city on June 1, 1891. Their older brother Fedor, twenty at the time of the trial, had been exiled along with their parents. Learning that the two had wintered in Irkutsk, Fedor traveled to

Kuz'ma Fedorovich Lisin (1842–1914?) with his followers from the village of Petropavlovsk on the Aldan River, 1897. GMIR, f. 2, op. 29, d. 387. (Copyright © GMIR.) Lisin, at this point about 55 years old, is seated third from left. He is the only one with a white kerchief in his hand, perhaps to signal his spiritual distinction. The man seated second from the right bears some resemblance to Andrei Latyshev.

Markha, outside Iakutsk, to take them to their destination in Troitsk (also known as Charan). "We had gotten as far as Iakutsk without a guide," Latyshev recalled, "but it was impossible to reach Charan without someone who knew the road, or, more exactly, the forest path. Sleepy forests, mountains, lakes, swamps—that is what you find on entering these thickets." Trekking for two weeks behind a laden cart through 250 miles of forest, "spending nights in the open air, listening to the howl of wild beasts," they finally arrived in the Skoptsy settlement of Petropavlovsk. Perched on the cliffs above the Aldan River, overlooking three wooded islands, Petropavlovsk is not far from the mouth of the Maia, which falls into the Aldan in a rush of foaming water at the site of a small village with an Orthodox church.[79] Steamboats plied these rivers with caution.

Upon arriving, the three brothers were welcomed by the local brethren and treated to a bath and tea. Crossing the Aldan in a small boat to the settlement of Troitsk on the opposite shore, they watched as the residents assembled to greet them. "Our brother Fedor shouted: 'Mommy! Leave the samovar. Guests are coming.' I was the first to jump out onto the bank, but I didn't know exactly where my father was. A withered, gray-haired old man came forward and called me by name. I guessed this was my father. My brother Fedor playfully asked my mother to point out her favorite Nikisha, who had left her when he was a child and was now a full-grown, almost thirty-year-old man. She started toward Andrei, but all cried out 'She didn't recognize him!' Then practically the entire village formed a procession to our parents' house."[80]

Recalling this transition many years later, from the far side of an apocalyptic historical divide, Latyshev explained why freedom in the world had lost its appeal. Unlike Prudkovskii, who lived to bemoan his unwilling inscription in God's heavenly flock, Latyshev had been released from their hold but yearned to return to his own kind. Though not at first. In his youth, he told Bonch-Bruevich in 1934, "I was not always thinking about the heavens. No. From the age of 18 until 30 I lived the life of a secular working man, drank wine, ate meat, went on sprees, boozed it up with my shopmates, but all the time something was pulling me toward another life, something did not seem sweet in all these amusements and binges. I was depressed and found no peace of mind. When I turned 30 I decided to visit my father, mother, and older brother in exile in the Iakutsk region. There I saw the life and labors of my old folks. Instead of cursing and swearing over the supposed privations of exile, on the contrary they worked and thanked God. As for me, I'm thinking: what's there to thank? This is Siberia!—60 degrees below zero, unbearable labor clearing the taiga for sowing grain. This and other privations should have filled them with horror, but they are joyful instead! And when I willy-nilly grew accustomed to looking and listening, I understood that here was life. Here it made sense to live the healthy life even for 100 years! Labor and joy together, love, faith, and support. Everything seemed to me patriarchal, dear and noble! without animal passions and without sin. It was then I began to think, to reflect more on heaven and whether it exists and whether there is life in heaven."[81]

Sheep from the Goats: A Writer's Calling

Latyshev was a man with a calling. His mission was to put the faith on record. He was a holy scribe. Compiling the profile of the Siberian settlements where he had spent fifteen years, he asked to be enrolled "in the lists of the truth-seekers."[82] He signed the first of his notebooks: "aspiring writer, Nikifor Petrov Latyshev" and later dubbed himself a "minor writer, an amateur of writing" and "an apprentice Skoptsy writer."[83] Embarrassed by his poor education, he feared that people would laugh at him and his mistakes, admitting that "the letter 'e' wanders about, not knowing where to settle down. Punctuation marks and others also end up in the wrong places."[84] He complained of his "lack of writer's talent" while admiring the cultural skills of the "Old Skoptsy" such as Men'shenin, "real intellectuals with a resemblance to human beings." By contrast, Lisin's followers seemed "all gray, though inside we are White and alive."[85] The humble words were perhaps designed to parry the disdain of truly educated people, such as Bonch-Bruevich. In fact, books and writing that led him to the Truest Truth were all that Latyshev lived for. When the Skoptsy had their portraits taken in worldly attire, they held small strips of white cloth in their folded hands: scraps of the white kerchiefs and white shirts that betokened salvation. When Latyshev sat for the camera, the white cloth could be seen protruding from behind a copy of the popular magazine *Niva,* balanced on his lap where the missing organ should have been (see page 6). It was the writer's calling that joined the secular and the spiritual domains. "I love to rummage around in books," Latyshev explained, "searching for the merest shadow of holy truth."[86]

His mission, like that of "all scholars, all searchers for truth," was "the transformation of the everlasting darkness of the world into God's Light."[87] Calling himself "the most sincere and truthful of writers," he

Group of sisters, followers of K. F. Lisin, in a Cossack village in the Kuban district. GMIR, f. 2, op. 29, d. 385. (Copyright © GMIR.) All the women, including the little girl, are holding white kerchiefs. The archives contain depositions and testimony presented during trials by female defendants but no texts written by women. Both Men'shenin and Latyshev mention their mothers, the first describing the intensity of his affection. The apostate Gerasim Prudkovskii gives a more detailed picture of the influence women might have exerted within the community. Some were recognized for their spiritual authority; Lisin included women among his close associates. But the Skoptsy whose compositions and letters survive were men.

said he was one of a kind. "Among the Skoptsy," he told Bonch-Bruevich, "I am the only one who has distinguished himself as a writer-philosopher. Among the Skoptsy I am even called by this suitable name." His ambition was not merely personal; others would benefit, too. "I wanted to shine nowhere else than in print," he confessed, but added: "This is the only way to make the Skoptsy interested in writing. Then you would be flooded with verses, miraculous prophesies, and other secrets of these people, because each would want to show his talent for self-expression."[88] "If I have written and continue to write it is exclusively . . . for the sincere love of God," he affirmed. "And at the same time, also to inform my listeners, if there should be any."[89]

The injunction to hide had become an injunction to reveal. "God's truth is concealed," Latyshev wrote, "not visible to everyone in general but hidden in sectarianism and moreover in exclusively Russian sectarianism. Here it has found itself a little nest, here it is accepted, here it lives among people who have adopted it—among the People of God, pure and unsullied (Revelation 14:4). But the question is: who will prove this? And who will have the guts to talk about this? For this is one persecuted, tried in court, deprived of liberty. . . . Where to find such a gutsy guy? And if you find him, who will believe him? And this truth will remain concealed—this truest most correct of truths. . . . Little is written about this truth, little is spoken, and it is DESPISED!. . . Experience has taught us that each Word of God spoken aloud leads unavoidably to the constable's whip or fleabag jail, in the company of bandits or the unavoidable recidivist pickpockets."[90]

"Every one of my thoughts comes from God's spirit, every word from God's Word," he insisted.[91] He "wanted to write a book to complement the Gospels."[92] But for the Word of God to be heard, someone must listen: "I will keep writing," Latyshev told Bonch-Bruevich, "if not to you then to someone else. I love in general to preach God's Cause. I would be happy to find someone kind and tolerant to talk with, who would ask questions, sincerely, without trying to trick me or mock me later."[93] Bonch-Bruevich was just this man. "Well, I talk with you completely frankly only because I don't think you're interested in having me discovered, beaten, or tortured for this. You are working for the sake of the Future—and may God give you a hand."[94]

The correspondence with Bonch-Bruevich reveals Latyshev's personality and the character of his faith. It also records the relationship between two culturally disparate, intellectually dedicated men. Though Latyshev dreamed of seeing his writing in print, the letters were "so-to-speak 'private,'" he said, not for publication, and "perhaps unnecessarily frank."[95] They expressed "what weighs on my heart."[96] His self-esteem had no doubt been enhanced by the notion that he had something valuable to offer. In his first letter, composed in late 1912, he tells Bonch-Bruevich: "If you, as researcher of the hidden secrets of Russian sectarianism, need this material, I will always be at your service and with the help of God I will show you the truth about the Skoptsy faith."[97] Bonch-Bruevich, in return, sends him two volumes of his documentary series. Having left Siberia with his family in 1906, Latyshev was at the time working in a machine-building factory in Aleksandrovsk, Ekaterinoslav province, where the Skoptsy were employed as watchmen, in recognition, as he explains, of their honest and sober ways. When the plant closed for the Christmas holidays, Latyshev had time to read and write.[98]

In the first of Bonch-Bruevich's volumes, he found the text of Tolstoi's letters to Men′shenin. If the latter had the self-confidence to initiate the exchange and meet the great man in person, Latyshev had just enough courage, in private, to scorn Tolstoi's response. "Burning with desire" to hear the reaction of "such a wise and great person" to "the convictions of a not-great person" such as himself and of people who follow Christ by mortifying the flesh, Latyshev was deeply disappointed. "Like all the great," Latyshev told Bonch-Bruevich, Tolstoi "cannot appreciate the simple wisdom extracted by the efforts of people of the simplest mind, knowledge, and position.... I cannot pass this over in silence because he himself took up the campaign to subdue nature.... I remember reading that L[ev] N[ikolaevich] asked, as a challenge to the nation, why he wasn't fettered and sent to farthest Siberia, as they had banished the brethren living in Jesus Christ. Why does he ask? Because Mr. Millionaire, and moreover with the flashy title of Count, is bored tinkering with the empty composition of novels and, of course, as a joke, takes up the cause, while losing neither goats nor hay."[99] Tolstoi, as everyone knew, had published a novel called *Resurrection* (1899). But Latyshev considered himself better qualified to write on that very theme and contemplated a volume called, "Well, why not: The Resurrection of Souls! Or the joy of those same souls! Something like that." After all, he reflected, "the publisher of *Niva* . . . paid a lot to the Great Thinker for the 'Resurrection' of one person alone! And here it will concern not only one but thousands of souls."[100]

For all his bluff and democratic indignation, however, Latyshev was easily slighted. His sense of cultural inferiority was acute. Why had Bonch-Bruevich not answered his last three letters, he asked in October 1914. Perhaps Bonch-Bruevich was trying to brush him off, like an "almost despicable mister." More likely, Latyshev feared, he may have brought this silence upon himself, with his "inappropriate and unnecessary compositions and lack of writer's talent." He reminded himself of the crow in Krylov's fable, flattered into showing off his voice: "Perhaps," he reflected, "but I don't want to believe all my own suppositions." Enough humble pie. If Bonch-Bruevich didn't answer this letter, it would be Latyshev's last: "Although I am a simple peasant guy, I would like to be a gentleman. Therefore I beg the most sincere pardon. Though I don't know how to behave with my betters, still I do not deserve reproach. I speak sincerely from the heart: I have not and do not deserve anything but the good!"[101]

Bonch-Bruevich quickly replied.[102] Latyshev was relieved. "I received your letter and I am very very happy that you have remembered me. And in fact I've been writing a lot, and in the process burned more than one candle to the quick before I managed to get some philosophizing onto paper. . . . It was painful of course to think I amounted to nothing! And suddenly, greetings, and even more precious to me—permission to write and send what I write. For me that is sheer happiness!" He had earned this place by his own spiritual labors. He had struggled before yielding to "the power of Holy Feelings and Convictions, but having become convinced, I place at the foot of the pedestal everything that has accumulated in all my years of existence. And what has not been in me? How many castles in the air have I not built? And where haven't I traveled in my imagination especially when I hungrily read through the World-Famous novelist-liars or the (false) prophets, not of God's Word, but of the word of logic, beauty, or elegance. It would seem that with so much read and seen one could calmly float along on the black sea (Skoptsy call the world the black sea), but no! thanks to having as a child already received the seal of righteousness (physical castration) as the pledge of righteousness, I have remained what I am, a Skopets among Skoptsy, and want to end my life in this faith. No one can make me believe in another faith and who would waste the effort on such a paltry character. Moreover, I despise anyone who persecutes people for their beliefs."[103]

Proud he may have been, but his choice was a hard one. It lent itself to misunderstanding. He took pains (as the parenthetical explanations in the above passage show) to translate the secret code of faith into accessible language, knowing how easy it was for outsiders to get the wrong impression from misleading or disturbing signs. "I myself have often come to the conclusion," he wrote, "that the Skoptsy seem rather silly and puzzling on the surface." When Bonch-Bruevich, despite Latyshev's coaching, wrote an article denouncing the sect's "pernicious notions," Latyshev was dismayed. He preferred to think that his correspondent was conforming to expected scholarly views rather than expressing a personal opinion. But in either case, the Skoptsy would not care. They were accustomed to being defamed, Latyshev wrote defensively, invoking the apostle Paul: "we are made as the filth of the world" (1 Corinthians 4:13). Therefore, Latyshev assured Bonch-Bruevich, "your condemnation does not offend us. I know very well that this is not your voice alone, but that of all people on earth, and so be it!"[104]

He was not being merely defensive. The Skoptsy welcomed persecution as a test of faith, a posture that made punishing them a difficult business. The same psychology led them to revel in their lowly state, as the most despised of men. In the same passage in which Paul addresses the brethren, he says: "God has set forth us the apostles last, as it were appointed to death: for we are made a spectacle unto the world, and to angels, and to men. We are fools for Christ's sake, but ye are wise in Christ; we are weak, but ye are strong; ye are honourable, but we are despised. . . . Being reviled, we bless; being persecuted, we suffer it: being defamed, we intreat: we are made as the filth of the world, and are the offscouring of all things unto this day" (1 Corinthians 4:9–13). To be despised and misunderstood was a mark of sanctity, a confirmation of the rightness of the way.

And yet, Latyshev, at least, aspired to a different kind of reception. He wanted to be heard, understood, and even appreciated for the message he had to offer. It was too bad, he told Bonch-Bruevich, that "people are people and deaf to everything Divine and thus to my heartfelt declarations." The public had no taste for the truth, especially truth with "the slightest sectarian odor." Jesus in his time had been branded a sectarian because the majority rejected his call. To this day sectarians inspired only hatred, though they were everywhere sober and God-fearing. Knowing that his truth would fall on deaf ears, Latyshev nevertheless showed "impatience to see my own thoughts, my own words in print." Latyshev was sorry Bonch-Bruevich seemed in no hurry: "You, too, respected Vladimir Dmitrievich, like all the others above all do not trust me, my words, my writings, my True Conviction, in short, my spiritual rebirth, resurrection. Therefore you look on all this (to you Mythical) from an entirely different angle. You find that all this is still not enough, you need something ever newer, something interesting, that agrees with the times, with the mood of the readers." People preferred to buy the lavishly printed works of Rasputin: "everyone on earth knows about him."[105]

It was not the waste of effort Latyshev would regret, but his failure to make God's Word known. If only Bonch-Bruevich were more attentive to matters of the soul, then, said Latyshev, "my words, my writings, would not in general remain only the Voice of one crying in the people's wilderness."[106] "Having become acquainted with your kind intentions and with you and trusting you," Latyshev wrote Bonch-Bruevich, "I hoped that you too would deign, if only partly, to believe in my Sincere desire, in my Love for God, my Openness to all that is pure, Sacred, and Good. But what is to be done? It's clear our beliefs are not yours and yours are not ours." Latyshev nevertheless valued Bonch-Bruevich's good opinion and his friendship, perhaps, above all. "Kindest Vladimir Dmitrievich, if you find in my letter and in general in my writings anything rather crude, please do not be offended. This is accepted in all levels of human sanctity. There's Grigorii Efimovich [Rasputin] on familiar terms with princes and counts and no big deal! He gets away with it! So don't ask more from a simple guy like me, please!"[107]

Sheep among Themselves

Latyshev insists that the truth will show the Skoptsy in a positive light. But he admits: "The point is not that everything about us must be positive, or else it's worthless. We ourselves know that among the Skoptsy there is both good and bad."[108] "There are some Skoptsy," he wrote in 1910, "especially the young ones, who regret being Skoptsy and do everything, including cosmetics and massage, to change their appearance not to resemble Skoptsy." But when speaking of the brethren, Latyshev prefers to "stress their good side, as I belong to the good kind." All the same, he wonders why "Skoptsy, who share the same cause, the same convictions, the same expectations, suffer[ing] persecution and contempt from the outside world, do not live peacefully among themselves."[109] Men'shenin had described some of the vices of Skoptsy life in Siberia. Latyshev also complained of internal conflicts. He had suffered their consequences in his personal life. Most critical had been the betrayal of Lisin and his followers by those who refused his call.

At least as painful had been the exiles' reception in Siberia. When Lisin's party arrived in Iakutsk, they had encountered the old-timers' resentment. As was their habit, those already established in the prosperous colonies of Spasskoe and Iliun'skoe asked the local authorities to send the newcomers farther on. "It seemed strange, bitter, and insulting," Latyshev wrote, recalling the experience of the group to which his parents belonged, to be treated harshly by "their own."[110] The problem, as Latyshev came to believe, was similar to the reasons for the original split. When the brethren became too involved in worldly affairs, they lost their spiritual bearings. Of the Old Skoptsy, who had rejected Lisin when he first appeared, Latyshev wrote, in a censorious tone recalling the fulminations of Nadezhdin or the populists' disdain: "They put everything into business, worry about profits. They fast once a week, but they are all fat, with big bellies like stuffed pigs. . . . Many in Romania, and even in

Russia, are money changers, traders, capitalists, sellers and buyers. . . . It's obvious their business affairs and 10 percent profits have confused them."[111]

Similarly, from living in the world, the colonists "began to forget about Holiness." When Lisin appeared among them, "walking with convicts in iron chains, one who by nature resembled Jesus Christ, with his head of beautiful curly hair, now disfigured, half-shaved and half-shorn," they did not recognize the Savior. He was too common, a mere tailor, not the Redeemer they had imagined.[112] Why, they asked, had he arrived on a raft and not on a ship, like a true king, if he really was one? And Latyshev imagined him to have replied, like a biblical prophet, that Jesus Christ would have chosen "an ass with long ears, instead of a pair of thoroughbred trotters, or a simple fishing boat, instead of a steamboat."[113] In the years that followed, Lisin's enemies expressed their continuing resentment by bringing charges against him for various alleged misdemeanors, of which he was always exonerated before the local courts.[114]

From the perspective of a believer, these conflicts were distressing, because they marked the fragmentation and decline of true belief. Naturally, purity was hard to maintain, but the difficult path was also the correct one. The Skoptsy, "separated from the whole world," stood "closest to God"; of this Latyshev remained certain. By "breaking with nature," they had been reborn and found salvation; they had made "the sacrifice of death for the sake of liberation from the slavery of darkness." But people continued to live in darkness, waver in their faith, and indulge the pleasures of the flesh; sects and schisms developed. Not all who had accomplished "the feat of making themselves outcasts" deserved the name Skoptsy, so far had they strayed from their calling.[115] When Lisin had challenged them to renew the faith, some refused to see the light that swept the spiritual horizon.[116]

The brethren not only disagreed on the issue of renewal, some following Lisin, others not. They also expressed a range of attitudes toward the community and its spiritual endeavor. We have encountered dramatic cases of apostasy, of which Prudkovskii's memoir is a case in point. But it is not surprising to discover other voices, more discreet but no less tormented, which registered alienation and dismay. Not all the papers that ended in Bonch-Bruevich's hands were composed in the spirit of celebration or with the intention of making the writer's name. The author of a "Deathbed Confession" and the "Biography of a Bereft and Anguished Life" mailed his unsigned manuscripts from Odessa in 1911.[117] He did not want to be known.

This is the story of a castrated man who resents his fate and chooses his words with intention, though he has a weak command of grammar and spelling and no use for punctuation at all. The epithet "bereft" evoked the melancholy tone of reportage on the exiled Skoptsy, a literature with which the writer was, by his own account, familiar. They were outside the law, wrote an observer from Tomsk in 1900, "these bereft and unfortunate Skoptsy."[118] Another, addressing the Eastern Siberia section of the Imperial Geographical Society in 1902, chose the same motif: "Among the bereft population of the bereft Iakutsk region those who should consider themselves the most bereft of all are the Skoptsy, sent there for an 'eternity' of exile."[119] Men'shenin commiserates with the misfortunes of the "already bereft Skoptsy-exiles"; he complains of administrative abuses that deprive the "bereft and unfortunate" Siberian Skoptsy of the benefits of the law.[120] This anonymous chronicler evokes the sense of pity, too, but on his own behalf. Toward his fellows he is ruthless. Like Prudkovskii, he wants to unmask the community's hidden vices, but he does not seem to have expected any advantage, except psychological relief, in putting his testimony to paper. No covering letter explains why he sent his outpourings to Bonch-Bruevich or what he thought their purpose might be.

Bitterly, the writer explains his "doubly unhappy life: on the one hand, surveillance and persecution by the authorities and the contempt of society; on the other, persecution by fanatics, or more precisely, spongers and blackmailers."[121] It all began in 1867, when, he says, he "had the misfortune of being castrated against my will." Brought to trial, he named his castrator, who was sentenced to hard labor. He himself was freed by the court of responsibility for his condition. Soon after his acquittal, letters began arriving that threatened to denounce him to the authorities as a castrator in his own right. The correspondents demanded he send money to the man who had gone to Siberia on his account. They also demanded payment for themselves. Over the years, he reports, he tried unsuccessfully to elude them by moving from place to place.[122]

Though he himself had clearly benefited from the judgment of a court, he criticized the terms of the law for failing to distinguish between true believers and those who fall victim to their wiles.

In legal terms, he had been lucky. But that had been the end of his luck. Only misery had followed. And in any case, he was the permanent victim of misfortune. To explain his position in the community, he divides the brethren into three groups. The first "publicly decry their irreversible fate; the second . . . correctly judge their situation of irreversible fate and with broken hearts keep silent and seem indifferent to everything around them but in their hearts they weep; . . . the third group . . . [are] fanatics proud of their shameful name and these are the ones harmful to the government and society and even to the second group; they harm the government as they are proud of their name and want others to have it too, it is easy to suppose they preach and castrate even to the point of violence, it's these who deserve to be persecuted by the government and deserve society's contempt." Those in the first group often fall into despair. Trying to detach themselves from the community, they take to eating meat and drink to excess, with harmful consequences for their health. The group with tears in their hearts reject the claim that castration leads to the heavenly kingdom, refusing to "attend gatherings of idiots dressed up in white costumes making a scarecrow of oneself and jump about moreover." Eager for enlightenment, they read Voltaire, David Friedrich Strauss, Ernest Renan, and Tolstoi but cannot apply what they learn, because they are barred from the world to which this knowledge applies.[123]

As Prudkovskii learned, it was not easy to break away and hard to find another home. The stigma of castration could neither be undone nor denied. The law did not accommodate apostates. The faithful were known for their duplicity; the sincerity of defectors was always in doubt. Skoptsy women in Siberian settlements who married outside the faith were prevented, for example, from joining husbands who lived elsewhere. Even after converting to Orthodoxy, they were still bound by the rules that limited the right of Skoptsy exiles to move about. Conversely, exiles permitted to return to their hometowns were required to carry passports that showed they were castrated. So were men such as the author himself, who managed to convince a court they had been castrated against their will. Loyal believers were ready, moreover, to use the laws that treated the community as a social menace to punish defecters, by denouncing them to the police.[124] Those, like the anonymous autobiographer, whose convictions had weakened often kept silent about their change of heart. As one observer had written in the 1890s, the Skoptsy who renounced the faith could find no haven: "Parted from those to whom they were joined by fanaticism and shared unhappiness, they cannot tie the knot that would bind them to the rest of the world. The artery is severed and circulation cannot be restored. The heart of the Skopets beats separately from the heart of the world."[125]

Like Prudkovskii, the anonymous writer bitterly denounces the company he cannot escape. Adopting the language of the alien world whose good opinion he courts, the apostate talks like an outsider. The fanatical types are "complete idiots," he says, "people who cannot tell black from white, some mentally incompetent." "During the Kharkov trial," he notes, "a doctor said the 142 defendants were mentally disturbed, otherwise it's impossible to imagine people in their right minds committing such acts upon themselves."[126] "Cloaked in eternal darkness," these benighted simpletons believe "the sun moves [and] Jonah ate the whale."[127] They follow leaders who play on their ignorance and "exploit the herd of the mentally ill." "Besides eternal darkness," he added, "there's also the psyche."[128]

No "thinking person" could look on castration as anything but a crime, the author concluded. But, alas, he complained, the laws that dealt with crime were singularly powerless against it. Exile only strengthened believers in their convictions. "Like the proletariat," they had nothing to lose and considered themselves martyrs.[129] Many a repentant, thoughtful brother ended in Siberia as well, because the courts were unable to distinguish fanatics from victims or from those who had lost their faith. Even missionaries failed at their task, being easily satisfied with external signs of conversion. What was needed, this writer insists, were schools: "It's obvious," he says, deploying the spiritual idiom he cannot avoid, "that light disperses the darkness."[130] The peasant needs books and time to read them. With priests and policemen standing in their way, the susceptible folk follow their fathers' example and welcome every sectarian who comes along, taking him for an Apostle.[131]

Nikifor Latyshev was among those who accepted the apostle. Yet he was a thoughtful and relatively well-read man for one of his station. Like his disgruntled colleague, he too could mobilize the cultural implements of the outside world. He demonstrates this facility in his very first exchange with Bonch-Bruevich in 1912, knowing it will establish his credibility if he can speak in the other's tongue. "I am not mentally ill," he writes, "as people who talk about God and the truth are usually considered."[132] Access to secular knowledge helps him span the gap between folk and elite, religion and reason, margin and center. But it does not distance him from his spiritual kind. He is bilingual. Like the author of the bitter confession of a "thinking man," Latyshev also uses the language of darkness and light, but he accepts its terms of reference. Its images are not metaphorical to him. In contrast to the apostate, moreover, Latyshev sees the shadow in a different place. His faith gives him hope and a sense of the future. "The enemy," he writes in 1915, "turned light into darkness." In the ages that followed, "weak-willed souls languished, wavering in the ocean of darkness." But some were lucky. In the obscurity and confusion, the Redeemer Kondratii Selivanov brought the Skoptsy "great joy, Forgiveness and Light in the Name of His Resurrection. . . . They finally found what they had been waiting for, found the straight pure bright road and took it. Various obstacles, traps laid by the enemy, and threats threw some off the path. The rest went in joy . . . toward the Eternal God,

Personal seals of Kuz'ma Lisin, "The Second Redeemer" (sketched from the original). "Tetrad' 'glagolov' skoptsov." GMIR, kollektsiia I, op. 6, d. 2, l. 17. (Copyright © GMIR.)

the True Holy God, in the context of the Holy and God-pleasing life."[133] Seeing the light was essential: "Illuminated means Holy!," he wrote in 1913.[134]

When Latyshev spoke of illumination, he had in mind not only the whole of the Skoptsy faith, from the moment of revelation by Kondratii Selivanov, but more particularly its renewal by Kuz'ma Lisin. Considering himself "the Second Redeemer," Lisin acquired a rubber stamp on which this title was embossed. Typical of the Skoptsy talent for selective borrowing, the stamp was a quaint appropriation of worldly, even commercial elements, but it marked a spiritual status that evoked ancient roots. The apostle styled himself the son of Sabaoth, Lord of Hosts. He and his followers reaffirmed the living connection with holiness in the form of so-called Utterances (Glagoly: literally, "verbs"). These were sometimes spoken by Lisin and transcribed by his helpers or pronounced and transcribed by the faithful, addressing their devotion to him. Repetitive and formulaic, they accompanied ecstatic worship and produced a sense of timelessness quite different from the narrative impulse that fueled Latyshev's writerly accounts. But they left room for the humble details of everyday life, which, like the formulas, also bound the congregations together.

On a sheet headed by two imprints of the stamp "Second Redeemer" and one with Lisin's own mark, "K. F. Lisin," a devotee had recorded the prophet's words:

I your True Father Holy Second Redeemer
Favored by the Almighty Creator, Sabaoth,
My Father, rejoice and celebrate my prophets
Filled with the bright spirits of their resurrected
Souls, together with my Own Dear Children I rejoice and
Celebrate and praise and honor Sabaoth, my
Almighty Father Creator, for arranging
and confirming for me the blessed place of rest.[135]

The congregation in a village in Kuban province heard the Holy Spirit on February 9, 1913. They received a greeting from the Redeemer addressed to "his Dear children and daughters of the resurrected souls, whose prophet Aksiniushka, full of the Holy Spirit, in the presence of witnesses, pronounced the Precious Word":

> *Christ is Risen, Christ is Risen, Christ is Risen.*
> *I beg thee my Merciful Creator*
> *Put me under thy Mighty Power*
> *and all my Members and My Holy*
> *Tongue and open thy Heavenly*
> *Depths and read thy secret book,*
> *I put my hopes in thee, my Merciful Father.*[136]

When the inspired words of the worship services were recorded, they were sometimes mixed with more practical messages to the emissary of the divine. One follower, writing on October 5, 1912, thanks Lisin for his letter, which the community had received on September 29, and says they held a prayer service the next day, after which Petr and Ivan Osipovich had returned to Tomsk but sent their greetings. "We your Own Children send you Almighty Creator our praise and Thanks for your mercy to us, which we do not deserve, and also for the PRAYERS that you OFTEN DIRECT on high TO THE ALMIGHTY CREATOR." The writer was off to Siberia, he said, to go fishing.[137]

For all his bookish pretensions, Latyshev regarded Lisin with the same respect and awe as the other brethren did and addressed him in the same reverential terms. He did not think the spiritual idiom incompatible with his literary persona. After the release from Siberia, Latyshev wrote a "Hymn of Praise," from himself and his mother, in which he exercised the inner language of the faithful. He sent a copy, however, to the archives, for the outside world to read.

> *Christ is Risen, Christ is Risen, Christ our Dear Father is Risen.*
> *In the name of the Father, Son, and Holy Ghost!*
> *Resurrected in my Soul through the Holy Spirit,*
> *called philosopher and evangelist, here I write, to my own*
> *Dear Father, the Second Redeemer, and most blessed Teacher,*
> *I write and wonder how I can properly thank*

God and the Dear Father Redeemer, for his great
Mercy toward me, for his great Love,
for the great Gifts, given me in Resurrection!
. . .
what can I, idle slave, bring Thee
Lord as a Gift for Your Love and Mercy
I search and search and find nothing with which to bring you joy
. . .
Thus I have come to the conclusion,
that I have nothing worthwhile of my own,
except myself. Therefore
Thou, my Heart-Seer, Thou my Father
of Love, my joy, take Me
as a Reward. Be my Adviser
Be my travel guide
lead me to eternity, to the Kingdom of Heaven
where Angels and Archangels
Cherubim and Seraphim and all the
Heavenly Powers, these are my desires,
Dear Father Redeemer, and all my life
is in these hopes. . . .
Signed by his own hand, NIKISHA.
And we will be a single
little flock. And he our pastor
will be the Light. Forgive and Bless
us living in Faith Love and Hope.[138]

The Skoptsy Vision

Attachment to the Second Redeemer had been reinforced by the thirty years the followers had shared with him in exile. When, in 1905, the Skoptsy received permission to depart from Siberia, Lisin's followers claimed he had predicted the event.[139] On the first day of that year, Lisin, by now a ripe sixty-six, had been sitting with the brethren, Latyshev recalled, chatting about "the resurrection of souls, his favorite theme," when he announced the conviction that he would soon be departing from Siberia, although how this would happen, he could not say. Though they accepted the Teacher's pronouncements "as the Sacred Word," Latyshev confessed, the faithful "were far from being convinced of this miracle, but this time it really was a miracle, though at the time it seemed inconceivable." Other sectarian exiles had been pardoned and released, but never the Skoptsy, and so the words of the Father Redeemer seemed only to challenge their faith, not promise deliverance. And yet the decree of June 25, 1905, in fact "fulfilled the words from on High of a year before. The unbelievers had to believe, those who rejected the Son of God, the Second Redeemer, had to be convinced that our Godly Cause (of the good, true Skopchestvo) is governed only by God through His Son, the Second Redeemer. However, many did not recognize this miracle."[140] Much to Latyshev's annoyance, the credulity of the faithful was selective.

Ten years later, in 1915, as Russia struggled through a debilitating war, Latyshev again invoked the power of prophesy. In 1902, he told Bonch-Bruevich, Lisin had delivered a sermon saying "that there would be a World War and now everything is coming true, word for word. He said that the Good Russian Tsar after serious ordeals, which Heaven visited on Russia for her sins, will triumph in the end. And we believe this. . . . The Holy Old Man has never said anything that did not come true." "I'll tell you and only you," Latyshev added, in his coquettish way, "that just as Our Dear Father Savior [Selivanov] saved Russia from Napoleon and blessed the Tsar Alexander the Blessed, so now at the present time Our Dear Father Savior [Lisin] has instructed all our communities to pray for the Tsar and for Russia, and this will be of great help."[141]

This was the Dear Tsar, Nicholas II, who had "granted [the Savior] freedom, liberating Him and his dear loyal little children from Siberia."[142] Nowhere in any of the pages filled by Latyshev's hand is there the slightest suggestion of disloyalty to the throne. Latyshev is perfectly aware that Bonch-Bruevich is not a religious man, but he seems to have no conception of what else his correspondent may believe. In short, as Kel'siev had correctly perceived almost fifty years before, the Skoptsy were faithful subjects of the empire. Their vision of heaven on earth had no political dimension. Indeed, it was precisely the earthly quality of political life that seemed to them shallow and unworthy. Latyshev's patriotism, with its unwavering trust in the sovereign's personal goodness, was no doubt sincere, but he was no champion of military glory.

In the midst of war, Latyshev reflected on human history and the vanity of earthly existence. "Generation after generation have died off. . . . Man's mind dominates down below, people have become Gods, the rulers of darkness. Everything the insatiable animal will desires it has obtained; it has used everything, achieved everything. What does it need now? . . . O, woe to people, woe to humankind in general! . . . All their wisdom, all their work, all their deceptions in the end are useless." These days patriotic men were summoning the Slavic races "to wake up and fight, so the bayonettes and swords would flash along the valley of the Danube." But, Latyshev objects, such patriots forget "that other nations, . . . also created in His image and likeness, have the same, if not better preachers of ideas, who no doubt have their own views and convictions and are also not loath to defend themselves with bayonettes and swords." Victory for the Slavs was not ensured; calls to conquest might end in subjugation. Wars had been fought before, to no avail; the dead were merely replenished: "The human lava flows from place to place and has no solid place either on earth or under the earth. . . . And all that in the name of acquired and invented so-called ideas, in the name of earthly rights. . . . Evil triumphs!"

What had become of the grateful subject who had prayed for the victory of tsar and fatherland? Latyshev no doubt felt the commoner's true affection for this monarch, who was not only great and august but had graciously released the Skoptsy from eternal exile. But he is not deeply concerned with such mundane affairs. From his perspective, war was a consequence of error on the part of men who did not understand "God's Holiness, God's life." In contrast to politics, the futile struggle for power and domination, "God's life is real, it calls and beckons to the ark of salvation."[143] And who has found a place on God's ship, this "ark of salvation"? Latyshev, having passed his fiftieth year, had no doubts. "In our day . . . the true adherents of Evangelical Christianity are the Skoptsy, both spiritual and sometimes also physical. They want to return to the spirit of their former original holiness, the holiness of the heavenly angels. . . . The world, the nation do not exist for them. The world remained where it was, they separated from it, becoming Godly! They gave themselves to God, trusting the man who is God for them, the all-forgiving God of grace." Ever the translator, Latyshev anticipates the outsider's disbelief: "People not initiated into God's secret will find it strange and ridiculous that a man who looks like a man is at the same time by the power of the spirit God, the absolver of sin, purifier of souls! . . . But this is so simple and miraculously possible (probably only for the Skoptsy)."[144] Wars were merely human; the Godly had escaped the common fate.

It was not simply their acceptance of the return of Christ that separated the Skoptsy from the rest of humankind. Recognizing the moral frailty of his brothers in castration, Latyshev still defended the act as the ultimate commitment to the holy life. The Skoptsy were right to insist that "one must conquer nature . . . prevent the multiplication of the same irresolute sinners." Unbelievers think it barbaric. "You can subjugate nature to the spirit without fire and blood," they say: "then why castration? What's the point of scorching the roots of sin?" Latyshev wished to answer such challenges in terms that were meaningful to the modern world, even if it was a world he scorned and disparaged. In his tirade against war, he showed himself abreast of current events and opinions. In defending the ritual that seemed to contemporaries a "savage" act, "too severe, unsuitable," he wished to speak as a man of his times, not the relic of an archaic creed. Displaying his familiarity with "worldly wisdom," he uses an analogy from science. Just as a physician protects his patient against disease and death, he argues, so "a person who wants to save himself from eternal ruin, from the eternal hell of torments, from eternal death in return for original sin, [will] protect himself by castration from the all-destroying stupidity of sinning, from the eternal shame committed, as is well known, by the first people on earth. . . . The Skopets by his successful innoculation, his death to nature and life for the sake of his soul, is forever separated from the voluptuous sin of nature, has conquered in himself the animal instincts once and forever, has switched to serving God, sacrificing himself to God, the Holy, True God."[145]

These lines were composed in December 1915. Two years later the earth had shifted under Latyshev's feet; the old regime was dust and ashes. As if in answer to the rhetoric of salvation, a new world had arisen in its stead. It was a moment of anxiety and expectation, for the Skoptsy, as for everyone else. Some commentators have argued that Communism represented the fulfillment of the apocalyptic, utopian vision embedded in folk dreams of paradise on earth. In the case of Soviet scholars, this observation reflects their sympathy for the socialist project and their desire to demonstrate its popular roots. For post-Soviet intellectuals, the motive is to disparage the revolutionaries' secular claims by insisting on the symbolic link between the sectarians' Heavenly Kingdom and the grandiose schemes of Bolsheviks at the helm. It is certainly the case that the populists—and Bonch-Bruevich, in their wake—hoped literally to annex heresy to revolution. It is also true that Great October promised to inaugurate the end of Time (History) and the triumph of Reason (Enlightenment) over Tradition (Darkness). It aspired to transform humankind into the New Man and New Woman of the collective age, to end bourgeois family life and install the era of Winged Eros (Aleksandra Kollontai's phrase), which was no eros at all, but a diffusion of energy throughout the body social, melding selfish desire into a communal whole. Did the Skoptsy project of physical and spiritual transfiguration anticipate—or even inspire, these designs? The story of how the sectarians, and in particular the Khlysty and Skoptsy, were perceived by Silver Age artists, intellectuals, and radicals, searching for models of symbolic expression and spiritual exaltation, deserves to be told.[146] But it is not our story. We are interested in the Skoptsy. Lest we ourselves succumb to the influence of metaphoric thinking, finding vestiges of holy castration in the rituals of the Communist regime, let us see how the flesh-and-blood adherents of the faith, Gavriil Men'shenin and Nikifor Latyshev in particular, made the transition to the new life.

5 🕊 LIGHT AND SHADOW

The people that walked in darkness have seen a great light: they that dwell in the land of the shadow of death, upon them hath the light shined.

ISAIAH 9:2

The people which sat in darkness saw great light; and to them which sat in the region and shadow of death light is sprung up.

MATTHEW 4:16

THE Skoptsy invented the mechanism of instant transfiguration at a moment of festering popular discontent. Catherine had recently colluded in the murder of Peter III and assumed the throne—an act of brash usurpation. Ten years after Peter's death, the disgruntled multitudes, invoking his name, followed Pugachev in a furious revolt against landlords and the throne. The powerless were hungering for earthly satisfaction. A similar impatience for inaccessible rewards can be discerned in the device of self-castration, which telescopes death and resurrection into one excruciating gesture of self-sacrifice, through which the Spirit is received and salvation granted. In stage-managing the anticipated finale of human existence, the Skoptsy took command of their fates, just as Pugachev had tried to intervene in the disposition of worldly matters.

A century and a half later, the facts of life and death had not altered. Succeeding generations of castrated believers had received the faith, replenished the earthly granaries with their labors, and then abandoned the vestiges of unwanted flesh for the disembodied existence of heavenly angels. As a community, however, the Skoptsy survived long enough to experience as dramatic a change in their earthly surroundings as they had managed to produce in the privacy of their souls. Not every millennial fellowship, persisting in expectation of universal renewal, gets such a chance. To the confessional groups that had suffered under the old regime, the new seemed to offer greater scope for the spirit.

This hope was an illusion. The Soviet state proved a blessing in disguise only in its role as the grave keeper of religious fervor. This book is a direct beneficiary of the regime's ideological arrogance and also of its collapse. It is nowadays easier than ever before to use the documentary record the Bolsheviks so pridefully amassed. Archivists may now display their scholarly expertise with the generosity of true colleagues. Sitting in a dank cubby high under the dome of St. Petersburg's Cathedral of Our Lady of Kazan, I fingered the material preserved and annotated by Bonch-Bruevich, detecting with excitement the sound of voices lost in the grand rumble of historical time. Among the odd-sized envelopes crammed with photographs of the brethren and their haunts were the portraits of Nikifor Latyshev, in childhood and manhood, identified in his own clearly legible hand, accompanying the papers in which he tells his story. The final chapter of his personal tale takes us back to the start, for the circumstances of the community's destruction are those that ensured the means for bringing it back to life.

Light Dawns

The earth may have shifted in 1917, but the end of empire was not accompanied by thunder and lightning, any more than the Second Redeemer had arrived in a halo of fire; the heavens did not immediately tremble. In February the monarchy was replaced by a committee of Duma deputies, who called themselves the Provisional Government. Respect for legal procedure combined with the lack of a formal mandate from the nation prevented them from ruling with conviction. Yet they set about immediately dismantling the legal structure of the old regime. The Skoptsy were no longer outlaws.

In the name of traditional piety, the autocracy had intervened heavily in the policing of spiritual affairs. Nineteenth-century Russian liberals criticized this policy, not only as disrespectful of individual rights, but as harmful to religion. Secular in outlook, they saw no contradiction between religious belief and modern principles of civic life. In protesting restrictive laws and rejecting the highly regulative strategy pursued since the time of Peter the Great, they argued for the extension of autonomy to religious institutions, on the one hand, and to individual believers, on the other, as a means of strengthening the nation's moral fiber. It was just such a program that was enacted by the Provisional Government on July 14, 1917, when it granted freedom of religious belief and the right to change confessional allegiance—or to profess no religion at all.[1]

When, in October, the Bolsheviks dislodged the liberals and their moderate socialist allies from their tentative hold on power and installed themselves at the head of the state, they did away with tsarist legislation altogether. Respecting neither religion nor the law, the new rulers focused single-mindedly on eliminating political opposition and disrupting the cultural and ideological allegiances that might challenge their monopoly on true belief. While adopting freedom of conscience as their slogan, their goal was to cripple the actively hostile Orthodox church and ultimately to discourage the practice of religion in any form.[2]

The Bolsheviks proceeded toward this objective with a mixture of pragmatic restraint and ideological belligerence. The first Soviet decree on religion, the Declaration of the Rights of the Peoples of Russia, issued November 2, 1917, immediately after the seizure of power, equalized the status of the various confessions, revoking the special privileges of the Orthodox church. In December 1917, additional decrees introduced civil marriage, which had not existed in tsarist times, and ended church-sponsored education.[3] The regime also confiscated church property. The autocracy had on occasion done the same, but for different reasons. Then, the state had endorsed, but also dominated, the religious domain. Secularization under the Soviets went further, of course, enhancing state power by seeming to liberate belief from any institutional constraint. The decree of January 23, 1918, on Separation of Church from State and School from Church endorsed "freedom of conscience," freedom of choice, freedom to abstain, and equality of belief before the law.[4] The high-minded rhetoric barely concealed the underlying repressive designs, which emerged more clearly with each successive decree. The July 10, 1918, Constitution of the Russian Republic (RSFSR), while affirming the "freedom of religious and antireligious propaganda," relegated the clergy to second-class citizenship.[5] In the short run, however, even some believers felt their lot enhanced. Insofar as these measures undermined the privileged position of the Orthodox church, indeed attacked its institutional well-being at the core, and insofar as they asserted the equality of creeds and the possibility of choosing among them, they benefited minority confessions and the sectarians in particular. Having no churches, nonconformists were immune from the attack on institutions. Long persecuted for attempting to spread their faith, they could now proceed unharmed.[6]

Early Soviet law reversed the underlying principle of tsarist policy, which had reinforced ecclesiastical authority while restricting individual belief. The distinction invoked by Soviet laws did not, however, constitute a recognition of individual civil rights as prerevolutionary liberal jurists had conceived them.[7] Reluctant to offend the devout common folk, the regime observed a thin line between anticlericalism and the assault on faith. Throughout the mid-1920s hotheaded atheists debated cautious pragmatists on the best methods to achieve the ultimate goal: a nation without religion.[8] The confusion of policy and Party line left room for believers who adapted themselves to the new dispensation. It has been argued that even the Orthodox folk practiced their faith at such a remove from official institutions that Soviet anticlericalism did not come as a shock. But many peasants and workers fiercely objected to attacks on the church and on the Orthodox religion.[9] Sectarians, though loyal subjects, were more likely even than ordinary folk to have decoupled their faith from its link to worldly power. They might have tended to view political change with a neutral eye and to expect some benefit from a system that formalized this detachment.

As with so many other aspects of Soviet life, Stalin's ascent was decisive. The Russian constitution was amended in 1929 to eliminate the right to proselytize: citizens no longer enjoyed the "freedom of religious and antireligious propaganda" granted in 1918 and reaffirmed in 1924, but only "the freedom of confession and of antireligious propaganda."[10] The latter formulation entered the Soviet constitution in 1936. As in tsarist times, when spiritual propaganda was monopolized by the state-supported Orthodox church, spiritual orthodoxy (in this case, atheism) was once again a state preserve. Religious activity was not banned but carefully regulated.[11] Indeed, 1929 seems to have constituted something of a high point in the trajectory of ideological consolidation and assault. In concert with the revised Russian constitution of that year, the League of the Godless, founded in 1925 as an organ of spiritual reeducation, renamed itself the League of the Militant Godless (Soiuz voinstvuiushchikh bezbozhnikov).[12] Despite its aggressively hostile tone, the league did not approve coercive measures that might antagonize the unenlightened. For one thing, such tactics did not work: the existence of "godless collective farms" and "godless shock brigades" had not defeated popular religious belief. By 1930 the Party itself was denouncing abuses on the antireligion front.[13] The league's journal, the brash and crudely illustrated *Bezbozhnik* (Unbeliever), closed temporarily in 1934.

Bonch-Bruevich experienced these shifts in personal terms. As Lenin's trusted associate, he had made the transition in 1917 from radical critic to inside power broker. When the religion decrees were being formulated, he served as administrator of the Council of People's Commissars, a position he retained until 1920. In the early years he set the tone for Party appeals that depicted religious nonconformists as victims of the old regime and urged them to endorse the new. In 1921 the Commissariat of Agriculture, appealing to sectarians as proto-Communists, attempted to involve them in collective farms. Certain leading Tolstoyans actively supported the regime and offered their services as conduits to the peasantry at large. Lenin himself welcomed such cooperation, supporting the return of Canadian Dukhobors, successful agriculturalists whose skills and collectivist ethos might benefit Soviet economic development. During the unsettled early years of the market-driven New Economic Policy (NEP), Bonch-Bruevich's attitude toward the sectarians was somewhat incoherent. On the one hand, he insisted that they belonged to the ideologically acceptable poorer peasantry; on the other, he described them as rural pacesetters, congenial by virtue of their spiritual nonconformism and useful as a model of economic success. In 1929 the League of the Militant Godless denounced as a vestige of idealistic populism any notion that sectarians were either oppressed or politically progressive. Bourgeois to the core, the league declared, they were not appropriate allies. Not surprisingly, Bonch-Bruevich, a good Party man, soon came around; by 1930 he was echoing the view that sectarians had outlived their heroic past and deserved no special regard.[14]

Seeing the Light

The fall of tsarism promised an end to persecution, and for this reason alone unorthodox believers were grateful. Before the year 1917 was out, Gavriil Men´shenin wrote in "ecstasy" to his old correspondent, no longer a dissident himself but now ensconced in the seat of power, "congratulat[ing]" him on "the revolution and on the fall of the old type of government." Asserting he now "liv[ed] and breath[ed] freedom," Men´shenin "greet[ed] the revolution with joy," glad he had lived "to see the new dawn of life."[15] In March 1919, Lisin's followers recorded the words of a prayer meeting, in which the Redeemer was said earlier to have predicted the advent of a new regime and new laws, which he advised his flock to welcome and obey, not as sacred in themselves but as the fulfillment of a prophesy.[16]

Did these expressions of welcome signal a meeting of utopian extremes, secular and sectarian? Did the Skoptsy understand the new dispensation as the analogue—or even enactment—of their own desire for the appearance of heaven on earth?[17] No doubt the collapse of the autocracy inspired many with awe. The use of religious imagery to express enthusiasm for the revolution was not peculiar to sectarians, let alone Skoptsy. Many ordinary people referred to the seemingly miraculous February events, in which the monarchy crumbled and the three-hundred-year-old Romanov dynasty was swept effortlessly from the stage, in terms of resurrection or even Christ's Second Coming.[18] No doubt some of these took the language literally. Yet once the Bolsheviks initiated their attack on the church and its teachings, many of the faithful opposed them as enemies of true belief.[19] The Skoptsy, for their part, had reasons to rejoice that were entirely this-worldly: their erstwhile oppressors had left the scene. In the uncertain conditions of sudden change, they wished to find favor with the new rulers of the land. They do not seem to have distinguished between the liberals who dismantled the old order and their radical successors, but they happened to have contacts with the Bolsheviks who had triumphed in the end and who—in the person of Bonch-Bruevich—had courted them precisely for their religious convictions. The Skoptsy had long been accustomed to expressing themselves in religious language; no reason to change now.

On this occasion, so conducive to the merging of pragmatic and apocalyptic modes, Men'shenin nevertheless took pains to separate his religious feelings from his worldly response. Despite some trouble with local authorities who threatened to confiscate his apartment for use as a radio station, Men'shenin assured Bonch-Bruevich of his continuing loyalty to the regime: "I call [the revolution] Great," he insisted in 1921, "because it is truly great. It has affected and struck man's body and soul."[20] But he had not abdicated his faith: "Although the new era denies the Great God of the universe," he wrote a year later, "I remain convinced of the Greatness of God."[21] What he appreciated was the policy of religious toleration. In 1924 he wrote, in the name of the entire community, to congratulate the Central Committee on its enlightened stand. In contrast to the old regime, "Soviet Power . . . has granted full freedom . . . to believers to worship God in their own way."

> In the name of all the members of the Skoptsy sect, I therefore convey our thanks and gratitude to Soviet Power for protecting us. May it enjoy prosperity and peaceful existence in all its blessed undertakings for the folk. We are all infused with the consciousness of deep feelings of respect.
> Let me add, that in the democratic spirit we Skoptsy submit fully to the Power that grants freedom of conscience. We are ready to respect the laws of the present Power. We have never harmed the people or the state. We always follow the path of that truth, unity, and brotherhood. Our life and feelings will always welcome Soviet Power.[22]

Despite the restrained tone of this formal statement, the Skoptsy idiom of heaven on earth was indeed perfectly suited to the new cirumstances of utopia triumphant. But the Skoptsy were masters of instrumental rhetoric. Writing in November 1920, Nikifor Latyshev chooses a vocabulary that can be read either as naive and otherworldly or as solidly rooted in the pragmatics of power in a world no less hostile for being ideologically transformed. Expressing the hope that in Bonch-Bruevich's "idea of Goodness and Light [Dobro i Svet] perhaps we too can find peace from former persecution and exile," he hails the advent of Soviet power as the coming of "Might and Light" (a rough translation of "Sovet i Svet," a typical Skoptsy pun) and the end of cruel mistreatment.[23] While emphasizing the elements their two projects shared, Latyshev had all along been conscious of the divergence between his own beliefs and Bonch-Bruevich's way of thinking. Now, when his fate depended most directly on maintaining his correspondent's goodwill, he reminds the Bolshevik of his own small role in the latter's achievement. He calls himself Bonch-Bruevich's "humble little helper in gathering the materials of enlightenment and the illumination of human darkness. With all my might I tried to be useful to you and your studies. I collected what I could and what I knew. During the day I worked at my job, at night and on holidays I wrote."[24]

In 1920, at the very moment, ironically, when Bonch-Bruevich was being removed from his position as administrator of the Council of People's Commissars and demoted to editing a newspaper, his humble friend from the common folk addressed him in his finest ceremonial prose, language fit for a king. It was a language in which ideology played no role, for ideology was risky. Metaphor and the cadences of the sublime provided safer ground, as they always had, in the Skoptsy experience. Claiming to rejoice in the Soviet conquest of the Crimea, Latyshev admits to having "little interest in national politics." "But all the same," he assures Bonch-Bruevich, "the balance is on your side: where there is greater human truth, more love for the downtrodden folk immured in darkness, where for the first time Human Kind has seen a breach in the shroud of Darkness, where—in a word, the people's leaders, not fearing the most powerful People and Nations on earth, have torn away that mightiest of veils—lies, deceit, and darkness. And shown people the Truth, Love, and the Light!" As for Bonch-Bruevich himself: "You have deservedly risen to the height of your calling, running the greatest enterprise in Russia, that of the People's State. You are busy building the Branch on which people may reach the Light of Enlightenment, the Light of healthy and normal human life."[25]

The motive behind the letter was not, of course, to celebrate the conquest of the Crimea, or even to cheer the triumph of enlightenment, but to seek assistance with the trials of everyday existence. Alas, nothing was perfect "on this gray earth." An elderly spiritual sister had sent him a book of verses and hymns. Not realizing that the Kingdom of Light had dawned, she still feared persecution by deacons and priests and sent him a string of anxious registered letters. The censor (now Soviet, but this provokes no comment) had concluded that "there must be something political here and ordered an investigation." A commissar had visited Latyshev's apartment, seized his correspondence, and written a report. Then he had taken Latyshev to the city and put him in prison, among a "den of various rabble—speculators, petty thieves, and bandits." "Bitterly insulted," Latyshev prayed for God's help. Having heard his version of things, two officials finally admitted his innocence, shook his hand in apology, and sent him home. The misunderstanding, "Grace be to God," had ended well. That was April. It was now November. The factory where Latyshev and his brother had been working as watchmen had closed and along with it the factory apartments. Could Bonch-Bruevich help him find a new place to live? As for the unpleasant incident, it was understandable: misapprehensions on both sides—a nervous old woman mistrustful of authority in any guise; low-level officials sensitive to political trouble but indifferent to religion as such. Nothing that could not be resolved, with God's help, and knowing they had at least one friend in high places.[26]

It is not clear from the record how often or successfully Bonch-Bruevich intervened in the lives of his correspondents. Sometimes it is obvious he could not or would not respond when the Skoptsy appealed for his aid, but the letter writing nevertheless continued, offering a chronicle of these uncertain years. For Latyshev and Men´shenin the mid-1920s presented a mixed picture. Preoccupied with gaining access to the historical archives, so he could at last refute the slanders concocted by the enemies of the faith, Men´shenin complained about archivists who stood in his way and other petty cares. In particular, he asked Bonch-Bruevich to intervene on behalf of Petr Zverev, who was arrested in 1926, when two hundred rubles were found in his possession. We have encountered Zverev before. In the 1890s, as a young man, he was exiled to Siberia with his father and brother, where they settled not far from the Latyshev clan. When the Zverevs returned to European Russia after 1905, they were the wealthiest family in the village. By 1917, Petr Zverev had become the coproprietor of a grain-trading firm, which lasted until

1920. He next ran a handicraft workshop employing twelve Skoptsy and then shifted to the metalware business. When arrested by order of the Tomsk political police (then, the GPU), Zverev denied any wrongdoing. He himself had suffered as a victim of tsarist oppression, he declared, on the same terms as the "fighters for the people's freedom," whom the Skoptsy encountered in Siberian exile and assisted with material support. The Tomsk brethren petitioned the authorities on Petr's behalf, urging he be freed on bail. They insisted on his good character "as a principled man who had suffered for our ideas in tsarist prisons and exile, along with many political activists." Despite the transparently absurd claims, Zverev seems to have survived the ordeal, for in 1929 he was seeking Bonch-Bruevich's advice on the possibility of forming a collective farm composed exclusively of the brethren.[27]

Zverev's misfortunes demonstrate the persistence of anticommercial attitudes even at the height of the market-driven New Economic Policy. The same hostility is evidenced in the extraordinary calamity experienced by the Latyshev family in 1924, which also testifies to the undisciplined character of local authority in the early Soviet years. In explaining the event to Bonch-Bruevich, five years after the fact, Latyshev brought his correspondent up to date on the family fortunes. By 1917, Nikifor and his older brother Andrei had moved to Aleksandrovsk in Ekaterinoslav province, where they found work in the local machine-building plant, and where they had "experienced all the horrors of the civil war." Having buried their parents in 1919, they moved to Kursk province in 1922. Following an established Skoptsy custom, they had accepted the offer of an elderly Skopets to become his heirs and run his household. There, in the village of Lower Ol'khovatka, they set up house with the old man and two aged spiritual sisters, Belianicheva and Barbatunova. The locals considered them a "laboring collective" and identified them as Skoptsy, or perhaps Old Believers. The villagers were also apparently convinced that Andrei Latyshev possessed a small fortune in gold, allegedly entrusted to him for safekeeping by his fellows during the civil war. As reported in the local newspaper, *Kurskaia pravda,* "criminal elements" therefore found the household an object of curiosity.[28]

What happened next belongs to the genre of rhetorical hyperbole encountered so often in hostile representations of the Skoptsy. This time, however, the fantastic elements were all too real. On the night of November 19–20, 1924, so the newspaper explained, a group of masked robbers entered the Latyshev brothers' house by climbing a ladder and shattering a windowpane. The "bandits" pursued Andrei to his hiding place under a cart and shot him point blank. Nikifor and the old folks tried to hide or flee but were rounded up and severely beaten. The robbers turned the stove inside out, searching for gold. Unappeased by offers of Soviet money, they trampled it under their heels. The two helpless old women they threw to the ground, kicking them with their boots and singeing their legs, bellies, and genitals with candles and cigarette lighters. The abuse lasted several hours. Convinced that Nikifor and the old man, both unconscious, were no longer of this world, the intruders sprayed the women with bullets and left them to bleed. Several weeks later the old man died; Nikifor and the women recovered but sustained permanent injuries and psychological trauma.[29]

The incident reflects the danger of violence in these unstable years. But more than simple violence, or even greed, was involved in the robbers' behavior. It was not enough to beat the old women (one was seventy). The desecration of their sexual parts suggests a form of black magic, in which the threatening gesture (self-inflicted castration) is turned back against the perpetrators. The criminals' macabre assault inflicted a distorted "baptism of fire" on the genitals of women too old to procreate or arouse sexual desire. In the scuffle, Belianicheva had somehow managed to unmask one of the men, whom she recognized as a member of the local volunteer militia. He was accompanied by two colleagues and an assistant, as well as an agent of the criminal investigation service and two neighbors. After a series of trials, three of the aggressors were acquitted, while the rest were convicted and sent to jail.

Despite the partial vindication, the effect on the victims was devastating. "Our health is ruined and we live in fear," Latyshev wrote Bonch-Bruevich after the verdict. "We even agreed to employ an entirely secular married man to live with us and run the household. But one way or the other, life and peace are shattered."[30] To escape the hostile atmosphere, Latyshev moved to the city of Osa in the former province of Perm (by then the Molotov region), on the Kama River, where he set up house in March 1928 with a spiritual sister, replicating not only the old

Skoptsy model of small-scale enterprise but also, as he now construed it, fulfilling the demands of the laborers' state. "We have everything we need," he boasted to Bonch-Bruevich in November 1928, "a small garden and two little cows, which feed us. We sell butter, cream, and milk. Our community is fine, everyone does factory labor or raises produce. We live an exemplary laboring life."[31] A year later his new situation had soured. Using his own savings, he had "rebuilt the compound, bought another cow, grain, hay for fodder, and so on. I began to think here's a place I can live out my days. But nothing doing. So long as the Sister saw me taking cash from my pocket she was oh so good and talkative, but when the cash ran out and it was hard to get more and nowhere to be found, she pulled a long face and seemed dissatisfied. Well, the house was hers and I came to her, not she to me. Well, whatever; she was discontent. And I am by character sensitive or whatever or I don't know what, with a soft and probably weak-willed soul, easily take offense, so I tinkered with the idea of moving again, somewhere more restful for my wimpy little soul."[32]

The Shadow Falls

While Latyshev worried about his personal affairs, Men'shenin was beginning to note the changed political atmosphere. In September 1927 he protested to Bonch-Bruevich about a propaganda play performed in Moscow which depicted the Skoptsy in a negative light. The intent to "insult any and all sects" reminded him of the methods used by the "tsarist-clerical gang," he complained, enlisting a Soviet-style slur.[33] Also during the fall of 1927, the GPU had rounded up a Skoptsy community outside Leningrad, consisting of 150 men and 8 women, some well along in years. Nine months later they still languished in confinement, Men'shenin objected: a clear injustice, reminiscent of the old regime.[34] In September 1929 the GPU had searched his own apartment while he was out, confiscating the notebooks prepared for Bonch-Bruevich's museum, as well as photographs and rare books on the Skoptsy. In early October he himself had been interrogated for four hours.[35]

By contrast, the year 1928 brought Latyshev some pleasure. It was then he discovered that Bonch-Bruevich's 1922 study of sectarians cited his precious notebooks, and his joy knew no bounds: "O! how happy and satisfied I am that my work, however minor, has been entered into History."[36] But the opportunity to tell the truth was no longer as bright as it had seemed with the onset of "Might and Light." Other Skoptsy were saying, Latyshev reported, that if Bonch-Bruevich were to publish his research now, he would, "like earlier scribblers, have to cast a shadow here and there to lower the prestige of the faith in the readers' eyes." A mere ten years after the revolution had raised the sectarians' hopes for tolerance and understanding, they were encountering the "same old persecution all over again."[37] This atmosphere only made them more reluctant to expose their beliefs. Though Latyshev said he had assured his fellows that "inquiry isn't inquest" (issledovanie ne sledstvie—another Skoptsy pun), they remained unconvinced. Still, the old folks—and he personally—were eagerly awaiting the promised tome.[38] Bonch-Bruevich owed it to them for supplying the raw material with which to set the record straight. That was an enterprise they still believed they shared, if not with the regime, then with him in particular, despite his association with worldly might.

This association notwithstanding, however, Bonch-Bruevich was also affected by the instability of the early Soviet years. The revolution had catapulted him and his comrades to power, but it caused ideological difficulties he had never experienced before. Wary of offending the guardians of political rectitude, whose own positions were far from secure, Bonch-Bruevich was forced to adjust his attitudes to the Party's shifting demands. It had by now renounced the posture of toleration for religious dissent which Bonch-Bruevich had helped define. He therefore had to demonstrate that he too had changed his mind. On the one hand, there was nothing to prove. Religion had never interested him for its own sake. As Latyshev and his fellows had always known, the Bolshevik dismissed it as something "mythical."[39] On the other hand, his quest for information about the stigmatized communities had established ties of mutual respect between him and his correspondents. In fact, the believers' trust was rewarded; their treasures were indeed in safe hands. Bonch-Bruevich saved the many letters he received: they constituted his repository of knowledge, the voices of natives speaking a soon-to-be-forgotten alien tongue.

By contrast, the Bolshevik kept few of his own replies. Perhaps the responses were perfunctory or formulaic, designed primarily to keep the connections alive. The files do, however, contain copies of the answers Bonch-Bruevich sent Men'shenin and Latyshev in 1928 and 1929, when they objected to the arrest and trial of several Skoptsy communities. Knowing that the mail was open to official scrutiny and therefore afforded a way of communicating his own attitudes, not only to his contacts in the vestigial world of religious faith but also to the ideological high command, Bonch-Bruevich may have utilized the museum archives to build a documentary history of his own true belief. The two Skoptsy had no doubt expressed their indignation in some expectation of being understood. Bonch-Bruevich had, after all, more than once come to the brethren's defense before different courts of law. But given his proud secularism and continuing public role, the response could not entirely have surprised them.

Bonch-Bruevich, of course, defended the honor of Soviet justice. The new regime did not prosecute anyone for what they believed. The arrested Skoptsy would have been charged with actions that violated human rights or harmed the social welfare. The same argument had been deployed in tsarist times to justify the same kind of harassment. The language was familiar as well. Bonch-Bruevich insisted that physical injury inflicted "under threat, or by some kind of material inducement, or by arousing religious fanaticism" was not to be condoned. Indeed, the encouragement of fanaticism was deplorable in itself.[40] The charge of economic exploitation, so emphasized in Nadezhdin's canonical tract, here emerged in Soviet guise. "You can put your hopes in anything, but you mustn't turn belief into a means of exploiting other people's labor, of seizing their wages, time, and human dignity."[41]

Defense of the need for repression led Bonch-Bruevich easily into an attack on the religious practices themselves. Castration served no purpose in any case, he scolded, but when practiced on children it was "inexcusable."[42] To Men'shenin he wrote in November 1928: "The twentieth century is time to call an end to propaganda for all kinds of genital disfigurement on so-called religious grounds. The circumstances that gave rise to such an idea in the eighteenth and nineteenth centuries, the customs and way of life created among the people by the autocracy and the dominant militant Orthodox church no longer exist. There is so much that is interesting, important, and necessary to engage one's energy and willpower, instead of trifles, like goading people into the fantastical 'kingdom of God' by all the methods invented by the unenlightened people of the seventeenth and eighteenth centuries."[43]

A year later, he wrote to Latyshev in the same vein, dwelling on child castration as the most extreme expression of what was wrong with Skoptsy belief. This emphasis allowed Bonch-Bruevich to wax indignant, while deflecting the brunt of his condemnation onto the status of the victim rather than the logic of the deed. "It goes without saying that Soviet Power can under no circumstances allow perversions to be performed here and there . . . by religious fanatics convinced that by mutilating people, and especially children, they will build God's kingdom on earth. Mutilation is mutilation, and it accomplishes nothing. That's my opinion. I understand the historical origins of this sect, I understand the situation of all of you who suffered under Nicholas I and II, Alexander III, II, and I. Doing what you did to yourselves you were often escaping terrible material conditions and through your ecstasy achieved the highest feelings. But now times are different, and if each can treat himself as he likes, he cannot do the same to underage children. This was not permitted before and cannot be permitted now."[44]

Arguing for the social determination of belief had allowed Bonch-Bruevich to defend sectarian benightedness in respectable Marxist terms as a product of historical circumstance and, in particular, as a response to injustice and oppression. The suffering peasantry, impoverished, exploited, and permeated with religious dogma, could be excused its flights of fancy. That some had the courage to concoct inventions of their own and reject those foisted upon them was only to their credit. Now, however, the same argument served to condemn, not absolve, the stubborn dissenters: the common folk was, by definition, no longer the object of oppression but master of its fate, no longer benighted but enlightened.

The tenor of Bonch-Bruevich's private communications can only be understood against the background of the assault on NEP that accompanied Stalin's turn toward forced industrialization and collectivization in 1928. The entrepreneurial spirit of the 1920s had never sat comfortably with Bolshevik maximalism; now trade, private property, and the accumulation of wealth were targeted for attack. Among the deeply exploited peasantry, it was said, some were fattening on the labor of others. These so-called kulaks (an old term with newly sinister implications) were as guilty of obstructing socialism as any landlord. At this juncture, the Skoptsy could no longer be viewed as spiritually befuddled enthusiasts or models of agricultural efficiency. They were now kulaks and exploiters.

This line of attack was not, however, entirely a product of the transition to Stalinism and the ferocious social warfare it unleashed. The themes had first been developed decades before, as we have seen, by Nikolai Nadezhdin, on the right, and by various commentators on the left. The populist view of sectarians as heroic nonconformists had shared rhetorical space with a radical critique of the Skoptsy as economic predators, not only in relation to feckless Orthodox peasants but also among themselves. Vladimir Iokhel´son, writing in 1894, used the disparaging term "kulak" to describe the wealthy Skoptsy of the Iakutsk region. Their coldhearted, insatiable avarice, he said, damaged the local communities, manipulating local markets to "take advantage of peasant need."[45] A study published in 1900 struck a similar note, describing how rich Siberian Skoptsy exploited the labor of their poor brethren (batraki) and excluded them from access to the land, resulting in a veritable class war within the community.[46] There was thus nothing original about the terms in which Soviet ideologues attacked the Skoptsy.

The trials of which Men´shenin and Latyshev complained provided an arena for political denunciation. They concerned three groups: one centered in the Leningrad area, one in Saratov (both tried in 1929–1930), and the last near Moscow (tried in 1931). The court proceedings and the propaganda literature the trials spawned characterize the defendants as kulaks, Nepmen, exploiters, speculators, predators, and hucksters.[47] They were portrayed at once as vestiges of the old order (religious obscurantists) and outcroppings of the latest policy shift (NEP profiteers). The familiar motif of conspiracy also resurfaced in the new context. Nadezhdin had railed against the far-flung network of spiritual and commercial ties that guaranteed economic success and tribal loyalty. Similar webs, he had pointed out, united the Jews in a sinister bond, which enabled them to sap the Russian nation.[48] Substituting revolutionary vigilance for overt anti-Semitism, Soviet ideologues retained the old images: the president of the Saratov People's Court wrote of a "clingy spider's web" spun by Skoptsy leaders to entrap new victims for their "fanatic predator-god."[49]

Webs and networks were not, alas, mere figures of speech. The verdict of the 1929 Leningrad trial insisted on the conspiratorial nature of the Skoptsy community. The sect, it ruled, "has the character of a formal organization. Its activities concern not only its ostensible goals but anti-Soviet ones as well. These activities occur in circumstances of strict conspiracy, involving only those already initiated into the sect." Devoted to an ideologically unacceptable mission, the congregations were linked, said the court, in a well-articulated system that escaped official control.

Nepmen–Skoptsy, Moscow. GMIR, fototeka, C-80-IV. (Copyright © GMIR.) Cf. N. Volkov, *Sekta skoptsov*, 2d ed. (Leningrad: Priboi, 1931), 106. Volkov used this photo to show how the Skoptsy had adapted to the modern commercial world, as indeed they had. Except for the white cloth (or shirttail) draped over the knee of the man on the right, they seem like ordinary fellows, quite pleased with themselves and unaware that their days as acceptable citizens were numbered.

The defendants were convicted, in the end, not only of inflicting physical injury (Article 142 of the 1926 Russian Criminal Code) but also of participation in organized counterrevolutionary activity (Article 58-10).[50]

The trial concluded with a speech by Nikolai Matorin (1898–1935), director of the Academy of Sciences Institute of Ethnography and head of the Leningrad division of the League of the Militant Godless.[51] Insisting on the class character of Skoptsy hostility to Soviet rule, he interpreted their support for NEP as a sign of bourgeois-capitalist sympathies.[52] The Skoptsy faith belonged to "the feudal and commercial capitalist eras," he explained, when it had originated "as an ideology of accumulation and retreat to one's greedy individual little world." These attitudes had unfortunately persisted into the Soviet period, although the community itself was splintering into antagonistic groups: kulaks and shop owners against the poor, exploited landless laborers. No longer were sectarians to be endorsed as the enemies of established religion; they must be denounced as its clearest exemplars: "Unmasking the Skoptsy," Matorin insisted, "we are at the same time unmasking the entire internal rot of the Christian creed, of Christian morality." Their prophesies, moreover, echoed "the same familiar anti-Soviet notes as in kulak and bourgeois agitation."[53]

In this context, Bonch-Bruevich was distinctive in avoiding the crudest terms of abuse (the word "kulak" is missing from these letters) and in his desire to sustain communication with the targets of ideological assault. His letter to Men´shenin in late 1928, denouncing Skoptsy fanaticism, is signed: "All the best. Write to me about everything."[54] His 1929 sermon to Latyshev concludes with the assurance: "I would be very happy if you let me know your opinion about what I have said in this letter."[55] He also seemed hesitant to renounce his long-standing belief (held dear for a quarter of a century by then) that Bolshevik orthodoxy was compatible with his interest in the unorthodox religious folk. Replying, in 1929, to a message from Petr Zverev, Bonch-Bruevich calls himself "an old Communist, a member of our Communist Party, to whose goals I have dedicated my life." As part of this commitment, he says, he had undertaken throughout his career to "understand the life of the popular masses, especially the peasantry and those called sectarians, and then honestly and objectively, without the least distortion, to describe that life." Wanting to keep the information pipeline flowing, he begs Zverev to keep him supplied with material about the Skoptsy, referring as always to the promised volume. For the past ten years Bonch-Bruevich had been distracted by other things. From 1921 to 1927 he had edited the journal *Zhizn' i znanie* (Life and Knowledge) and was at this point director of the State Museum of Literature. Now, he told Zverev, he wanted to resume his scholarly work.[56] The long-awaited book was never, in fact, published. When a study of the Skoptsy did appear in 1930, it was not at all what Bonch-Bruevich and his contributors had envisioned.

That outcome was not under Bonch-Bruevich's control. But he was not entirely candid when cultivating Zverev's good graces. He wished to have his ideological cake and eat it too: archives full and commissars happy. Knowing full well that policy had shifted, he nevertheless deflected Zverev's complaints about the hostile attitude of the Soviet press, on the grounds that journalists were often ill-informed about the "complicated issues of folk life, especially concerning the sects." At the same time, Soviet rule must be respected. It was unacceptable, he told Zverev, to "hide from the law and do one's dirty deeds," under the pretext of sectarian faith, as the Baptists had recently been caught doing. Having defended the Baptists before 1917 as unfairly maligned, Bonch-Bruevich now claimed they were agents of "Black Hundred White Guard . . . counterrevolutionary Polish intelligence."[57]

A strange passage from the correspondence with Men'shenin suggests that Bonch-Bruevich's bad faith was not entirely opportunistic but reflected inner conflicts on his side. Reminding Men'shenin in 1929 that, with the conclusion of NEP and the onset of the first Five Year Plan, the era of private property was over, Bonch-Bruevich uses images the Skoptsy themselves might have chosen, as if confirming a link that still might span the widening ideological divide: "It is finally time to rid ourselves of this ancient serpent-seducer," the Bolshevik warned, "which we must really beat over the head, because this is in fact the very flesh that weighs us down."[58] Given Bonch-Bruevich's condemnation of Skoptsy belief, his appropriation of metaphors peculiar to them suggests an unmastered ambivalence on his part—not in relation to their world, but to his own. The serpent of Skoptsy discourse represented the organ of desire and impregnation. Bonch-Bruevich's borrowed images thus suggest an intuition that the Soviets, in abolishing private property, were amputating the source not only of temptation and pleasure but also of fecundity and abundance.

No doubt this ambivalence emerged only because it was unmastered. Bonch-Bruevich was not a man of independent mind, and the time for political disagreement was in any case over. In regard to his contacts in the field, there was less and less room to maneuver. By 1929 complacency toward religious dissenters was no longer acceptable. At the opening of the Leningrad trial, Nikolai Matorin had offered his personal hospitality to Bonch-Bruevich should he wish to travel up from Moscow. Soon Matorin was assailing Bonch-Bruevich's "liberal-populist approach" and his "assessment of many aspects of sectarian activity" as "deeply misguided."[59] A politically more acceptable interpretation, consonant with the rhetoric of the recent trials, was provided by Nikolai Volkov, at the time a graduate student in the Academy of Sciences Institute of Ethnography. Born in 1904, of peasant origin, Volkov had joined the Party in 1921.[60] He was admitted to the institute ten years later on the recommendation of the Party section of the Leningrad regional division of the League of the Militant Godless, which vouched for his "ideological reliability."[61] There, under Matorin's guidance, he prepared an "ethnographic" study of the Skoptsy, first published in 1930, which bore the stamp of "correct science."[62]

It was a science that explained everything in economic terms. "The mystical covering of Skoptsy belief in fact conceals entirely real economic interests," Volkov declared. These were the interests of merchants and kulaks, whose voracious appetite for wealth could be satisfied only by the cruel exploitation of the oppressed and needy masses. Enticed by promises of salvation, impoverished peasant recruits were bound for life by the indelible stigma: "The brand of physical mutilation prevented them from rupturing the fatal bond."[63] Echoing the views of turn-of-the-century radicals, Volkov emphasized the element of conflict between rich and poor.[64] Unburdened with children among whom they would have had to divide their gains, rich Skoptsy grew ever richer. In Siberia, the wealthier settlers exploited the laboring masses.[65] Citing a passage in which Nadezhdin describes the mutual support that held the sect together, Volkov criticized the bureaucrat for misrepresenting the actual conditions of Skoptsy life and failing to apply a materialist analysis.[66] Volkov nevertheless relied on nineteenth-century sources such as Nadezhdin and Pelikan for information about Skoptsy rites and the physical consequences of castration. As a Bolshevik, however, he preferred a social to a physiological explanation. "Such negative traits as egotism, cunning, and greed, typical of the Skoptsy masses, can better be explained as a result of the social environment in which . . . the members are mainly recruited: the venal huckster and peasant-kulak who join the sect lend it the psychological features of their class."[67]

Volkov derives not only his themes but also his style from the standard genre of denunciation. Like earlier texts, this one offers graphic first-person accounts of castration. One pretends to describe the group ritual performed on four men and a ten-year-old boy. The scene is narrated as the boy's recollection in adulthood. It has the requisite elements: the knife, the streaming blood, the crude bandaging and salves, the suspense while waiting one's turn, the shock, the recovery. Another believer recalls the lead nail inserted into his urinary canal, which was kept in place during the eight painful months of healing. This procedure is described in Pelikan's study, which includes an engraving of the tools and equipment used for the job. Volkov also produces an account of female castration, in which a man purports to recall his experience as a young boy, witnessing his mother help in severing another woman's breasts.[68] In the first edition, Volkov concedes that deaths from these procedures were relatively rare.[69] The concession is missing from the later edition. The early edition also includes photographs from the 1929–30 trials, showing castrated men and women in naked, frontal poses. The subjects regard the camera with the same stolid gaze that appears in snapshots the Skoptsy had taken of one another over the years. These were clearly unwilling subjects of the camera's eye, and their emotions—whether dignity, shame, sadness, or regret—can only be imagined.

Like everything else in Volkov's book, the images are designed to elicit sympathy for the suffering of the common folk (even if self-inflicted) and indignation at the effects of ignorance (religion) and eco-

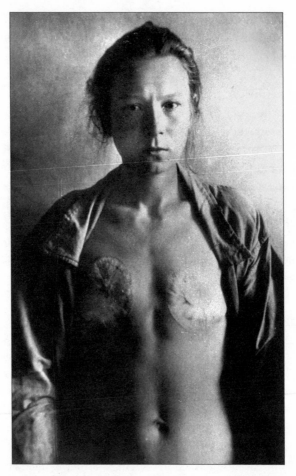

Female Skopets with major seal, 1928. GMIR, fototeka, C-
68/3-IV. (Copyright © GMIR.) Cf. N. Volkov, *Sekta
skoptsov,* 2d ed. (Leningrad: Priboi, 1931), 82. This harrowing portrait was taken by the authorities in the course of
preparing the 1929 trials. Volkov uses it to arouse the
reader's indignation. This and the following image are the
only two photographs reproduced in the present book
(with the exception perhaps of the Nepmen) in which the
subjects did not willingly participate. Unlike the stereo-
typical medical drawings in Pelikan's text, these documents for the prosecution capture the individual personality along with the anatomical features.

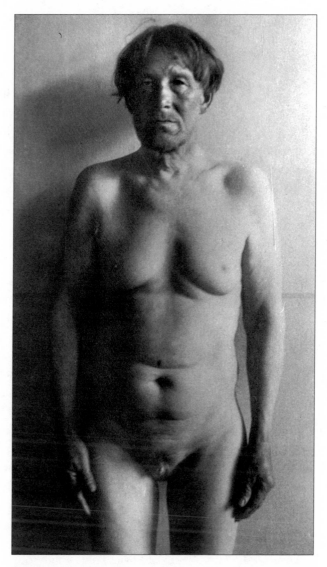

Skopets with major seal, 1928. GMIR, fototeka, C-665/25-IV.
(Copyright © GMIR.) Similar photos, also from the 1929 trials,
appear in Volkov's book. This middle-aged man has a craggy
peasant face but soft fleshy torso. Despite the appearance of
breasts (not unknown among ordinary men of a certain age), this
person is unequivocally of the masculine gender. If further proof
were needed that desexing did not obliterate gender among the
Skoptsy, either in social or biological terms, here it is.

nomic oppression. The latter was explained, as it was in the everyday politics of Soviet life, as the fault of "bourgeois-kulak" elements in the
countryside. As an elaboration of current political themes, the work, not
surprisingly, served the author in good stead. Volkov submitted the first
edition, along with the manuscript chapters on fascism and sterilization
included in the 1937 version, for the candidate's degree in ethnography.
Two academic reviewers endorsed the application and approved his "his-
torical-materialist" approach. "Facts in hand," wrote one, Volkov "ruthlessly destroys the bourgeois conception of this phenemenon [the
Skoptsy] and attempts independently to interpret the broad factual
material from the position of Marxist-Leninist methodology."[70]

Confident as they were in 1930–31 of their hold on Truth, both
Volkov and his mentor soon enough lost their grip. Arrested as a terror-
ist and enemy of the people, Matorin died in 1935, in his thirty-seventh
year.[71] Volkov was expelled from the Party in 1937 for "contacts with
enemies of the people, getting drunk with enemies of the people, and
relaxed vigilance."[72] He was at the same time dismissed from the Institute
of Ethnography. After volunteering for the front in 1941, he was
wounded, captured, and spent almost four years as a prisoner of war.
Readmitted to the institute in 1945, he was arrested for anti-Soviet activity two years later and dismissed once again.[73] Within days of the death of
Joseph Stalin in early March 1953, Nikolai Volkov also died, at the age of
forty-nine. He had spent his last years in a forced labor camp in the Kirov
district (formerly Viatka province), not far from Nikifor Latyshev's one-
time home in the former province of Perm. He was rehabilitated in
August 1989.[74]

The Kingdom of Heaven

If insistence on the Great Truth of Soviet science did not guarantee
its proponents either long life or spiritual solace, how did the spokesmen
of otherworldly transcendence fare? Men'shenin died in 1930 at the age
of sixty-eight, just as Volkov and Matorin were hitting their stride. Latyshev lasted until 1939, when he disappears from the record in his seventy-
fifth year, an aged but not unhappy man. The Soviet regime was a source
of aggravation, but his spirit prevailed. Feisty and argumentative as ever,
he kept Bonch-Bruevich apprised of his ordeals and state of mind. Their

epistolary relationship, ideologically fraught on both sides, survived the dangers and hardships of the 1930s.

Latyshev's anger over the Skoptsy trials of 1929–30 and Bonch-Bruevich's scolding did not put an end to the flow of words and the frank expression of opinion. Working with the vocabulary of Soviet political speech, Latyshev used it to establish his moral bona fides and define himself in acceptable terms. Yet the defensive maneuvers did not weaken but rather bolstered his commitment to his own, forever stigmatized identity. In February 1932 he and the members of his household were arrested and dispossessed of all their worldly goods.[75] In April they were interrogated by agents of the political police, who asked "where I lived, what I did, was I rich or poor. I told the simple truth, that I was never rich and have no tendency toward that class, being satisfied with my quiet, modest life. I am no threat to the Soviet regime and no criminal, never been involved in anything criminal, and despise those who misbehave." The interrogator "tried with all his might to make criminals of everyone with whom I once lived, thinking to pin something criminal on me, too, to justify their illegal action in seizing all our property."[76]

Calling himself "a worker-proletarian, a laboring Soviet citizen," Latyshev denounced the seizure as unjust. In the same "un-Soviet" manner, he said, the authorities had described Mariia Bochkareva, herself but a "poor proletarian," as a wealthy woman, though her "entire fortune consisted of a small house and one cow." Even the house was no longer hers. Latyshev claimed to have bought it from her. The investigators declared such transfers invalid under Soviet law. Then why, Latyshev demanded, when he signed the deed in 1931 had the state charged a fee for stamps and registration? The injustice galled him, and he wanted Bonch-Bruevich to think he'd had the courage to take the evildoers to task. "What a pity," he claimed to have admonished his interrogators, "that in Soviet Russia the innocent are treated so rudely. Only wreckers behave this way." He himself was loyal: "Of course one mustn't talk," he admitted to Bonch-Bruevich. "One must examine the situation carefully and not disgrace the Soviet regime. It has enough enemies already. And my injury plays into the hands of its enemies. Though I am not a Communist, I deplore the behavior of those who don't understand the behests of Lenin and other clever and noble Communists."

Bonch-Bruevich declined to intercede on Latyshev's behalf but advised him to bring his complaint to the higher powers, because local authorities must obey the law like anyone else.[77] Obsessed with his case, Latyshev had not yet unburdened his heavy heart. Apologizing, though with little conviction, for sending yet another letter in the same vein, Latyshev kept the chronicle going. "I'm very sorry, most esteemed Vladimir Dmitrievich," he wrote in February 1933, "that the great, mighty, Russian revolution, in which all the best forces, minds, and noblest people took part, should behave this way toward those who are poor ALTHOUGH completely insignificant. It seems to me a great mistake. Everyone has a right to live, the insignificant no less than the great, the powerful as well as the powerless.... I myself am a real son of the proletariat who should not be slighted."

Latyshev also reported on conditions of everyday life: "I spent the summer growing things in the garden, planted several tomato plants, and lived on what I sold.... At present I'm working as a carpenter in the organization 'Red Star,' earning a little, maybe 80–100 rubles a month on piecework. Produce is fantastically expensive. Rye bread, flour at 100 a pud [measure equal to about 16 kilograms], and there isn't any. No more bread or produce rations to organizations. There is no bread. None in the villages either. The collective farmers come to town in search of bread to buy. People are terribly hungry. We eat nothing but potatoes now and at 25–30 rubles a pud we can't really afford them and a pud doesn't last long. People are in a horrible state and there's little joy anywhere." The lamentation concludes with a characteristic mix of ingratiation and asperity: "Forgive me for bothering you. I would like to praise the goodness of the highest Soviet authorities in the presence of the people of the entire world, and all the more so to you, most respected Vladimir Dmitrievich. But clearly it's not fated to be."[78] Indeed, the year 1933 brought even worse news before it was over. In August, Latyshev received a letter from his home village, reporting that his brother Fedor, by then almost eighty, had died in early May, of starvation. The local situation had been "very bad," he learned, "in the village at least 500 or 600 people died."[79]

This correspondent hastened to add that the harvest had since improved and the collective farms were being promised abundant supplies of bread.[80] Latyshev himself did not seem to fear the consequences of complaining. Indeed, he considered it a duty to record his humble experiences for the historical record. A loyal citizen had this right, and Latyshev was emphatically loyal. But to whom or what? He never betrays any interest in the particulars of socialism. There was no natural affinity between the Skoptsy way of life and the new social order. The sect did not hold property in common and neither preached nor practiced economic equality. Many, indeed, were devoted to the acquisition of wealth. Latyshev took his prosperous fellows to task for losing sight of higher things and said that among the "real ones by calling, all this beautiful solid stuff plays no role." Yet he managed to construe the community's material success as a positive achievement. "What they acquire by their efforts," he had written in 1910 of the thriving Skoptsy exiles, "serves only to show the world, look at us, spending our time working and earning material sustenance, and at the same time serving the Lord God and His Holy Cause."[81] There were, however, some points of convergence between the Godly and the Godless: each spoke of enlightenment, of a new era dawning; each proclaimed the righteousness of the injured and insulted; each believed they held the key to moral rectitude and the virtuous life. Being himself of the downtrodden, as Latyshev would have said, also gave him license to speak with a clear civic conscience.

But, in fact, the socialist project filled him with no special warmth. He saved his feeling for a particular person and his ambition for a loftier aim than any system could offer. Here is where his true loyalty lay. Bonch-Bruevich had done for Latyshev's cause, Latyshev wrote in December 1933, what "no other person on earth would have done. And I am very very pleased that it was precisely you who did this, with your good and great soul, a good Communist, who desires all the best for humanity." He, Latyshev, was but a "minor player, though one who loved the Good, the High and the Glorious, and mainly the Useful." Bonch-Bruevich had invited him, Latyshev, "negligible" as he might be, to share in the cause of enlightenment. Still eager to add his own "mite to the worthy cause," he wished that "every writer, every ordinary man, could boldly, openly, and honestly explain in writing, for history's sake, his views and opinions on the past, the present, and most important the future of humanity in all its varied beliefs and ways of understanding."

Clearly, he meant himself. At once humble and exalted, Latyshev believed in his own special gifts and used the posture of humility to bind himself in fellowship and clientage to his patron. "Forgive my philoso-phizing," he wrote coyly, still in December 1933. "Nonentity that I am, I sometimes think I let fall into my apparently silly words precious stones or drops of Light, but I don't have the will or help to bring them to the surface for history."[82]

If Latyshev insisted on his partnership in a spiritual cause that tran-scended time and place, he also portrayed himself in more specific, Soviet terms. Still employed at "Red Star," he boasted of the "honest and upright" work that earned him the occasional award, like the champions of socialist labor. Indeed, his standing as toiler, as the lowest of the low, seemed to authorize the expression of candid reproofs. "My health is broken from grief, sorrow, and work beyond my strength," he com-plained. The dreadful year of 1933 was only just coming to a close. "I am literally in the grip of complete poverty, often unable to buy a pound of bread, which a worker needs." Indeed, material want was a constant theme: "All improvements, all various cultures, games and amusements, are accomplished at the expense of us unfortunates and on our backs. But what is to be done? One half triumphs, the other groans in convul-sions of hunger and cold. I am a drop of these last. I have been working in the carpenter and cooperage shop at 'Red Star,' whose turnover reaches hundreds of thousands of rubles, while the conditions for work-ers are horrid; we manage somehow to work and live half-starving. In the shop it's cold, frost on the floor and walls. Not one window is solid, the holes are barely covered up by boards, and in such conditions we live."[83]

If suffering was a recurrent theme, so was injustice: the unresolved conflict over his confiscated property. The story, as he recounts it, has something of the irony and absurdity of Mikhail Zoshchenko's tales. Latyshev seems to relish the chance to bring characters to life and to portray himself in the grip of a tragicomic fate, as though Nikolai Gogol's Akakii Akakievich, from the story "The Overcoat," had seized the pen and exacted the revenge he could otherwise muster only as a vision from the other world. Perhaps that is how Latyshev saw himself, as an emissary from the beyond. Though tormented by his plight, he seems almost to welcome the excuse to turn his worries to literary ends. In

October 1933 he reports being interrogated "good and proper" by the regional procurator. Witnesses affirmed that he had "never traded in anything but had worked in factories. In short, the procurator decided they had cleaned out an innocent man and thus destroyed my life, which was already none too joyful." The Regional Executive Committee (RIK) was ordered to return his property. But Latyshev doubted they would ever find what had been "plundered." In fact, they were ignoring the procurator's orders. The income inspector, "a careerist, runs around like a bloodhound, asking everyone he meets, who's this Latyshev, was he formerly rich or poor. Tries to find the crimes I committed, but to his dismay there aren't any and never were. I don't dare ask the procurator how it will all turn out. . . . So I wait, pine away, despair, and grieve over the new life in Russia—on earth. If they're treating me like this, nothing much is new!" His elderly female companion had "up and died, this spring, partly from bitterness, mostly from hunger. All summer there was horrible hunger here. In the organizations, the shop employees and workers received no bread ration at all. Some tried to dry out wood: spruce, linden leaves, and various substitutes. Now some bread's appeared. I get 8 kilos a month, workers 12. And for that thanks a lot!" "Forgive me," he concluded, "for bothering you with my case, with my impoverished, bereft life."[84]

Apologies notwithstanding, two months later Latyshev was posting the next installment. Back at the procurator's for more information, he announced he had come "to find out whether the sixteenth anniversary of Soviet Power hadn't brought me the happiness of returning my practically worthless property." But there was nothing for him. "What kind of procurator is this? Why, I ask myself, should he be sorry?" The higher-ups, in Latyshev's not so humble opinion, were "ready to let the unfortunate perish so long as their authority doesn't suffer." The procurator was not a bad man but had no clout and told him to appeal to Sverdlovsk or even to Moscow. Alas, the procurator was "weak, timid, and scrawny, while the guys from the RIK are fat and greasy and consider themselves equal in dignity to Moscow."

In real life, the story did not end well, but it was worth telling. "So, dear, respected Vladimir Dmitrievich," Latyshev concluded, "forgive me for all this, but I speak without guile or trickery but only for history's sake to state the truth and my own opinion—sometimes stupid, sometimes sensible. I would like for everyone who does any thinking at all to record for history his views and opinions of the new life." Such thoughts were not, however, to be shared with everyone. Bonch-Bruevich constituted a kind of sacred ear, a trusted confessor: "You are the only one I deeply trust. You I consider over 19,000 kilometers high. To study the stratosphere is good, but to love a person and men in general is worth even more." Latyshev had not misplaced his faith. On the envelope Bonch-Bruevich wrote: "Not answered. Skoptsy."[85] This one for the file. He, too, put History first.

In the end Latyshev's small-scale campaign for justice, Soviet-style, came to naught. The regional authorities flaunted the law; the procurator, however sympathetic, was "a quiet one" whose powers were "puny." Alas, Latyshev was no "exception and not the first to fall victim of a mistake by the schemers and activists whose heads are spinning from success." In March 1930, Stalin had used the phrase "dizzy from success," in a tirade published in *Pravda,* which every citizen would have known and Latyshev now consciously echoed. "It would be nice," he went on in a less subservient vein, "if in my case, insignificant citizen that I am, Soviet Russia would correct its illegal mistake and ensure that local authorities took even the slightest account of revolutionary legality and carried out decrees from higher up. If they don't return the property, I'll submit to my fate and die from hunger. If strength permits, I'll write to [Petr] Smidovich in the Central Executive Committee. He knows my case. Maybe I'll even complain to Justice Commissar [Nikolai] Krylenko. Then I can take off to join my ancestors, where there's no sadness or lamentation, only joy! To be rid of all this dizziness!"[86]

As time passed, Latyshev relinquished his obsession with recovering his goods. Material conditions may also have improved. In 1934 he sent Bonch-Bruevich some general reflections on the Skoptsy sect, his own life, and the transition to the new world. "Nowadays here in Soviet Russia the question of God is practically extinct. The clergy of the dominant Orthodox religion has almost disappeared, you don't see them anymore. Baptists, Shtundisty, Egovisty, and other religious cults have also gone into hiding. You don't hear their songs or meetings as before. The Skoptsy have almost all died out. Sometimes I read in the newspapers or in some antireligious publications about the sectarians. Makes me wonder: are there any?"[87]

Far from regretting this turn of affairs, Latyshev praises the "benevolent" Soviet regime for using cultural means, rather than repression and Siberian exile, to detach people from their "unrealizable dreams" and attach them to reality. He does not in this passage mention the prison terms to which the brethren had only recently been condemned. Nor does he seem to regret the loss of these dreams, which he now describes as mistaken: "No religion or sect on earth," he writes, "has correctly understood its own actual true convictions. They erred in thinking up their OWN teachings, which were not God's." More generally, he seems to reject the very possibility of realizing religious principles on earth: "It's impossible indeed to transform the living world by worldly means into God's world." Having lost their spiritual direction, the faithful busied themselves with material well-being. He wondered "to what extent people might have been mistaken when seeking the light, not seeing and not knowing what Light is and what Light consists of."[88]

These enigmatic reflections do not indicate that Latyshev has wavered in his religious faith. They might possibly be construed as a rueful meditation on the shortcomings of Communism as an all-too-worldly enterprise, mistaken by some for a spiritual quest. They clearly reflect his desire to go on thinking about important things, to pursue his calling as a writer. In this connection, he apologizes for his lowly station, as he has repeatedly over the years. Out of touch with scientific literature, he explains to Bonch-Bruevich, he is afraid of reinventing the wheel.) But he insists, as he always has, on the value of his testimony as a man of the people, as a self-made intellectual. He continues writing precisely because "the world already wants to forget what we with our dim education dream about." "But all the same," he continues, "I'm sometimes pleased with myself for occasionally soaring higher than all the scholars on earth. I wonder where I get such rich ideas! But for all that, I tell them to no one—no one except the one person who wins my heart by his goodness and decent, upright dealings with me. With ordinary people I am humble and silent. No use—people won't understand and won't appreciate the convictions so dear to my dim life that cling to me body and soul."[89]

22~/III
19/38 г.   К № 14028   3

Многомилостивому ?

Для всех добрых, строгому для
всех злых врагов народа, которые ненавидят
добро и в своем зле ищут славы только себе
Забывая что добрая Слава дается народом
добрым, честным справедливым и довольным.

В силу этого всепобеждающаго добра, я и
пишу Вам как великому из великих, благо
родному во всех отношениях Сверх-человеку
Иосифу Виссарионовичу Сталину свою ис-
креннюю чистую от своего доброго Сердца благо
дарность, за то что, Вы, призрели сирот, на-
кормили голодных и одели нагих :—

Ваше высокоблагородное Сердце и великая
душа (жизнь) Сделали то что не один в мир
человек немог даже мечтать о таких великих
и благородных действиях и поступках вашего
все-побеждающаго добра и дела..

Letter from N. P. Latyshev to I. V. Stalin (December 22, 1938), sent to V. D. Bonch-Bruevich. GMIR, f. 2, op. 5, d. 49, l. 3–12ob. (Copyright © GMIR.) The letter is addressed: "To the one most gracious toward those who are good, but strict toward the evil enemies of the people who hate what is good and in their evilness seek glory only for themselves, forgetting that virtuous glory is given to the nation of people that is good, honest, just, and satisfied" (l. 3). The letter ends with a plea to the State Museum of Literature "if possible to keep in its archive my Mite of Praise and Gratitude to the Great, Glorious Benefactor, the highest Soviet Government,

Latyshev seems to have given up on the project of bringing heaven to earth. But he has not given up on transcendence. The writer from the people continues to register his thoughts and feelings, trusting that they will endure. Still living in two worlds, Latyshev persists in recording the details of everyday existence, while keeping his sights on Higher Things. His final communication with Bonch-Bruevich consists of two letters, one bidding him farewell and another, dated December 22, 1938, the one addressed to Joseph Stalin. Its ostensible purpose is to pay tribute to the Almighty Earthly Power, while also reporting on the moral condition of the realm. More important, however, since the letter is not sent to Stalin but intended for archival safekeeping, it is designed to speak to Eternity.

Addressing Stalin as one "most gracious to those who are good," he mixes archaisms and current idiom in a parody of self-abasement. "I write to you, Iosif Vissarionovich Stalin, as the Greatest of the Great, a superman of complete nobility, to thank you with the purest sincerity, with all the goodness of my heart, for sheltering the orphans, feeding the hungry, and clothing the naked!"[90] Himself having hungered and watched others die, was Latyshev indulging the Skoptsy habit of confusing the exalted with the gruesome? Was he simply allowing the grandiloquence of sacred speech to invest his final words with an otherworldly luster? Over the years, he had often indulged in ironic bravado with respect to the business of the world and had left a record of his fulminations in the archives. It is unlikely that the old man would now suddenly toe the official line. Perhaps he wished in this respect to obey the rhetorical conventions of the day, which demanded Stalin be addressed in unctuous terms. He might also have followed the Skoptsy model of adoration addressed to the spiritual leader. One is reminded of the "Hymn of Praise" Latyshev had written to the Second Redeemer, sometime during World War I, in which the faithful ask Lisin to accept their "deepest bow and the best wishes born of our love."[91]

In addressing Bonch-Bruevich, Latyshev speaks not in formulas but

---

headed by the Great, Glorious, Noble, and Inspired Leader of the entire people and all humanity, Iosif Vissarionovich Stalin. Glory to them all, forever and ever, until the end of time! This is my Mite to the Great!" (l. 120b.).

with emotional directness. The phrases of greeting directed at Stalin are, by contrast, abstract and unconvincing. "Your noblest of hearts and great soul (life) have accomplished what no one else on earth could even dream of—in such great and noble deeds and actions of your all-conquering GOODNESS AND CAUSE! Your all-conquering feat of a noble knight has caused enemies everywhere to tremble. Your good, noble heart has compelled the entire living world to honor and love YOU. In tribute to your great glory, even I, a physical nonentity perhaps, but spiritually ennobled, dare in turn to recognize your glory and sense of justice."[92]

The tone begins to change when Latyshev turns from tribute to complaint, from ceremony to the circumstances of his own life. In particular, he thanks the great leader for getting him admitted to the old-age home where he is now ending his days. This "grain of generosity" in the "ocean of [Stalin's] good and merciful deeds" was especially noteworthy in relation to a being as lowly and despised as the writer: "in the eyes of all humanity, a ruined creature, having lost the right to any form of PLEASURE or SATISFACTION, a person, in short, unworthy of attention." In applying to the home, Latyshev had indicated his "diagnosis of unfitness, figuring that if the great of mind and noble character were to notice this mark of shame or crime, I would be in a fix. But it turned out as I had expected and forever hoped it would! As in all your actions you stand at the height of your greatness, so regarding this small affair you showed your true greatness, your fine soul and golden virtuous heart, which urged you not to neglect even THIS PHENOMENON! Thus you showed the entire world your love for all the insulted and downtrodden by life, including me."[93]

Latyshev attributes his admission to the old-age home to the gracious intervention of Stalin himself. There he finds the kind of luxury which formerly only the nobility, clergy, and merchants enjoyed. But not everyone who benefited from the "transition to enlightenment" lived up to its standards. And on this subject the philosopher and evangelist begins to hit his stride. Alas, some people retained the habits acquired in the "darkness of bygone times." They could not relinquish "those filthy, vile sins—drunkenness, fighting, hooliganism, thievery, and other shameful passions." The sponsors of enlightenment "build culture and bring humankind rebirth, raising people by a different plan, in a different system of life. But following their old habits, some crawl back into the filthy swamp."[94] Some of the residents were mild and industrious; others were idle and debauched, taking advantage of the state's goodwill.

Who was he, lowest of the low, to judge others? But his abasement also constituted his virtue, no less in current than in outmoded terms. Soviet idiom favored the downtrodden. It also rewarded those who conformed to worldly expectation, as Skoptsy conduct had always done. But the stigma of castration had survived the destruction of religion and the inversion of the social hierarchy, as Latyshev's experience had shown. "Wherever I have lived, worked, or held a post, supervisors and mates have considered me a model worker, polite to everyone. But that wasn't enough for them to consider me their equal (by nature). I suppose it's because they are creators of life and in that respect I am dead, though this is not fair. Plenty of people capable of reproducing humankind have voluntarily refused this great honor. Moreover, I received castration as a child and for a long time had nothing to do with those who did this in their right minds and by religious conviction. From the perspective of nature it's just as harmful either way."[95]

Seeking a place for himself in the new social and ideological dispensation, boasting of humility and moral perfection in a single breath, Latyshev encountered the same old hostility. He speculated on the cause. People might be thinking: "Why aren't you like the rest of us? Perhaps you are more cunning, smarter than us. Perhaps in this way you want to be better than us. Therefore you're not as honorable as the rest of us. Perhaps that's it. On this account I wrack my brains wondering how I'm worse than others. Judging by my life, my proper life, I'm a great guy! My exemplary decent behavior admits me everywhere. What qualities are missing for me to be accepted as human. Better be a drunk, hooligan, roué, drifter, loafer, or malingerer—but not castrated! Nothing is more shameful among humankind. I've felt this on my own hide for 75 years."[96]

Such constant humiliation made him all the more sensible to the "act of grace and small favor rendered by the GREATEST OF THE GREAT, the Kindest of the Kind, the Most Glorious of the Glorious, the Leader and Transformer Iosif Vissarionovich Stalin! How this entire event affected my soul, how much satisfaction it gave me! It seems I'm guaranteed for old age." In exchange for the charity involved in admitting him to the government home, Latyshev felt obliged to contribute to the regime's project of moral improvement. "If I didn't see shameful drunkenness, hooliganism, and other forms of vice," he wrote, "I couldn't ask for anything better. But this scourge (of course, not of all humanity) ruins my mood, and not only mine. Many complain (especially the old women who seek refuge in these homes), unhappy with those who offend this peace. I wonder, why put everyone in one place: old men, cripples of various kinds, mental cases, alcoholics, and incorrigible petty thieves, *than which there's nothing worse!*" Why not divide them up? "The invalids sometimes joke that they dumped us here out of a sack: two or three ardent partisans, several nut cases, a few cripples, and some completely healthy lazybones."[97]

Latyshev was on the side of the "Great Benefactor." Too bad ordinary folk did not always conform to Stalin's wishes, making it harder for him to achieve his "great plans," and giving comfort to the "enemies of the people," who oppose "the rational new life." Indeed, he was afraid his own frankness in "unmasking the misbehavior of unsuitable elements, enjoying the benefits conferred by the Highest Government," might get him into trouble. All the more so as "the people think I'm cut off from the whole. For my steady behavior I was nominated to the commission to organize the festival of the October Revolution. The chairman of the editorial board cried, 'Comrades, Latyshev is a good man but he seems to be an Evangelist.' I didn't try to disprove this, so instead of me they chose someone else. I'm not surprised. In this company, the biggest drunkard shouts loudest of all."[98]

More criticism, more advice: administrators lack training, inmates need constructive activity, immorality reigns. In an era when "relaxed vigilance" could prove fatal (as both Matorin and Volkov found out), Latyshev exercised his civic responsibility with particular gusto. Not from humility but from the deep conviction that he qualified as a moral witness on this earth and had standing in the next one. In closing, Latyshev readied himself for the beyond by designating his words as historical testimony: "I beg the State Literary Museum," he wrote Bonch-Bruevich, "if possible to keep in its archive my Mite of Praise and

Gratitude to the Great, Glorious Benefactor, the highest Soviet Government, headed by the Great, Glorious, Noble, and Inspired Leader of the entire people and all humanity, Iosif Vissarionovich Stalin. Glory to them all, forever and ever, until the end of time! This is my Mite to the Great!"[99]

Latyshev sent the letter to Bonch-Bruevich in March 1939, accom-

N. P. Latyshev, sketch of Joseph Stalin. Envelope postmarked: Orlovo, Melit[opol] District, 16-4-36. GMIR, f. 2, op. 5, d. 48, l. 8ob. (Copyright © GMIR.) "I seem to boast that I also have people who respect even someone like me. Drawn by Latyshev."

panied by his note of farewell.[100] The Guardian of Historical Records, his intellectual companion of opposing but honest views, had treated him with respect, allowing Latyshev to realize his spiritual destiny. To talk to God he needed someone high up and far away, but human. Someone for whom he could write. While still awaiting the End of Time, the Last Judgment, and the Kingdom of Heaven on earth, Latyshev had achieved transcendence. He owed this feat to Bonch-Bruevich's stubborn devotion to historical memory, to the Bolshevik's grandiose self-designation as the repository of human misunderstanding. For Bonch-Bruevich, Latyshev's views must have offered a benchmark against which to measure the extent of the progress the new order had achieved. The believer's error set the regime's truth in stark relief. From Latyshev's perspective, Bonch-Bruevich's religion project had not extinguished but conserved the glimmer of Light in the Darkness. And if the Christian managed to surround the language of political submission with the aura of the divine, it was only to further his own sacred ends. In classic Skoptsy mode, Latyshev's final letter combines a moralist's concern for proper conduct in this world with the holy man's thirst for grace.

"Most Gracious, Most Respected Vladimir Dmitrievich," he wrote. "I have sent the State Museum of Literature in your name my letter to the Greatest Person in the world. There I expressed as best I could my heartfelt gratitude for everything that makes this great person GREAT and deserving of renown.... [E]verything I said was sincere and from the bottom of my pure and noble heart. Further, knowing that among humanity I am nothing in comparison to others I hesitated to send it to the addressee. I beg you to accept it for the State Museum, to preserve as a document. In 100 or 200 years it will speak of how the common folk understood the Greatness of the Great and at the same time how they saw in humanity what the Great could not see: everything bad and unfitting that humanity sometimes concocts.

"But you have been silent about whether I should have troubled myself with what doesn't concern me and is beyond my strength to deal with. Perhaps you have thought that a man who already feels the end drawing near doesn't know what he's up to, for good or for ill. For this, Vladimir Dmitrievich, I beg your forgiveness. You know I'm an odd duckie. Sometimes I imagine something sensible and say it. Sometimes

I'm simply afraid to offend you by confiding my views, opinions, and suppositions. My life is clearly on the wane, my health is fragile, I feel my years. But when it comes to eternity I have no worries, there's no blot on my record!

"There's only one thing still unaccounted for: I haven't thanked you the way one should thank noble and kind people. But still I want to do something, so I can die in peace concerning all you have done for me, and you have done a lot for me. Will I be able at the end of life to satisfy my sincere wish, my vow? For the time being I seem healthy, but I expect I'll die on my feet! All the better! Less bother!"[101]

Unable to stop himself, Latyshev repeats to Bonch-Bruevich the same complaints he has sent Stalin himself, about the disorders and moral disarray in the old-age home. But reporting from the front of ordinary life is what allows Latyshev to exercise his central identity: the writer. It connects him to the world of meaningful exchange. "I myself realize I'm only bothering you," he writes, "but for me it's the greatest pleasure to communicate—especially with you, a kind and noble person. Indeed, I love and respect only those who are noble, intelligent, and charitable. That's all I've needed all my life. The rest is only dust and rot.

"If I sent the letter to you it's because I didn't know how else to leave my opinion about the good and the bad. Thus, Vladimir Dmitrievich, don't take offense, forgive me the liberty I took, thanks to your noble relation to me, in sending you everything that happened in my life for the judgment of future people. I fully realize that this isn't the end of the world! All manuscripts and letters some thousand years from now will be considered historical documents. In that far-off time they will seem wise and useful. Forgive me and farewell! Latyshev, N. P. March 6, 1939." Then, as though he could neither let go of the relationship that had kept him alive nor admit that the end of life was upon him, he added a final thought—half wish, half request, below the signature and date: "It would be nice to read something very very intelligent, something old, but there's nothing like that around. It's almost impossible to live or breathe . . ."[102]

Latyshev had gone from peasant to proletarian. He had run a small farm, worked as a carpenter and factory watchman. He ended his days in an old-age home. Sailing his personal ship on the waters of an inhospitable world caught in the throes of revolution, he did not lose his spiritual bearings. What kept him on course and helped him navigate the shoals, allowing him to maintain his faith and survive a lifetime of danger and persecution, was his writer's calling. This he embraced against all odds, as the core of his being and his link to the beyond. When in 1929, aging and needy, he had been looking for a job, he asked if Bonch-Bruevich could find him a little something to do. "As for writing," he feigned, "I'm not a writer. I have neither talent nor calling. I manage a bit, but in the long run I'm afraid of ruining my eyes. Something like janitor, cleaning up, sweeping, keeping watch during the day, tidying the rooms, making tea." But he always returned to the same theme: did Bonch-Bruevich have "some kind of job in Moscow for an aged writer? I'm no great writer but if my needs were met I might write something serious. And I would be able personally to explain many things to you for your book and research." Perhaps "dear Mikhail Ivanovich Kalinin" could help him get a pension for the five years he had served as a factory watchman in Alek-sandrovsk, protecting state property. Alert to the linguistic environment, he suggested ingeniously that he might "count as a peasant-agricultural-ist in Kursk province, according to the new law of 1928 or 1929. I'm a homeless, helpless old man of 65, having the legal right to a pension of 65 rubles a year. These are the facts. Do what you can for a poor writer-peasant, or just because I'm an old man." Old he was, though ten years still awaited him. But a "writer-peasant" he had always been and remained until the end.[103] A writer and man of God, a voice from the outer edge of two different social regimes, witness to the power of holi-ness in the popular imagination.

Holiness, however, of a special kind. What has happened to the cen-tral trauma of castration, in this long and deeply personal tale? By the time Latyshev had rounded out his years, extremity of a different sort permeated his world. The mental and physical trials of Siberian exile had once been incorporated into sacred stories of sacrifice and endurance. The faithful had focused their anger and indignation not on the regime as a whole, but on petty officials and local administrators, saving their loyalty for the sovereign himself, in the venerable tradition of popular monarchism. However much they might welcome pain and deprivation as elements in their striving toward the divine, and however much they

felt themselves singled out as God's chosen people, the Skoptsy nevertheless rejoiced when their worldly torments diminished. They happily
abandoned the harsh abode of the Iakutsk region, eagerly accumulated
material goods, and greeted the end of the old regime with little regret,
it seems. Insofar as they hailed the new order, they did so as an instinctive
reflex of submission to whatever power governed their lives. They also
responded to the possibility that those now in control might simply
ignore them.

The Skoptsy, like everyone else, soon found themselves surrounded
and affected by death and suffering of massive proportions. But the ago-
nies of the Soviet years were not intended for them in particular. Some
were sentenced to prison on the pretext of economic crimes, but this
was in the context of a general assault on faith of all kinds and on the
policies and social forms of the NEP years. The fate of the Latyshev
brothers illustrates the extent to which, in political terms, the Skoptsy
had lost the status of symbolic monstrosities to which unique measures
of prophylaxis must be applied. Andrei Latyshev was murdered in 1924 in
the course of a freak act of violence, reflecting the persistence of old
stereotypes about Skoptsy wealth, which gained new force in the moral
uncertainty of the NEP years. The assault was not the direct consequence
of official policy but rather a reflection of the relative weakness of the
new state. Fedor Latyshev, for his part, died of starvation in 1933, along
with hundreds of thousands of other peasants. Nikifor witnessed one
elderly spiritual sister after another give up the ghost, in hunger and
despair, but he himself held on. To the end of his days he complained of
local malfeasance, while praising those on high. This habit conformed
entirely to Soviet mores.

Did his rhetorical celebration of "Might and Light" and his paeon
to the Greatest of the Great reflect the sense that his ship had indeed
reached port? The horrors of the Soviet regime resulted from the pursuit
of a cause justified in terms of human salvation, just as the agony of castration was linked to salvation of a spiritual kind. There are formal, as
well as psychological and even intellectual, parallels between revolutionary and religious exaltation. But the Skoptsy, as Skoptsy, did not participate in the worldly project that enveloped their lives. They remained, as
Latyshev eloquently testified, on the periphery, "cut off from the
whole."[104] If not in ideological then in social terms, they were still a

gruesome human mystery, beyond the comprehension of the ordinary folk, whose spiritual landscape and everyday life they largely shared. Even in the microcosm of the old-age home, in which every resident had his or her quirk or fault, an old fellow like Latyshev, a useful, literate jack-of-many-trades, was not fully accepted. Yet, as the Skoptsy had often been, he was also left alone. This persistent exclusion, as well as the distancing the brethren chose for themselves, lent them an acute and mournful perspective on the common lot.

The Skoptsy hunger for transcendence was fully satisfied by the radical nature of their defining act; they did not translate their project into worldly terms. Despite his devotion to Bonch-Bruevich and his servile hymn to the mightiest one of all, Latyshev was no enthusiast for the Bolshevik cause. The secular mode that interested him, and that seemed to have attracted the other semieducated brethren as well, was not politics but the culture of letters. The Word of God entailed the production and realization of metaphor. The language of sacred verse and sacred tales, the "Utterances" of collective worship, the volume of holy lore published in Tomsk: these bound the faithful together. They also fostered habits of expression that sought wider range. The Skoptsy despised the world as the arena of sin and impurity, a realm driven by the chronological imperatives of birth, aging, and death. They did not wish to transform it into a different kind of place. Yet some of them ultimately felt the need to leave traces in the profane sands of time, to reach beyond their allotted span through the medium of language addressed to human ears. The mystery of castration connected them to God but also turned them into special witnesses of the human condition. It reduced the play of metaphor to the finality of physical enactment, yet castration was only the opening move in a complex spiritual destiny. In some ways it was a beginning, not an end. In at once embracing the intellectual company of the Archivist on High and yearning for earthly readers, Latyshev did not betray his faith. This quest was a continuation, by other means, of the mission that gave meaning to his life. Having lived as a sheep among the goats, he left for the heavenly pastures, his calling fulfilled. And we know that his faith in the historical record was not misguided.

NOTES

Note: For brevity, "ibid." is used throughout to refer to the item directly preceding it in the same note.

Introduction: The Archives of Eternity

1. Letter from N. P. Latyshev to I. V. Stalin (December 22, 1938), GMIR, f. 2, op. 5, d. 49, l. 80b.–90b. (quote, 90b.).

2. Letter from N. P. Latyshev to V. D. Bonch-Bruevich (February 23, 1933), GMIR, f. 2, op. 5, d. 43, l. 10b. See Sarah Davies, *Popular Opinion in Stalin's Russia: Terror, Propaganda, and Dissent, 1934–1941* (Cambridge: Cambridge University Press, 1997).

3. G. P. Men'shenin, the community spokesman, commented, when asked about the name "Skoptsy": "There is no other appropriate name. 'Skoptsy' is not an insult. I know my brethren are never ashamed of this name." Letter from G. P. Men'shenin to V. D. Bonch-Bruevich (January 22, 1928), OR-RGB, f. 369, k. 301, ed. khr. 27, l. 40.

4. Letter from N. P. Latyshev to V. D. Bonch-Bruevich (March 6, 1939), GMIR, f. 2, op. 5, d. 49, l. 5–50b.

5. On his career, see P. Nikolaev, "Literaturnye vospominaniia V. D. Bonch-Bruevicha," in V. Bonch-Bruevich, *Vospominaniia* (Moscow: Khudozhestvennaia literatura, 1968), 5; M. I. Shakhnovich, "V. D. Bonch-Bruevich: Issledovatel' religiozno-obshchestvennykh dvizhenii v Rossii," *Ezhegodnik Muzeia istorii religii i ateizma* 7 (1963), 293–300; Eberhard Müller, "Opportunismus oder Utopie? V. D. Bonč-Bruevič und die russischen Sekten vor und nach der Revolution," *Jahrbücher für Geschichte Osteuropas* 35 (1987), 509–33. On the founding of the museum, see John Shelton Curtiss, *The Russian Church and the Soviet State, 1917–1950* (Boston: Little, Brown, 1953), 255.

6. A. I. Klibanov, "V. D. Bonch-Bruevich i problemy religiozno-obshchestvennykh dvizhenii v Rossii," in V. D. Bonch-Bruevich, *Izbrannye sochineniia*, vol. 1: *O religii, religioznom sektantstve i tserkvi* (Moscow: Akademiia nauk, 1959), 21.

7. O. D. Golubeva, *V. D. Bonch-Bruevich—izdatel'* (Moscow: Kniga, 1972), 7–9, 16. On the volumes, see Shakhnovich, "Bonch-Bruevich," 296–97.

8. On the relatively recent date of both the Skoptsy and the reinvigorated spiritual elders (startsy), see Viktor Zhivov, "Skoptsy v russkoi kul'ture," *Novoe literaturnoe obozrenie*

18 (1996), 396–400; Vladimir Lossky, "Les starets d' Optino," in Vladimir Lossky and Nicholas Arseniev, *La paternité spirituelle en Russie aux XVIIIème et XIXème siècles* (Bégrolles-en-Mauges: Abbaye de Bellefontaine, 1977); and Robert L. Nichols, "The Orthodox Elders (*Startsy*) of Imperial Russia," *Modern Greek Studies Yearbook* 1 (1985), 1–30.

9. Letter from N. P. Latyshev to I.V. Stalin (December 22, 1938), l. 4.

10. See Vladimir Bonch-Bruevich, *Sokhraniaete arkhivy* (Moscow: Gosudarstvennoe izdatel'stvo, 1920). In this pamphlet Bonch-Bruevich exhorts local officials to preserve the contents of government and personal archives dating from the old regime. They must not interpret orders to recycle used paper as an excuse to mangle historical documents. The revolution has an obligation to future generations to preserve the past. It destroys the old social order but guards its cultural achievements. The pamphlet was written on Lenin's suggestion: Golubeva, *Bonch-Bruevich*, 110.

1. Myths and Mysteries

1. See Robert O. Crummey, *The Old Believers and the World of Anti-Christ: The Vyg Community and the Russian State, 1694–1855* (Madison: University of Wisconsin Press, 1970); Manfred Hildermeier, "Alter Glaube und neue Welt: Zur Sozialgeschichte des Raskol im 18. und 19. Jahrhundert," *Jahrbücher für Geschichte Osteuropas* 38:3 (1990), 372–98; 38:4 (1990), 504–25; and Roy R. Robson, *Old Believers in Modern Russia* (DeKalb: Northern Illinois University Press, 1995). For numbers, see, Peter Waldron, "Religious Reform after 1905: Old Believers and the Orthodox Church," *Oxford Slavonic Papers*, n.s., no. 20 (1987), 115; members of Orthodox church estimated at 88 million, 112.

2. Gregory L. Freeze, "The Rechristianization of Russia: The Church and Popular Religion, 1750–1850," *Studia Slavica Finlandensia* 7 (1990), 101–36; Waldron, "Religious Reform," 113.

3. Article 196, *Ulozhenie o nakazaniiakh ugolovnykh i ispravitel'nykh 1885 goda*, ed. N. S. Tagantsev (St. Petersburg: Gosudarstvennaia tipografiia, 1901), 225.

4. Archpriest T. I. Butkevich, *Obzor russkikh sekt i ikh tolkov*, 2d ed. (Petrograd: Tuzov, 1915).

5. N. P. Latyshev, "Prodolzhaia nachatoe mnoiu opisanie" (January 4, 1915), GMIR, f. 2, op. 5, d. 264, l. 6.

6. On this sect, see John Eugene Clay, "God's People in the Seventeenth Century: The Uglich Affair of 1717," *Cahiers du monde russe et soviétique* 26:1 (1985), 69–124; and idem, "Russian Peasant Religion and Its Repression: The Christ-Faith (Khristovshchina) and the Origins of the 'Flagellant' Myth, 1666–1837" (Ph.D. diss., University of Chicago, 1989). For description of the Skoptsy ritual, including the term "spiritual bath," see testimony in N.Varadinov, *Istoriia Ministerstva vnutrennikh del*, vol. 8: *Istoriia rasporiazhenii po raskolu* (St. Petersburg: II Otdelenie Sobstvennoi Ego Imperatorskogo Velichestva Kantseliarii, 1863), 256. For recent discussion of the relationship between Khlysty and Skoptsy, see A. A. Panchenko, "Zametki i materialy k issledovaniiu fol'klora russkikh

misticheskikh sekt," in *Mifologiia i povsednevnost'*, ed. K. A. Bogdanov and A. A. Panchenko (St. Petersburg: Russkii Khristianskii gumanitarnyi institut, 1998), 146–57.

7. N. P. Latyshev, "Prodolzhenie" (December 26, 1915), GMIR, f. 2, op. 5, d. 265, l. 70b.; Latyshev, "Prodolzhaia nachatoe mnoiu opisanie," l. 1–10b.

8. Latyshev, "Prodolzhaia nachatoe mnoiu opisanie," l. 20b.–3.

9. Latyshev, "Prodolzhenie," l. 470b.

10. Letter from G. P. Men´shenin to V. D. Bonch-Bruevich (March 28, 1910), GMIR, f. 2, op. 5, d. 66, l. 10b.

11. See Kathryn M. Ringrose, "Living in the Shadows: Eunuchs and Gender in Byzantium," in *Third Sex, Third Gender: Beyond Sexual Dimorphism in Culture and History*, ed. Gilbert Herdt (New York: Zone Books, 1994), 85–109; Shaun Marmon, *Eunuchs and Sacred Boundaries in Islamic Society* (New York: Oxford University Press, 1995).

12. Latyshev, "Prodolzhaia nachatoe mnoiu opisanie," l. 5.

13. See Daniel F. Caner, "The Practice and Prohibition of Self-Castration in Early Christianity," *Vigiliae Christianae* 51 (1997), 396–415 (quote, 399). I thank Dr. Robert Conner for mentioning this article.

14. Latyshev, "Prodolzhenie," l. 48.

15. Caner, "Practice and Prohibition," 403, 407. See also Ringrose, "Living in the Shadows," 100–101, and Elizabeth A. Clark, *The Origenist Controversy: The Cultural Construction of an Early Christian Debate* (Princeton: Princeton University Press, 1992), 246–47. For more on the significance of bodily marking in early Christianity, see Susanna Elm, "'Pierced by Bronze Needles': Anti-Montanist Charges of Ritual Stigmatization in Their Fourth-Century Context," *Journal of Early Christian Studies* 4:4 (1996), 409–39.

16. See Peter Brown, *The Body and Society: Men, Women, and Sexual Renunciation in Early Christianity* (New York: Columbia University Press, 1988), 164–69; also John Meyendorff, Introduction to Gregory Palamas, *The Triads*, ed. John Meyendorff (Mahwah, N.J.: Paulist Press, 1983).

17. [Nikolai Nadezhdin], *Issledovanie o skopcheskoi eresi* (n.p.: Ministerstvo vnutrennikh del, 1845), 203.

18. For this interpretation, see P. I. Mel´nikov, "Belye golubi," chaps. 1–12, *Russkii vestnik*, vol. 80, bk. 3 (1869), 320. Modern Russian coincides with the English version, in which Herod asks "where Christ should be born" (gde dolzhno rodit´sia Khristu). On earlier popular "Christs," see V. N. Mainov, "Skopcheskii eresiarkh Kondratii Selivanov: Ssylka ego v Spaso-Evfimiev monastyr´," *Istoricheskii vestnik*, bk. 4 (1880), 757–58.

19. See John Meyendorff, *Byzantine Theology: Historical Trends and Doctrinal Themes*, 2d ed. (New York: Fordham University Press, 1983), 159–65 ("Redemption and Deification"); idem, Introduction to Palamas, *Triads*; S. S. Khoruzhii, "Analiticheskii slovar´ isikhastskoi antropologii," in *Sinergiia: Problemy asketiki i mistiki pravoslaviia*, ed. S. S. Khoruzhii (Moscow: Di-Dik, 1995), 42–150.

20. On folk Orthodoxy, see Pierre Pascal, *The Religion of the Russian People*, trans. Rowan Williams (Crestwood, N.Y.: St. Vladimir's Seminary Press, 1976; French ed.,

1947), 10–13, 19–21; A. Siniavskii, *Ivan-durak: Ocherk russkoi narodnoi very* (Paris: Syntaxis, 1991); A. A. Panchenko, *Issledovaniia v oblasti narodnogo pravoslaviia: Derevenskie sviatyni Severo-Zapada Rossii* (St. Petersburg: Aleteiia, 1998). On links between Skoptsy practices and folk Orthodoxy, see Panchenko, "Zametki i materialy."

21. On the danger of sectarian misunderstandings, see Meyendorff, *Byzantine Theology*, 177, and Mainov, "Skopcheskii eresiarkh," 757. On Old Belief, see Boris A. Uspensky, "The Schism and Cultural Conflict in the Seventeenth Century," in *Seeking God: The Recovery of Religious Identity in Orthodox Russia, Ukraine, and Georgia*, ed. Stephen K. Batalden (DeKalb: Northern Illinois University Press, 1993), 106–43.

22. Testimony of Ivan Andreianov, in Varadinov, *Istoriia*, 8:256.

23. Latyshev, "Prodolzhenie," l. 560b.–57.

24. Aleksei Elenskii, quoted in Mel′nikov, "Belye golubi," chaps. 13–18, *Russkii vestnik*, vol. 81, bk. 5 (1869), 259, 262; also in N. P. Liprandi, *Delo o skoptse kamergere Elenskom* (Moscow: Universitetskaia tipografiia, 1868), 12 (reference to 2 Corinthians 3:6). For more on rejection of reading and Scripture, see testimony of Ivan Andreianov, in Varadinov, *Istoriia*, 8:256.

25. On access to Scripture, see the article on Ukrainian peasants by the priest A. F. Khoinatskii, "Bibliia i narod v ikh vzaimnykh otnosheniiakh mezhdu soboiu, v predelakh iugozapadnogo kraia Rossii," *Drevniaia i novaia Rossiia*, vol. 2, no. 7 (1878), 173–201. On sacred verses, see L. F. Soloshchenko and Iu. S. Prokoshin, "Slovesa zolotye," in *Golubinaia kniga: Russkie narodnye dukhovnye stikhi XI–XIX vekov*, ed. L. F. Soloshchenko and Iu. S. Prokoshin (Moscow: Moskovskii rabochii, 1991), 5–33. For doubt that the illiterate founders of the sect could have derived their notions from Scripture, see testimony quoted in P. I. Mel′nikov, "Materialy dlia istorii khlystovshchiny i skopcheskoi eresi," pt. 1: "Solovetskie dokumenty o skoptsakh," *Chteniia*, bk. 1, pt. 5 (1872), 157–58. Mel′nikov solves the puzzle by deciding that Selivanov was not a commoner at all; see "Materialy," pt. 3: "Pravitel′stvennye rasporiazheniia, vypiski i zapiski o skoptsakh do 1826 goda," *Chteniia*, bk. 3, pt. 5 (1872), 60.

26. Quotes from "Poslanie," in V.V. Rozanov, *Apokalipsicheskaia sekta: Khlysty i skoptsy* (St. Petersburg: Vaisberg i Gershunin, 1914), 158–59, 161, 163–64.

27. Witness testimony in "Obvinitel′nyi akt" (Kharkov), RGIA, f. 821, op. 133, d. 233, l. 15 (p. 3). Initiation ceremony (privod) described in Nadezhdin, *Issledovanie*, 219–26; also P. I. Mel′nikov, "Materialy," pt. 2: "Solovetskie dokumenty o skoptsakh," *Chteniia*, bk. 2, pt. 5 (1872), 109–18. On two-handed crossing, see ibid., 85, and Varadinov, *Istoriia*, 8:261.

28. Comparison made by Nadezhdin, *Issledovanie*, 183 (sekta triasuchek). When the Skoptsy learned of the Shakers, they recognized this affinity themselves; see N. M. Iadrintsev, *Russkaia obshchina v tiur′me i ssylke* (St. Petersburg: Morigerovskii, 1872), 257. Some suggested that Mother Anne had originated as Annushka, a house servant of Prince Vorontsov: V. Kel′siev, "Sviatorusskie dvoevery," pt. 1, *Otechestvennye zapiski*, vol. 174, no. 10, sec. 1 (1867), 609.

29. See John Money, "The Skoptic Syndrome: Castration and Genital Self-

Mutilation as an Example of Sexual Body-Image Pathology," *Journal of Psychology and Human Sexuality* 1 (1998), 113–28; Eli Coleman and John Cesnik, "Skoptic Syndrome: The Treatment of an Obsessional Gender Dysphoria with Lithium Carbonate and Psychotherapy," *American Journal of Psychotherapy* 44:2 (1990), 204–17. On homosexuality, see Aleksandr Etkind, "Russkie skoptsy: Opyt istorii," *Zvezda* 4 (1995), 140. The evidence for this idea comes from testimony presented to Dosifei, the superior of the Solovetskii monastery in the 1820s and 1830s. Dosifei reported that the Skoptsy confided to his care entered into sexually perverse relations with one another. Either Dosifei imagined something that did not exist, in order to defame the men, or they may actually have formed such sexualized companionships. Such intimacies might also have appeared among the monks and other detainees. Given the ample description of family life pertaining to the vast majority of Skoptsy faithful who were never in monastic confinement, this one source cannot sustain any reliable conclusions. For Dosifei's comments, see Mel´nikov, "Materialy," pt. 1, 162.

30. Daniel Rancour-Laferriere, *The Slave Soul of Russia* (New York: New York University Press, 1995).

31. John T. Alexander, *Bubonic Plague in Early Modern Russia: Public Health and Urban Disaster* (Baltimore: Johns Hopkins University Press, 1980), 193–95, 299.

32. On branding connected with the Pugachev events, see "The Captain's Daughter," in *The Complete Prose Tales of Alexandr Sergeyvitch Pushkin* (New York: Norton, 1966), 416 ("As we approached Orenburg, we saw a crowd of convicts with shaven heads and faces disfigured [obezobrazhennye] by the hangman's pincers"); 390–91 (Bashkir, whose tongue has been cut out as punishment). See also Abby Schrader, "Branding the Exile as Other: Corporal Punishment and the Construction of Boundaries in Mid-Nineteenth-Century Russia," in *Russian Modernity: Politics, Knowledge, Practices,* ed. David L. Hoffmann and Yanni Kotsonis (London: Macmillan Press, 1999).

33. Valerie A. Kivelson, "Through the Prism of Witchcraft: Gender and Social Change in Seventeenth-Century Muscovy," in *Russia's Women: Accommodation, Resistance, Transformation,* ed. Barbara Engel, Barbara Clements, and Christine Worobec (Berkeley: University of California Press, 1991), 89–91.

34. Emmanuel Le Roy Ladurie, "The Aiguillette: Castration by Magic," in *The Mind and Method of the Historian,* trans. Sian Reynolds and Ben Reynolds (Brighton, Eng.: Harvester Press, 1981; French ed., 1978), 84–95.

35. Nik. Gavrilovich Vysotskii, *Pervyi skopcheskii protsess: Materialy, otnosiashchiesia k nachal´noi istorii skopcheskoi sekty* (Moscow: Snegireva, 1915), 4–5 (Quaker), 213 (new kind). Officials first dubbed them Quakers in 1734: Mel´nikov, "Materialy," pt. 1, 120–21.

36. Vysotskii, *Pervyi,* 2–3. The peasants all have the same surname, which is also the name of the village: Maslov. They are distinguished by their patronymics: Petrov, Vasil´ev, Porfenov.

37. On earlier persecution of Christ Faith, see I. P. Iakobiia, "Ob ugolovnoi nakazuemosti prinadlezhnosti k izuvernym sektam," *Zhurnal ministerstva iustitsii,* no. 5 (1912), 101–2. On the thirteen serfs, see Mel´nikov, "Materialy," pt. 3, 59.

38. Vysotskii, *Pervyi*, 7–13 (quote, 13).

39. For property inventories, including various barns, stocked granaries, livestock, bathhouses, and beehives, see Vysotskii, *Pervyi*, 24–30, also 119–25.

40. Vysotskii, *Pervyi*, 36–37 (list). At the end of the eighteenth century, the odnodvortsy were consolidated with the state peasantry. See "Chetvertnye krest´iane, chervertnoe zemlevladenie," *Entsiklopedicheskii slovar´* (St. Petersburg: Brokgauz-Efron, 1903), 38:726–36; also Aleksandr B. Kamenskii, *The Russian Empire in the Eighteenth Century*, trans. and ed. David Griffiths (Armonk, N.Y.: M. E. Sharpe, 1997), 109; and Elise Kimerling Wirtschafter, *Social Identity in Imperial Russia* (DeKalb: Northern Illinois University Press, 1997), 31.

41. Vysotskii, *Pervyi*, 16–17, 99–102, 175–76, 211–12.

42. Vysotskii, *Pervyi*, 87. On difficulty determining exactly when the break occurred, see ibid., xviii.

43. Vysotskii, *Pervyi*, 33–35; 41 (other witnesses confirming Andrei and Kondratii as castrators); 88–93 (Blokhin's testimony repeated); 218 (gelding); 264 (for number 62).

44. Vysotskii, *Pervyi*, 14 (quote), 22, 30–31, 35, 37–38 (quote), 45–46, 58. On fortune-telling in traditional culture, see Faith Wigzell, *Reading Russian Fortunes: Print Culture, Gender, and Divination in Russia from 1765* (Cambridge: Cambridge University Press, 1998), chap. 2.

45. Vysotskii, *Pervyi*, 41–42, 221, 264, 295.

46. Vysotskii, *Pervyi*, 44–45, 48–49 (quote).

47. Vysotskii, *Pervyi*, 56.

48. Vysotskii, *Pervyi*, 55–58, 102–3, 175, 198, 263.

49. Vysotskii, *Pervyi*, 76–77.

50. Vysotskii, *Pervyi*, 79–83, 176; for testimony of another couple and their daughter, 111–13.

51. On the relationship between church and state in this case, see Vysotskii, *Pervyi*, Introduction.

52. Synodal decree no. 4053, July 16, 1722: "O nedeistvitel´nosti samovol´nogo stradaniia, navlekaemogo zakonoprestupnymi deianiiami [On the illegitimacy of self-inflicted suffering, incurred by criminal actions]," *Polnoe sobranie zakonov Rossiiskoi Imperii*, ser. 1 (n.p.: II Otdelenie Sobstvennoi Ego Imperatorskogo Velichestva Kantseliarii, 1830), 6:742–46.

53. Vysotskii, *Pervyi*, 53–54 (May 25, 1731, decree against sorcerers); 18 (1722 decree applied to Khlysty and Skoptsy).

54. On the stake, flogging, excising tongues, applied as late as 1730s, see Ardalion Popov, *Sud i nakazaniia za prestupleniia protiv very i nravstvennosti po russkomu pravu* (Kazan: Imperatorskii universitet, 1904), 334–39.

55. Vysotskii, *Pervyi*, 213–14. For comment on this designation, see Iakobiia, "Ob ugolovnoi nakazuemosti," 105.

56. Vysotskii, *Pervyi*, 213–14.

57. Vysotskii, *Pervyi*, 265, 195.

58. Vysotskii, *Pervyi*, Introduction, xviii. Mel′nikov calls him Kondratii Ivanovich Selivanov, from the village of Stolbov: Mel′nikov, "Belye golubi," chaps. 1–12, 389.

59. On confused identity, see Nadezhdin, *Issledovanie*, 124; more completely, Mainov, "Skopcheskii eresiarkh," 759–61 (recounts others' confusion but adds some of his own). Even more confused: N. V. Reutskii, *Liudi bozh′i i skoptsy: Istoricheskoe issledovanie* (Moscow: Grachev, 1872), 104, 106, 125; also Mel′nikov, "Materialy," pt. 3, 60–61.

60. Mel′nikov, "Belye golubi," chaps. 1–12, 389. For Popov, see also Reutskii, *Liudi bozh′i*, 106.

61. Vysotskii, *Pervyi*, 228–45 (tabulation of those sought or questioned).

62. Reutskii, *Liudi bozh′i*, 110; Mel′nikov, "Materialy," pt. 3, 63. In these two accounts, he is said to have been informed by a local woman; another account has him informed by two boys who had been castrated and told their relatives: K. V. Kutepov, *Sekty khlystov i skoptsov* (Kazan: Imperatorskii universitet, 1883), 142.

63. This was Nadezhdin's idea: *Issledovanie*, 124.

64. Kutepov, *Sekty*, 116–17.

65. Mel′nikov, "Materialy," pt. 3, 97.

66. Reutskii, *Liudi bozh′i*, 125, says that Selivanov was a surname common in the area, which Andrei Ivanov may have adopted.

67. Unless otherwise indicated, all citations to "Strady" refer to the exact reprint of Nadezhdin's version, under the title "Strady Kondratiia Selivanova," in Rozanov, *Apokalipsicheskaia*, 134–52.

68. On the living and former Saviors, see Mel′nikov, "Materialy," pt. 2, 68.

69. "Poslanie," in Rozanov, *Apokalipsicheskaia*, 161.

70. "Strady," in G. P. Men′shenin, ed., *Poeziia i proza sibirskikh skoptsov* (Tomsk: Levenson, 1904), 27; variation in Mel′nikov, "Materialy," pt. 2, 67; also "Strady," in Rozanov, *Apokalipsicheskaia*, 134.

71. "Strady," in Men′shenin, *Poeziia i proza*, 29.

72. "Poslanie," in Rozanov, *Apokalipsicheskaia*, 163.

73. Mel′nikov, "Materialy," pt. 3, 143 (crown); others from "Strady," in Rozanov, *Apokalipsicheskaia*, 143, 145, 151.

74. The snake appears in Mel′nikov, "Materialy," pt. 3, 143; also "Prezhde stradanii istinnogo ottsa pokhozhdeniia," in Men′shenin, *Poeziia i proza*, 26; "Strady," in ibid., 28. On the "abyss," see Nadezhdin, *Issledovanie*, 203, and E. V. Pelikan, *Sudebno-meditsinskie issledovaniia skopchestva i istoricheskie svedeniia o nem* (St. Petersburg: Golovin, 1872), 4, 143.

75. "Strady," in Rozanov, *Apokalipsicheskaia*, 142 (tovar). Rozanov provides annotations for Selivanov's symbolic terms, as do earlier commentators: e.g., Nadezhdin, *Issledovanie*, 113, where he calls their language "figurnyi iazyk." "Figurnyi" means figured, ornamented; close to "figural′nyi," figurative, metaphorical, also ornate.

76. Siniavskii, *Ivan-durak*, 172 and 400 (Christ-purity-castration), 214–16 (saints). On theological issues concerning the sounds and meanings of names in relation to the divine, see Irina Paperno, "On the Nature of the Word: Theological Sources of

Mandelshtam's Dialogue with the Symbolists," in *Christianity and the Eastern Slavs*, vol. 2: *Russian Culture in Modern Times*, ed. Robert P. Hughes and Irina Paperno (Berkeley: University of California Press, 1994), 290–91.

77. On the Jesus Prayer, see Meyendorff, Introduction to Palamas, *Triads*, 2–4.

78. On folk versions of religious belief, see Linda J. Ivanits, *Russian Folk Belief* (Armonk, N.Y.: M. E. Sharpe, 1989), 19–37, 136–53. Citations in following passages from "Strady," in Rozanov, *Apokalipsicheskaia* (pages in parentheses).

79. Michael Cherniavsky, *Tsar and People: Studies in Russian Myths* (New Haven:Yale University Press, 1961), 97; on mitigation under Peter III, see Iakobiia, "Ob ugolovnoi nakazuemosti," 104–5.

80. Mel'nikov, "Materialy," pt. 3, 148.

81. "Prezhde," in Men'shenin, *Poeziia i proza*, 19.

82. On images of offal and wolves in saints' lives, see Siniavskii, *Ivan-durak*, 198, 205.

83. D. N. Bludov, "Obshchaia ob″iasnitel′naia zapiska," in *Proekt ulozheniia o nakazaniiakh ugolovnykh i ispravitel′nykh, vnesennyi v 1844 godu v Gosudarstvennyi Sovet, s podrobnym oznacheniem osnovanii kazhdogo iz vnesennykh v sei proekt postanovlenii* (St. Petersburg: II Otdelenie Sobstvennoi Ego ImperatorskogoVelichestva Kantseliarii, 1871), lii.

84. For an eighteenth-century engraving showing the victim of flogging in the posture of the cross, see M. I. Piliaev, *Staryi Peterburg: Rasskazy iz byloi zhizni stolitsy*, 3d ed. (St. Petersburg: Suvorin, 1903), 343, pl. 5.

85. On 1797 escape and capture, see Mel'nikov, "Materialy," pt. 3, 48.

86. On age, see Nadezhdin, *Issledovanie*, 153; see also Mel'nikov, "Materialy," pt. 3, 49, also 87 (mystery of Selivanov's grave).

87. Kutepov, *Sekty*, 197.

88. Nadezhdin, *Issledovanie*, 125–26 (illiteracy), 280 (illiteracy likening Selivanov and Shilov to Christ's Apostles); Mel'nikov, "Belye golubi," chaps. 13–18, 282 (denying illiteracy); Kutepov, *Sekty*, 199 (Selivanov as writing the "Passion").

89. Nadezhdin, *Issledovanie*, 162 (illiterate); I. P. Shul′gin, "Dlia istorii russkikh tainykh sekt v kontse XVIII veka," *Zaria*, no. 5, pt. 8 (1871), 37 (writing).

90. Quote from "Prezhde," in Men'shenin, *Poeziia i proza*, 12.

91. For view that "Strady" was recited by Selivanov and transcribed by his followers, see Mel'nikov, "Materialy," pt. 3, 141. For the "Epistle," see testimony of Ivan Andreianov, in Varadinov, *Istoriia*, 8:252.

92. [V. I. Dal′], *Issledovanie o skopcheskoi eresi* (n.p.: Ministerstvo vnutrennikh del, 1844), 147–86. This text is reproduced in Nadezhdin, *Issledovanie*, Appendix, 1–26, and reprinted in *Sbornik pravitel′stvennykh svedenii o raskol′nikakh*, ed. V. Kel′siev, vol. 3 (London: Trübner, 1860). It is virtually the same as "Prezhde" and "Strady," taken together, in Men'shenin, *Poeziia i proza*, 27–34. A less polished version appears as "Stradanii sveta, istinnogo Gosudaria Batiushki, stranstvovanii i trudov drazhaishego nashego Iskupitelia iVselenskogo Uchitelia Oglashenie," in Mel'nikov, "Materialy," pt. 3,

142–54. For an allegedly archival text from the early 1830s, see Mel′nikov, "Materialy," pt. 1, 133–41.

93. View of Nadezhdin, *Issledovanie;* also Reutskii, *Liudi bozh′i,* 100 (citing text), and Kutepov, *Sekty,* 127–36, 143.

94. Reutskii, *Liudi bozh′i,* 93–94; Mel′nikov, "Materialy," pt. 2, 65–66, 71.

95. Nadezhdin, *Issledovanie,* 101.

96. Following summary based on Nadezhdin, *Issledovanie,* 101–10.

97. Nadezhdin, *Issledovanie,* 198.

98. Phrases cited in Nadezhdin, *Issledovanie,* 107.

99. Mel′nikov, "Materialy," pt. 3, 94. Apparently the church itself referred to Napoleon as the Antichrist: ibid.

100. On Elenskii, see Liprandi, *Delo.* On Tatarinova, see Iurii Tolstoi, "O dukhovnom soiuze E. F. Tatarinovoi," in Petr Bartenev, ed., *Deviatnadtsatyi vek: Istoricheskii sbornik,* bk. 1 (Moscow: Ioganson, 1872), 220–34; and F. Fuks, "Iz istorii mistitsizma: Tatarinova i Golovin," *Russkii vestnik,* vol. 218 (January 1892), 3–31. For a sensible discussion, see Kutepov, *Sekty,* 175–78. Also: Aleksandr Etkind, *Khlyst: Sekty, literatura i revoliutsiia* (Moscow: Novoe literaturnoe obozrenie, 1998), 544–47. For a fantastical view of Tatarinova, including castration of followers, sexual orgies, and her illegitimate child, see Mel′nikov, "Materialy," pt. 3, 177–78.

101. Kutepov, *Sekty,* 182, 186–89, 195. On "bozhestvennaia kantseliariia" and "Izvestiia na chem skopchestvo utverzhdaetsia," see Mel′nikov, "Belye golubi," chaps. 13–18, 258–68.

102. Mel′nikov, "Materialy," pt. 3, 106–7.

103. Mel′nikov, "Materialy," pt. 3, 165–66.

2. Reports and Revelations

1. "Nastavlenie Spaso-Evfim′evskogo Monastyria Arkhimandritu Parfeniiu" (June 17, 1820), RGIA, f. 797, op. 3, ed. khr. 12668, l. 6; quoted in [Nikolai Nadezhdin], *Issledovanie o skopcheskoi eresi* (n.p.: Ministerstvo vnutrennikh del, 1845), 156.

2. P. I. Mel′nikov, "Materialy dlia istorii khlystovshchiny i skopcheskoi eresei," pt. 3: "Pravitel′stvennye rasporiazheniia, vypiski i zapiski o skoptsakh do 1826 goda," *Chteniia,* bk. 3, pt. 5 (1872), 227–28. On protecting belief and punishing actions, see I. P. Iakobiia, "Ob ugolovnoi nakazuemosti prinadlezhnosti k izuvernym sektam," *Zhurnal ministerstva iustitsii,* no. 5 (1912), 105–6.

3. K. V. Kutepov, *Sekty khlystov i skoptsov* (Kazan: Imperatorskii universitet, 1883), 17, 205; P. I. Mel′nikov, "Belye golubi," chaps. 13–18, *Russkii vestnik,* vol. 81, bk. 5 (1869), 253; Mel′nikov, "Materialy," pt. 3, 80.

4. Piletskii was arrested in 1837 along with the rest of Tatarinova's group and confined to Spaso-Evfim′ev monastery: F. Fuks, "Iz istorii mistitsizma: Tatarinova i Golovin," *Russkii vestnik,* vol. 218 (January 1892), 31.

5. Nadezhdin, *Issledovanie,* 71.

6. Mel'nikov, "Belye golubi," chaps. 13–18, 272–73.

7. On repentence, see Kutepov, *Sekty,* 219–21; V. N. Mainov, "Skopcheskii eresiarkh Kondratii Selivanov: Ssylka ego v Spaso-Evfimiev monastyr'," *Istoricheskii vestnik,* bk. 4 (1880), 767. See also "Kantseliariia novgorodskogo i S. Peterburgskogo mitropolita po Vladimirskoi Eparkhii Delo: O pomeshchenii i soderzhanii v Suzdal'skom monastyre starika nachal'nika sekty skoptsov" (1820–24), RGIA, f. 815, op. 16, ed. khr. 824.

8. Quoted in P. I. Mel'nikov, "Materialy," pt. 4: "Pravitel'stvennye rasporiazheniia, vypiski i zapiski so vremeni Imperatora Nikolaia do Svoda zakonov, 1825–1833," *Chteniia,* bk. 4, pt. 5 (1872), 26.

9. Decrees from 1807 to 1820, in *Sobranie postanovlenii po chasti raskola* (St. Petersburg: Ministerstvo vnutrennikh del, 1858), 33–61. Skoptsy were found in Orel, Smolensk, Kaluga, Tula, Riazan, Tambov, Kursk, and Voronezh: Kutepov, *Sekty,* 149–50.

10. Mel'nikov, "Materialy," pt. 3, 259, 262, 265.

11. "O ne rasprostranenii polozheniia Gg. Ministrov 4 Avgusta 1816 g. na tekh Skoptsov, kotorye oskopleny do sostoianiia sego postanovleniia i kotorye ne skloniali drugikh v svoiu sektu" (January 7, 1819); "O rasprostranenii polozheniia Komiteta Gg. Ministrov 4 Avgusta 1816 g. na tekh Skoptsov, kotorye budut pokazyvat', chto oni oskopleny v maloletstve neizvestnymi im liud'mi ili sluchaino" (January 30, 1826), in *Sobranie* (1858), 59, 94–96.

12. Mel'nikov, "Materialy," pt. 4, 33; "O nakazanii Skoptsov" (March 14, 1812), in *Sobranie* (1858), 39.

13. Mel'nikov, "Materialy," pt. 3, 218–31.

14. "Kasatel'no presecheniia vrednykh deistvii Skoptsov" (April 18, 1847), in *Sobranie* (1858), 480–81 (quote, 481).

15. Iakobiia, "Ob ugolovnoi nakazuemosti," 105–6.

16. On the origins and ideological complexity of this slogan and on the instrumental view of religion it expressed, see Andrei Zorin, "Ideologiia 'Pravoslaviia-Samoderzhaviia-Narodnosti': Opyt rekonstruktsii," *Novoe literaturnoe obozrenie,* no. 26 (1997), 71–104. On Peter the Great's view of religion as an instrument of state, see N. S. Suvorov, *Svetskoe zakonodatel'stvo i tserkovnaia distsiplina v Rossii do izdaniia Ulozheniia o nakazaniiakh ugolovnykh i ispravitel'nykh 1845 goda* (St. Petersburg: Strannik, 1876), 29–30.

17. On the link between intolerance and growth of the modern state, see R. I. Moore, *The Formation of a Persecuting Society: Power and Deviance in Western Europe, 950–1250* (Oxford: Blackwell, 1987); on Nicholas I, see Richard S. Wortman, *Scenarios of Power: Myth and Ceremony in Russian Monarchy,* 2 vols. (Princeton: Princeton University Press, 1995), 1:part 4; and David W. Edwards, "The System of Nicholas I in Church-State Relations," in *Russian Orthodoxy under the Old Regime,* ed. Robert L. Nichols and Theofanis George Stavrou (Minneapolis: University of Minnesota Press, 1978), 154–69.

18. The State Council first distinguished degrees of harm in 1830: Ardalion Popov, *Sud i nakazaniia za prestupleniia protiv very i nravstvennosti po russkomu pravu* (Kazan:

Bor'ba za veru: Istoriko-bytovye ocherki i obzor zakonodatel'stva po staroobriadchestvu i sektantstvu (St. Petersburg: Gosudarstvennaia tipografiia, 1912), 35−37, 375−92; on the decrees, see Waldron, "Religious Reform," 116−17.

40. On the decree, see below, Chapter 3. On renewed repression, see Coleman, "Most Dangerous Sect," chapt. 4; Waldron, "Religious Reform," 137; V. D. Bonch-Bruevich, "Presledovanie sektantov," *Sovremennyi mir,* no. 7 (1911), 252−82; and Iasevich-Borodaevskaia, *Bor'ba za veru,* 375−92.

41. Mel'nikov, "Materialy," pt. 4, 27−28; Kutepov, *Sekty,* 215.

42. Iakobiia, "Ob ugolovnoi nakazuemosti," 106−7. See also Kutepov, *Sekty,* 225−26, and Karl Konrad Grass, *Die russischen Sekten,* vol. 2: *Die Weissen Tauben oder Skopzen* (1914; rpt. Leipzig: Zentral-Antiquariat der Deutschen Demokratischen Republik, 1966), 450−80. On regulations and persecution under Alexander I and Nicholas I, see N. Varadinov, *Istoriia Ministerstva vnutrennikh del,* vol. 8: *Istoriia rasporiazhenii po raskolu* (St. Petersburg: II Otdelenie Sobstvennoi Ego Imperatorskogo Velichestva Kantseliarii, 1863), 69−624.

43. "Ob otdache vsekh vnov' oskopivshikhsia v arestantskuiu rotu i o priniatii dlia preduprezhdeniia skopchestva nravstvennoi mery" (November 2, 1849), in *Sobranie* (1858), 517−18.

44. "O privedenii v ispolnenie vravstvennoi mery nad nekotorymi vnov' oskopivshimisia v Orlovskoi gubernii i o priniatii sego pravila v rukovodstvo na budushchee vremia" (January 14, 1850), in *Sobranie* (1858), 526−27.

45. A. M. Bobrishchev-Pushkin, *Sud i raskol'niki-sektanty* (St. Petersburg: Senatskaia tipografiia, 1902), 75−76.

46. "Dnevnik ekaterinburgskogo kuptsa V. P. Kliukvina o svoem prebyvanii v sekte skoptsov," RGIA, f. 1005, op. 1, ed. khr. 70 (1826−27); l. 8ob. for his return to Orthodoxy from Old Belief. For the edited text, see "Iz arkhiva S. D. Nechaeva: Donesenie V. P. Kliukvina o skoptsakh," pt. 1, *Bratskoe slovo,* vol. 2, no. 9 (1893), 717−35; pt. 2, ibid., no. 10 (1893), 770−87. The journal was edited by the same Professor Subbotin who testified at the Kudrin trial.

47. Testimony of Ivan Andreianov (1826), in Varadinov, *Istoriia,* 8:247−66.

48. Mel'nikov, "Materialy," pt. 4, 38. On Perovskii, see Daniel Orlovsky, *The Limits of Reform: The Ministry of Internal Affairs in Imperial Russia, 1802−1881* (Cambridge: Harvard University Press, 1981), 32−35.

49. *Skopcheskoe delo,* sten. Lipskerov, 91. See also Kutepov, *Sekty,* 30−31.

50. [Nikolai Nadezhdin], *Issledovanie o skopcheskoi eresi* (n.p.: Ministerstvo vnutrennikh del, 1845). On print run: 50 copies noted in Kutepov, *Sekty,* 17; 25 copies in G. I. Rodzevich, "Skoptsy v Rossii: Bibliograficheskii ukazatel' literatury o nikh," *Antikvar: Bibliograficheskii listok,* no. 2 (1902), 60.

51. N. K. Kozmin, *Nikolai Ivanovich Nadezhdin: Zhizn' i nauchno-literaturnaia deiatel'nost', 1804−1836* (St. Petersburg: Aleksandrov, 1912); A. N. Pypin, *Istoriia russkoi etnografii* (St. Petersburg: Stasiulevich, 1890), 1:234−74; Nathaniel Knight, "Constructing the Science of Nationality: Ethnography in Mid-Nineteenth-Century Russia" (Ph.D.

diss., Columbia University, 1994), chap. 3. Nadezhdin's views on narodnost´ are reprinted in N. I. Nadezhdin, "Ob etnograficheskom izuchenii narodnosti russkoi" (1847), *Etnograficheskoe obozrenie*, nos. 1–2 (1994), 107–17, 124–39.

52. V. I. Dal´, *Zapiska o ritual´nykh ubiistvakh: Rozyskanie ob ubienii evreiami khristianskikh mladentsev i upotreblenii krovi ikh* (St. Petersburg: Suvorin, 1913). This edition, issued during the Beilis trial, was a reprint of the original 1844 text, with an introduction. The Suvorin edition was republished in Moscow in 1995 by "Vitiaz´."

53. [V. I. Dal´], *Issledovanie o skopcheskoi eresi* (St. Petersburg: Ministerstvo vnutrennikh del, 1844). For the story of this assignment and its outcome, see P. I. Mel´nikov (Andrei Pecherskii), "Vladimir Ivanovich Dal´: Kritiko-biograficheskii ocherk," *Polnoe sobranie sochinenii Vladimira Dalia* (Moscow: Vol´f, 1897), 1:i–xc; and A. A. Il´in-Tomich, ed., "Perepiski V. I. Dalia i M. P. Pogodina," pt. 1, in *Litsa: Biograficheskii al´manakh*, no. 2 (Moscow–St. Petersburg: Feniks-Atheneum, 1993), 343–45. Nadezhdin's report is longer (384 pages of text, compared with Dal´'s 146). It reflects the same attitudes and sometimes quotes verbatim from the earlier text but also adds new material and new arguments.

54. Letter dated spring 1844, in Il´in-Tomich, ed., "Perepiski," 343.

55. Mel´nikov (Pecherskii), "Vladimir Ivanovich Dal´," 1:xc (quote); lxxxvi–lxxxix.

56. Nadezhdin, *Issledovanie*, 189; Dal´, *Issledovanie*, 32, 120.

57. Nadezhdin, *Issledovanie*, 197. The phrase "legkie lodochki" comes from Skoptsy verses: P. I. Mel´nikov, "Materialy," pt. 1: "Solovetskie dokumenty o skoptsakh," *Chteniia*, bk. 1, pt. 5 (1872), 79.

58. Nadezhdin, *Issledovanie*, 270–71. Dal´ talks of eradication (iskorenit´) and extermination (unichtozhenie), *Issledovanie*, 145–46.

59. Nadezhdin, *Issledovanie*, 324–25, 334 (2:400).

60. Grass, *Die russischen Sekten*, 2:888, 891–92. On Grass, see Roger Comtet, "A propos du livre du Karl Konrad Grass, *Die russischen Sekten* (Dorpat–Leipzig, 1907, 1909, 1914)," *Revue des études slaves* 69:1–2 (1997), 183–200. Grass lived 1870–1927.

61. Nadezhdin, *Issledovanie*, 366–67. Dal´ says Skoptsy have irreparably lost their humanity: *Issledovanie*, 146.

62. On Nadezhdin's misreading of symbolic language and the dated character of his tract, see comments of Kudrin defense lawyer, in *Skopcheskoe delo*, sten. Lipskerov, 122.

63. Nadezhdin, *Issledovanie*, 272, 284 (quote), 287 (quote). Same terms in Dal´, *Issledovanie*, 146 (sore), 118–19 (secret society, brotherhood). Dal´ argued that their wealth made them politically dangerous, allowing them to exercise influence over the popular masses (126).

64. Nadezhdin, *Issledovanie*, 316. "Yellowish cast" from Dosifei's testimony, also in Mel´nikov, "Materialy," pt. 1, 160.

65. "O merakh k pregrazhdeniiu sekty Skoptsov" (March 11, 1836), in *Sobranie* (1858), 210–12.

66. E. V. Pelikan, *Sudebno-meditsinskie issledovaniia skopchestva i istoricheskie svedeniia o nem* (St. Petersburg: Golovin, 1872), 69, 71–79.

67. Nadezhdin, *Issledovanie*, 352 (neistovstvo). Opinion repeated, almost word for

word, in Efim Solov'ev, *Svedeniia o russkikh skoptsakh* (Kostroma: Gubernskaia tipografiia, 1870), i.

68. Pelikan, *Sudebno-meditsinskie*, 87.

69. Nadezhdin, *Issledovanie*, 336 (zapoi). Such reasoning became a cliché: see Solov'ev, *Svedeniia*, 78–80.

70. Nadezhdin, *Issledovanie*, 337–41; on offering loans and excusing debts on condition of castration, see Pelikan, *Sudebno-meditsinskie*, 95. For persistence of accusations of bribery and enslavement of children, see A. A. Levenstim, "Fanatizm i prestuplenie," pt. 2, *Zhurnal ministerstva iustitsii*, no. 8 (1898), 6. For poverty as motive for joining and wealth as source of community's strength, see Solov'ev, *Svedeniia*, ii–iii, 17.

71. Pelikan, *Sudebno-meditsinskie*, 103–6.

72. Pelikan, *Sudebno-meditsinskie*, 129, 133–34, 136.

73. See Laura Engelstein, *The Keys to Happiness: Sex and the Search for Modernity in Fin-de-Siècle Russia* (Ithaca: Cornell University Press, 1992), chap. 8.

74. Pelikan, *Sudebno-meditsinskie*, 148–49, 162 (quote), 164. On tradition of accusing marginal religious groups of sexual licentiousness, see Daniel F. Caner, "The Practice and Prohibition of Self-Castration in Early Christianity," *Vigiliae Christianae* 51 (1997), 400; on charges of ritual killing of children, see Susanna Elm, "'Pierced by Bronze Needles': Anti-Montanist Charges of Ritual Stigmatization in Their Fourth-Century Context," *Journal of Early Christian Studies* 4:4 (1996), 411–13.

75. Nadezhdin, *Issledovanie*, 349.

76. Nadezhdin, *Issledovanie*, 347–48 (on conflict between rich and poor among the Skoptsy); A. Orlov, "Missionerstvo, sekty i raskol: Khronika," *Missionerskoe obozrenie*, no. 10 (1902), 516 (kagal'noe obshchestvo, kagal'nye bogatstva).

77. The first trial to follow the legal reforms of 1864 was that of the wealthy merchant Maksim Plotitsyn of Morshchansk: see Grass, *Die russischen Sekten*, 2:480–513. On divisions, see Gur'ev, *Sibirskie skoptsy*, 24; also V. I—n [Iokhel'son], "Olekminskie skoptsy," pt. 2, 315–16.

78. Nadezhdin, *Issledovanie*, 347–48, 351–52, 361–62 (quote), 363. Dal' also emphasizes the danger of their accumulated wealth but does not use the overtly anti-Semitic language: *Issledovanie*, 126.

79. Baron von Haxthausen, *The Russian Empire, Its People, Institutions, and Resources*, trans. Robert Fairie, 2 vols. (London, 1856; rpt. London: Frank Cass, 1968), 1:254. (Original, German ed., 1847–52.)

80. Mel'nikov, "Belye golubi," chaps. 1–12, *Russkii vestnik*, vol. 80, bk. 3 (1869), 332, 384–87 (affirming Haxthausen's reports and adding his own testimony). A. P. Shchapov, "Umstvennye napravleniia russkogo raskola," *Delo* (1867), no. 10, 319–48; no. 11, 138–68; no. 12, 170–200; rpt. in *Sochineniia A. P. Shchapova* (St. Petersburg: Pirozhkov, 1906), 1:636.

81. Major cases: Maksim Plotitsyn in Tambov (1838–68); 58 Finnish Skoptsy in St. Petersburg (1870); Kudrins in Moscow (1871); Lisin case in Melitopol (1876). Partial list in Levenstim, "Fanatizm i prestuplenie," pt. 1, *Zhurnal ministerstva iustitsii*, no. 7 (1898), 33–78; pt. 2, 3–4.

82. *Skopcheskoe delo*, sten. Lipskerov, 5–6 (audience and list of defendants). For jurors,

see "Dopolnitel'nyi spisok," in "Materialy po delu riada lits . . . osuzhdennykh za prinadlezhnost' k sekte skoptsov i sovrashchenie v nee drugikh lits. Prav. Senata ugol. kass. dep., delo po 1 stolu: Moskovskii okruzhnoi sud," RGIA, f. 1363, op. 9, ed. khr. 10 (1871), l. 32.

83. "O dozvolenii skoptsu Kudrinu prozhivat' v Moskve" (November 17, 1860), in *Sobranie* (1875), 575–76.

84. *Skopcheskoe delo*, sten. Lipskerov, 17, 21, 23.

85. *Skopcheskoe delo*, sten. Lipskerov, 31, 38–39, 44.

86. *Skopcheskoe delo*, sten. Lipskerov, 143.

87. V. I. Kel'siev, ed., *Sbornik pravitel'stvennykh svedenii o raskol'nikakh*, 4 vols. (London: Trübner, 1860–62). On the context for his interest in the sects, see Michel Mervaud, "Une alliance ambiguë: Herzen, Ogarev et les Vieux-Croyants," *Revue des études slaves* 69:1–2 (1997), 119–34.

88. V. Kel'siev, "Sviatorusskie dvoevery," pt. 1, *Otechestvennye zapiski*, vol. 174, no. 10, sec. 1 (1867), 583–619.

89. On Romania as refuge, see N. P. Latyshev, "Nachalo moego povestvovaniia" (1910), GMIR, f. 2, op. 5, d. 261, l. 160b. For figures, see Grass, *Die russischen Sekten*, 2:459. Apparently some Skoptsy were brought to trial in 1835 by the local court but were acquitted (ibid., 457–58). Men'shenin guessed that in 1917 there had been some 1,500 Skoptsy in Romania, but ten years later perhaps only 300–400: letter from G. P. Men'shenin to V. D. Bonch-Bruevich (January 22, 1928), OR-RGB, f. 369, k. 301, d. 27, l. 42–43.

90. Kel'siev, "Sviatorusskie dvoevery," 600.

91. Kel'siev, "Sviatorusskie dvoevery," 583 and 587.

92. Kel'siev, "Sviatorusskie dvoevery," 599, 592 (quotes).

93. Kel'siev, "Sviatorusskie dvoevery," 619.

94. Kel'siev, "Sviatorusskie dvoevery," 600.

95. Shchapov, "Umstvennye napravleniia," 580–647. On A. P. Shchapov, see Franco Venturi, *Roots of Revolution* (New York: Grosset and Dunlap, 1966), 196–201; also Daniel Field, *Rebels in the Name of the Tsar* (Boston: Houghton Mifflin, 1976), 92–103.

96. His observations offended the Skoptsy themselves, when they happened upon them: see N. M. Iadrintsev, *Russkaia obshchina v tiur'me i ssylke* (St. Petersburg: Morigerovskii, 1872), 256–57.

97. Shchapov, "Umstvennye napravleniia," 608, 611, 621, 623, 629.

98. Shchapov, "Umstvennye napravleniia," 632, 634, 636.

99. Shchapov, "Umstvennye napravleniia," 629, 635–36, 647.

100. Shchapov, "Umstvennye napravleniia," 636.

101. V. I—n [Iokhel'son], "Olekminskie skoptsy: Istoriko-bytovoi ocherk," pt. 1, *Zhivaia starina* (1894), 203; ibid., pt. 2, 306–8. On Iokhel'son, see Yuri Slezkine, *Arctic Mirrors: Russia and the Small Peoples of the North* (Ithaca: Cornell University Press, 1994), 125.

102. V. I—n [Iokhel'son], "Olekminskie skoptsy," pt. 2, 303–4.

103. Pelikan, *Sudebno-meditsinskie,* 117–18 (account). On the use of similar horror stories to generate moral indignation in mid-nineteenth-century Anglo-American culture, see Karen Halttunen, "Humanitarianism and the Pornography of Pain in Anglo-American Culture," *American Historical Review* 100:2 (1995), 303–34. For a similar example in the anti-Skoptsy literature, see the description of castration performed on a young boy in N. V. Reutskii, *Liudi bozh'i i skoptsy: Istoricheskoe issledovanie* (Moscow: Grachev, 1872), 108.

104. [G. E. Prudkovskii], "Golos iz mogily zhivykh mertvetsov: Zapiski skoptsa," pts. 1–3, *Zhurnal romanov i povestei,* no. 1 (1881), 1–70; no. 2 (1881), 71–126; no. 1 (1882), 127–78. The journal was published by the editors of *Nedelia,* a mouthpiece of cultural populism: N. A. Rubakin, *Sredi knig* (Moscow: Nauka, 1911), 1:209 and 216. The "living dead" (khodiachie mertvetsy) was a common pejorative for the Skoptsy: for example, Nadezhdin, *Issledovanie,* 316. The first two parts of the memoirs were published anonymously, but the author's name appears on the last part. The first page of *Zhurnal romanov i povestei,* no. 3 (1881), in the collection of the Public Library in St. Petersburg, carries a penciled inscription in old orthography, presumably a librarian's hand, that identifies the author by his full name as a member of the sect. He is said to have died in 1909 in extreme poverty. His other manuscripts were burned by fellow Skoptsy during the 1905 revolution. References to the memoirs are indicated by part and page, e.g., (1:32). Prudkovskii's birthdate is unclear. The memoir, written between 1878 and 1880, says he was castrated at age ten, lived exclusively among the Skoptsy until age thirty, and worked on a riverboat for ten years (1:1–2, 51). By 1878 he had discovered his mission to unmask the sect's iniquities, applied for a passport to travel, and been refused (2:82, 110). Taking all this into account, one can say he was probably born in the 1830s.

105. On castration of children brought into the sect by their parents, see below, Chapter 3, and Pelikan, *Sudebno-meditsinskie,* 38; Nadezhdin, *Issledovanie,* 210–11.

106. On this custom, see S. M. Tolstaia, "Simvolika devstvennosti v polesskom svadebnom obriade," in *Seks i erotika v russkoi traditsionnoi kul'ture,* ed. A. L. Toporkov (Moscow: Ladomir, 1996), 197.

107. St. Barbara opposed her father by rejecting the pagan gods in favor of Jesus Christ. Dedicating herself to God, she refused to marry. Unable to prevail, her father handed her over to the Roman governor, who had her exposed naked in public, beaten, and her nipples removed. Finally, her own father wielded the sword that cut off her head. He and the governor were then struck dead by lightning. See "Zhitie i stradanie sviatoi velikomuchenitsy Varvary," in *Zhitiia sviatykh, na russkom iazyke,* ed. Dimitrii Roskovskii (Moscow: Sinodal'naia tipografiia, 1903), 4:75–88.

108. See Engelstein, *Keys to Happiness,* 114–27.

109. On the Skoptsy use of "sheep and goats," see testimony of Ivan Andreianov (1826), in Varadinov, *Istoriia,* 8:264.

110. Andreianov testimony, in Varadinov, *Istoriia,* 8:250.

111. Though many survived, it is unclear how many did not: compare Nadezhdin, *Issledovanie,* 212 (often fatal), and Pelikan, *Sudebno-meditsinskie,* 80 (rarely).

112. "For the kingdom of heaven's sake," from Matthew 19:12. On the testimony of children, see Pelikan, *Sudebno-meditsinskie,* 95–97. The loyalty of children is illustrated by the case of two boys confined to a monastery as a means of persuading them to talk, who were released after six years of stubborn silence: "O pomeshchenii v monastyr' oskoplennogo po novomu sposobu krest'ianskogo mal'chika" (December 27, 1851), in *Sobranie* (1858), 563–64; "Ob oskoplennykh meshchanskikh detiakh" (December 9, 1858), in *Sobranie* (1875), 561–63.

113. For Men'shenin's case, see G. P. Men'shenin, "Zametki bolee vydaiushchie sobytiia [*sic*] i raznogo roda sluchai iz zhizni v Rossii i Sibiri" (1900), GMIR, f. 2, op. 5, d. 272, l. 21.

114. Tagantsev, ed., *Ulozhenie* (1901), 227. Art. 147, in *Svod zakonov Rossiiskoi Imperii,* ed. I. D. Mordukhai-Boltovskii, 5 vols. (St. Petersburg: Deiatel', [not before 1913]), 5:244.

3. Boundaries and Betrayals

1. Letter from N. P. Latyshev to V. D. Bonch-Bruevich (before December 18, 1912), GMIR, f. 2, op. 5, d. 28, l. 10b. N. P. Latyshev, "Nachalo moego povestvovaniia" (1910), GMIR, f. 2, op. 5, d. 261, l. 26. Letter from N. P. Latyshev to V. D. Bonch-Bruevich (December 27, 1912), GMIR, f. 2, op. 5, d. 29, l. 4 (novoe skopchestvo).

2. N. P. Latyshev, "Prodolzhenie" (December 26, 1915), GMIR, f. 2, op. 5, d. 265, l. 6.

3. Latyshev, "Nachalo," l. 30, 35, 37ob. (quote).

4. Latyshev, "Nachalo," l. 27ob. (horse), 42ob.–43.

5. N. P. Latyshev, "To chto ia khotel by peredat' chitaiushchemu miru" [between 1906 and 1913], GMIR, f. 2, op. 5, d. 263, l. 2–20b. See also "Sudebnoe sledstvie po delu o krest'ianakh Lisine i dr., obviniaemykh v rasprostranenii skopchestva: Obvinitel'nyi akt" (Tavricheskaia gubernskaia tipografiia, 1875), GMIR, f. 2, op. 5, d. 223, l. 27 (p. 67). Likening their treatment to that of bandits, Latyshev was invoking Luke 22:52, where Jesus reproaches the guardians of the temple for coming against him "as against a thief." In this hour, Jesus adds, theirs is "the power of darkness" (Luke 22:53). Thanks to Peter Brown for this connection.

6. [—], "Ratsionalizm na iuge Rossii," *Otechestvennye zapiski,* 3 (1878), 209 ("protsess-monstr," respect). Latyshev, "To chto," l. 20b. (spectacle). Porfirii Mochul'skii, "Ekspertiza po delu o skoptsakh, razbiravshemusia v g. Melitopole v sentiabre mesiatse sego 1876 goda," pt. 1, *Tavricheskie eparkhial'nye vedomosti,* no. 23 (1876), 747. The 128 mentioned by Mochul'skii does not correspond with the 136 on the list in GMIR, f. 2, op. 5, d. 223.

7. "Sudebnoe sledstvie po delu," l. 20 (p. 52).

8. For mention of the principal trials, see K. V. Kutepov, *Sekty khlystov i skoptsov* (Kazan: Imperatorskii universitet, 1883), 235, 265–68 (Berdiansk, 1864; Kaluga, 1868; Iuganov, 1869; Kudrin, 1869; Kursk, 1869; Plotitsyn in Morshchansk, 1869; Tula, 1869; Kaluga, 1871; Moscow, 1873; Kazan, 1874; Kronstadt, 1874; Ufa, 1874; Melitopol, 1875;

Penza, 1876; Orel, 1879; Samara, 1879; Saratov, 1880); repeated in V. D. Bonch-Bruevich, "Spisok protsessov skoptsov" (n.d.), GMIR, f. 2, op. 5, d. 137; Dmitrii Skvortsov, *Ocherki tverskogo raskola i sektantstva* (Moscow: D. A. Bonch-Bruevich, 1895), 107–16 (Tver, 1888); *Skopcheskoe delo: Protsess Kudrinykh i drugikh 24 lits, obviniaemykh v prinadlezhnosti k skopcheskoi eresi*, stenographer A. Ia. Lipskerov, ed. A. P. Sokolov (Moscow: Ioganson, 1871). Two in which famous lawyers participated: A. F. Koni, "Po delu ob oskoplenii kupecheskogo syna Gorshkova" (1873), *Sobranie sochinenii*, vol. 3: *Sudebnye rechi* (Moscow: Iuridicheskaia literatura, 1967), 136–57; V. D. Spasovich, "Delo o skoptsakh Plotitsynykh i dr." (1869), in *Sochineniia V. D. Spasovicha*, vol 5: *Sudebnye rechi (1867–74)* (St. Petersburg: Rymovich, 1893).

9. "Statisticheskie svedeniia o sektantakh (k 1 ian. 1912 g.)," Departament dukhovnykh del, Ministerstvo vnutrennikh del, RGIA, f. 1276, op. 2, d. 597 (1906–14), l. 383 (p. 49).

10. RGIA, f. 821, op. 133, d. 233, l. 9a–55, 93, 98–100 (Kharkov, 1910), l. 102–15 (Ufa, 1911), l. 135–38 (Orenburg, 1910); ibid., d. 234, l. 48–59 (Perm, 1915), l. 62–73 (Ekaterinburg, 1915), l. 82–88 (Riazan, 1915). See also GMIR, f. 2, op. 5, d. 165, 178–213, 215, 228 (Ufa); d. 214 (Kharkov).

11. On "stinkers," meaning both goats and women, see V. Kel´siev, "Sviatorusskie dvoevery," pt. 1, *Otechestvennye zapiski*, vol. 174, no. 10, sec. 1 (1867), 600.

12. In the Melitopol case, 38 percent belonged to groups of four or more relations (9 clans), 60 percent to groups of three or more; 84 percent were related to at least one other person. Among defendants in the six cases, at least 80 percent were related to someone else in the same community. The figures involved in these cases concern only the persons apprehended. It is possible, of course, that loners—or men in general—more easily escaped detection than members of kin-based households. The picture of communities centered around a number of core households is not affected by this possibility.

13. Data on both sexes exist for four communities: Riazan, Orenburg, Ufa, and Kharkov, in which the average age is identical (39, 36, 43W/45M, 46), the mean comparable (35W/41M, 32W/32M, 41W/47M, 46), as are the ranges (17–90/19–65, 16–60/18–62, 30–65/18–64, 14–77/14–85). In the Melitopol case, 7 of the 50 males and 10 of the 85 females were younger than 18. When the youngsters are excluded, the average age of adults is 40 for men, 37 for women (teens included: 36.6 and 34). The mean without teens: 43 for men, 33 for women; with teens: 39 men, 30 women. The spread without teens: 18–74 men, 18–75 women; with teens: 10–74 men, 14–75 women.

14. Of the 136 Melitopol defendants, 63 percent were female. Of these, 85 percent were related to another defendant, compared with 84 percent of the men. The 350 tried in the six cases were divided almost evenly between male and female. Of the women, 81 percent were related to another defendant, compared with 79 percent of the men. These figures probably underestimate the density of family ties. For example, in the Melitopol case, the two Krasnikov brothers were listed among the accused, but their mother, also a believer, was not, and their father had been exiled several years before. What appears

on the list as a sibling pair is in fact half a family foursome. For these additional facts, see Latyshev, "Nachalo," l. 11.

15. "Sudebnoe sledstvie po delu," l. 11 (p. 26).

16. "O sudebnykh presledovaniiakh skoptsov" (Perm, 1915), RGIA, f. 821, op. 133, d. 234, l. 56ob. (testimony of Ustin'ia Bogdanova).

17. Latyshev, "Nachalo," l. 38.

18. In the breakaway part of the Melitopol community, there were at least three female prophets: Latyshev, "Nachalo."

19. "Obvinitel'nyi akt po delu o sekte skoptsov" (Kharkov: "Khudozhestvennyi trud," n.d.), RGIA, f. 821, op. 133, d. 233, l. 24.

20. In Melitopol: of defendants 18 or older, 32 percent of the women were physically altered, compared with 57 percent of the men. In the six later cases taken together: 39 percent of women, 60 percent of men. Among the Kharkov defendants alone: 47 percent of women, 86 percent of men. The Riazan case (extracted from the six cases) is an exception: 82 percent of women, but only 64 percent of men. There were also twice as many women as men in this community. In Melitopol, among children aged 10 to 19, 7 of 9 boys were castrated, compared with none of the 13 girls—though all belonged to families. In Kharkov, all 7 of the boys were castrated, but only 1 of 6 girls. Again, Riazan was different: here both males under 21 were castrated, but so were the 3 girls under 21.

21. The relatively low level of castration among adult males may have reflected the unusual background of this group: those arrested had recently been converted by the prophet Lisin to a stricter version of the faith. The low level thus reflects the lax practices of the community from which they had only recently separated.

22. See *Skopcheskoe delo*, sten. Lipskerov.

23. "Obvinitel'nyi akt" (Kharkov), l. 24.

24. Latyshev, "Nachalo," l. 140ob. (serye muzhiki).

25. In the Kharkov case, Negrebetskii, called the "Savior," and Razinkova, called "Goddess" (boginia), were not castrated: "Obvinitel'nyi akt" (Kharkov), l. 150ob. (p. 4).

26. On rejecting castration, see P. I. Mel'nikov, "Materialy dlia istorii khlystovshchiny i skopcheskoi eresei," pt. 1: "Solovetskie dokumenty o skoptsakh," *Chteniia*, bk. 1, pt. 5 (1872), 78.

27. Latyshev, "Prodolzhenie," l. 470b.–48 (sanctification), 53 (justify). On the Melitopol defendants as "spiritual," see "Ratsionalizm," 209.

28. Latyshev, "Nachalo," l. 10.

29. "Protokol obyska v dome Ivanovykh" (February 7, 1911), GMIR, f. 2, op. 5, d. 208; on indoor plumbing in early twentieth-century Russian cities, see Barbara Alpern Engel, *Between the Fields and the City: Women, Work, and Family in Russia, 1861–1914* (Cambridge: Cambridge University Press, 1994), 209–10.

30. "Svidetel'skie pokazaniia po delu Daletskikh," GMIR, f. 2, op. 5, d. 215, l. 9 (V. K. Ivanov).

31. "Obvinitel'nyi akt" (Riazan), Moskovskaia Sudebnaia Palata (March 17, 1915), RGIA, f. 821, op. 133, d. 234, l. 84 (p. 5).

32. Clipping from *Peterburgskie vedomosti* (September 24, 1910), RGIA, f. 821, op. 133, d. 233, l. 10.

33. Latyshev, "Nachalo," l. 350b.

34. "Obvinitel'nyi akt" (Kharkov), l. 19 (p. 11) (postniki), l. 140b. (p. 2) (shtund); "Obvinitel'nyi akt" (Riazan), l. 82 (p. 1) (Masons, Khlysty); N. Varadinov, *Istoriia Ministerstva vnutrennikh del*, vol. 8: *Istoriia rasporiazhenii po raskolu* (St. Petersburg: II Otdelenie Sobstvennoi Ego Imperatorskogo Velichestva Kantseliarii, 1863), 139 (Molokans). For "speckled shirts," see Kel'siev, "Sviatorusskie dvoevery," 592.

35. Jeffrey Burds, "A Culture of Denunciation: Peasant Labor Migration and Religious Anathematization in Rural Russia, 1860–1905," *Journal of Modern History* 68 (1996), 815.

36. Latyshev, "Prodolzhenie," l. 50b.

37. Latyshev, "Nachalo," l. 490b.

38. "Ratsionalizm," 208.

39. "Svidetel'skie pokazaniia po delu Daletskikh," l. 1–10b. (Vasilii Oshurko).

40. Latyshev, "To chto," l. 2–20b.

41. Testimony in "Obvinitel'nyi akt" (Orenburg, October 2, 1910), RGIA, f. 821, op. 133, d. 233, l. 1350b.

42. Latyshev, "Nachalo," l. 28.

43. "Obvinitel'nyi akt" (Kharkov), l. 25 (p. 23).

44. "Obvinitel'nyi akt" (Kharkov), l. 21 (p. 24).

45. "Obvinitel'nyi akt" (Kharkov), l. 26–260b. (pp. 25–26). For another example with apiary and axe, from the Ufa case, see "Protokol doprosa: Grigorii Koloskov" (February 12, 1911), GMIR, f. 2, op. 5, d. 90.

46. "Obvinitel'nyi akt" (Kharkov), l. 19–190b. (pp. 11–12; quote, 190b.). The Riazan case provides another example of the local priest knowing about the Skoptsy and neglecting to report them: "Obvinitel'nyi akt" (Riazan), l. 85 (p. 7).

47. "Obvinitel'nyi akt" (Kharkov), l. 150b. (p. 4).

48. "Obvinitel'nyi akt" (Riazan), l. 82–83 (pp. 1–3).

49. Timofei Ivanovich Butkevich, "Ekspertiza po Ostrogozhskomu protsessu skoptsov" (July 3, 1910), GMIR, f. 2, op. 5, d. 139, l. 10b.

50. Letter in "Protokol osmotra naidennykh veshchei pri obyske u skoptsov" (n.d.), GMIR, f. 2, op. 5, d. 212, l. 2–3.

51. On Siberia, see mention in Latyshev, "To chto," l. 8, 100b. Family listed in village census: "Imennye spiski skoptsov i skopcheskikh selenii Iakutskoi oblasti, Olekminskogo okruga" (1902; notes as late as 1909), GMIR, f. 2, op. 5, d. 250, l. 240b. Later success: "Tetrad' 'glagolov' skoptsov," GMIR, kollektsiia I, op. 6, d. 2, l. 420b. (firm name). Zverev's own account: P. P. Zverev, "Zaiavlenie na prediavlenie mne obvinenie, po st. 138 U. K." (May 27, 1926), GMIR, f. 2, op. 5, d. 249, l. 2. Zverev remembers leaving in 1908, but Latyshev, writing closer to the events, remembers his family and the Zverevs leaving

in 1906.

52. Letters from Iakov Pavlovich Zverev to G. P. Men'shenin (November 15, 1911; December 31, 1911), GMIR, f. 2, op. 5, d. 115, 116.

53. "Proekt ustava blagotvoritel'nogo obshchestva vo imia presviatoi Bogoroditsy v g. Iassakh" (with cover letter dated July 29, 1911), GMIR, f. 2, op. 5, d. 294, l. 1–16. On the almshouse and pensions in the Siberian village of Markha, see "Imennye spiski," l. 27.

54. Letter in "Protokol osmotra," l. 1–2.

55. On Kiriukhin and his role, see Chapter 4.

56. "Sudebnoe sledstvie po delu," l. 44, 67–68.

57. Latyshev, "To chto," l. 20b.

58. Luke 23:42, reported in Mochul'skii, "Ekspertiza," 749.

59. Skopcheskoe delo, sten. Lipskerov, 16.

60. Mochul'skii, "Ekspertiza," 747. Also A. Zabelin, "Dvizhenie vpered v sekte skoptsov," Drevniaia i novaia Rossiia, no. 2 (1878), 137.

61. Latyshev, "Nachalo," l. 110b.

62. Latyshev, "Nachalo," l. 430b.–440b.

63. "Obvinitel'nyi akt" (Orenburg), l. 137. One among other examples from Kharkov: "Obvinitel'nyi akt" (Kharkov), l. 26 (p. 25).

64. "Protokol doprosa: Evdokiia Driamova" (February 2, 1911), GMIR, f. 2, op. 5, d. 186.

65. "Protokol doprosa: Nikolai Rabeev" (February 2, 1911), GMIR, f. 2, op. 5, d. 204. Bogorodskaia can be translated as "Virgin Mary."

66. "Protokol doprosa: Agaf'ia Sycheva" (March 6, 1911), GMIR, f. 2, op. 5, d. 201.

67. "Protokol doprosa: Grigorii Koloskov." For earlier examples of this same device, see E. V. Pelikan, Sudebno-meditsinskie issledovaniia skopchestva i istoricheskie svedeniia o nem (St. Petersburg: Golovin, 1872), 120; Appendix A, 11; Appendix B, 18–21, 25–27.

68. "Protokol doprosa: Nikifor Daletskii" (January 30, 1911), GMIR, f. 2, op. 5, d. 182.

69. "Protokol doprosa: Larion Koloskov" (January 30, 1911), GMIR, f. 2, op. 5, d. 191.

70. "Protokol doprosa: Stepan Kornoukhov" (February 1, 1911), GMIR, f. 2, op. 5, d. 194.

71. "Protokol doprosa: Arkhip Kulikov" (February 1, 1912), GMIR, f. 2, op. 5, d. 195. He says "oskopilsia," which leaves ambiguous whether it was done to him or by himself.

72. "Obvinitel'nyi akt" (Kharkov), l. 170b.–18 (pp. 8–9).

73. "Obvinitel'nyi akt" (Kharkov), l. 18–180b. (pp. 9–10).

74. "Obvinitel'nyi akt" (Kharkov), l. 210b., 220b. (quote) (pp. 16, 18).

75. "Obvinitel'nyi akt" (Kharkov), l. 27 (p. 27).

76. "Obvinitel'nyi akt" (Kharkov), l. 29 (p. 31).

77. "Protokol doprosa: Iakov Labutin" (February 2, 1911), GMIR, f. 2, op. 5, d. 197.

78. Letters from Ia. S. Labutin to V. D. Bonch-Bruevich (May 2, 1912), GMIR, f. 2,

op. 5, d. 20; (August 16, 1912), d. 21; telegram, with Bonch-Bruevich's reply (October 21, 1912), d. 22; telegram (October 22, 1912), d. 23.

79. I. A. Amenitskii, "Doklad po voprosu o priglashenii v sudebnoe zasedanie po delu Ivanovykh i dr. obviniaemykh po 95 st. Ug. Ul. v kachestve eksperta g.V. D. Bonch-Bruevicha," GMIR, f. 2, op. 5, d. 138; "Uchebnyi komitet pri Sviateishem Sinode: Otnoshenie v Ufimskii Okruzhnoi Sud" (July 7, 1912), ibid., d. 224; Ufa Circuit Court, letter to V. D. Bonch-Bruevich, confirming his appearance (November 5, 1912), ibid., d. 102.

80. "Prigovor po delu skoptsov v g. Ufe" (Ufa Circuit Court, November 12, 1912), GMIR, f. 2, op. 5, d. 178, l. 3–30b. See newspaper report, "Delo skoptsov," *Russkoe slovo*, no. 265 (July 16, 1912), GMIR, f. 2, op. 26, d. 73, l. 140b. Bonch-Bruevich is mentioned as witness for the defense.

81. From the procurator of the Ekaterinburg Circuit Court to the governor of Perm province (October 30, 1915), RGIA, f. 821, op. 133, d. 234, l. 62–72.

82. Records of the Perm case (May 27, 1915 to February 11, 1916), RGIA, f. 821, op. 133, d. 234, l. 48–59.

83. Aleksandr Petrovich Dulkin, procurator of the Kharkov Circuit Court, to A. N. Kharuzin (November 3, 1910), RGIA, f. 821, op. 133, d. 233, l. 55–550b. On not-guilty verdict, see Dulkin to Ministry of Internal Affairs, Department of Spiritual Affairs (October 10, 1910), ibid., l. 52. On rearrest, see Kharkov governor to Ministry of Internal Affairs, Department of Spiritual Affairs (August 25, 1911), ibid., l. 93.

84. Procurator's appeal to the Senate: "Protest prokurora Khar'kovskogo okruzhnogo suda na opravdatel'nyi prigovor po delu I. N. Negrebetskogo . . . ." Prav. Sen. ugol. kass. Delo po 3 stolu (November 16, 1910), RGIA, f. 1363, op. 4, ed. khr. 978 (1910–11), l. 1–40b. Senate ruling: "Pravitel'stvuiushchii Senat: Ukaz Khar'kovskomu Okruzhnomu Sudu" (January 28, 1911), GMIR, f. 2, op. 5, d. 177, l. 1–20b.

85. "Skopcheskii protsess v Khar'kove," *Kolokol*, no. 1351 (November 23, 1910), RGIA, f. 821, op. 133, d. 233, l. 9a.

86. On retrial, see "Khar'kovskii okruzhnoi sud: Obvinitel'nyi akt po delu obviniaemykh v skopchestve" (December 23, 1911), GMIR, f. 2, op. 5, d. 231. Invitations to Bonch-Bruevich to appear as expert witness: "Khar'kovskii okruzhnoi sud: Povestka ekspertu V. D. Bonch-Bruevichu" (July 27, 1912 to August 31, 1913), GMIR, f. 2, op. 5, d. 104, l. 1–5. "Delo skoptsov," *Utro*, no. 2112 (October 17, 1913), GMIR, f. 2, op. 26, d. 73, l. 200b.–21.

87. S. Utin, procurator, Khar'kovskaia sudebnaia palata (November 4, 1910), RGIA, f. 1405, op. 543, ed. khr. 457.

88. See Peter Waldron, "Religious Reform after 1905: Old Believers and the Orthodox Church," *Oxford Slavonic Papers*, n.s., no. 20 (1987), 134–37.

89. Objecting that penal sanctions were inappropriate: I. P. Iakobiia, "Ob ugolovnoi nakazuemosti prinadlezhnosti k izuvernym sektam," *Zhurnal ministerstva iustitsii*, no. 5 (1912), 131.

90. Latyshev, "Prodolzhenie," l. 6ob.

91. Latyshev, "Nachalo," l. 50.

92. Latyshev, "Prodolzhenie," l. 8.

93. "O raspredelenii vnov' otkryvaiushchikhsia v Sibiri skoptsov" (July 7, 1835); "O merakh k presecheniiu rasprostraneniia sekty skoptsov v Sibiri" (February 17, 1836); "O nakazaniiakh za rasprostranenie skopcheskoi eresi" (June 10, 1850); "Ob otmene ssylki skoptsov v Zakavkazskii krai" (June 10, 1854), in *Sobranie postanovlenii po chasti raskola* (St. Petersburg: Ministerstvo vnutrennikh del, 1858), 184–85, 202–3, 541–44, 623.

94. "O privedenii v ispolnenie prigovorov sudebnykh mest o ssylke skoptsov" (October 24, 1861), in *Sobranie postanovlenii po chasti raskola* (St. Petersburg: Ministerstvo vnutrennikh del, 1875), 584–85. Also, Aleksandr Bychkov, *Ocherki iakutskoi oblasti*, pt. 2: *Skoptsy v ssylke* (Irkutsk: Makushin, 1902), 7–8, 18; N. A. Gur'ev, *Sibirskie skoptsy, ikh ekonomicheskoe i pravovoe polozhenie* (Tomsk: Orlov, 1900), 15, 60.

95. A. F. Sanin, "K bytiiam skopcheskikh stradov" (October 2, 1905), GMIR, f. 2, op. 5, d. 355, l. 45.

96. N. Latkin, "Iakutskaia oblast'" and "Iakutsk," in *Entsiklopedicheskii slovar'* (St. Petersburg: Brokgaus-Efron, 1904), 82:618–27, 628–30.

97. Bychkov, *Ocherki*, 14–15; Latyshev, "To chto," l. 6.

98. Bychkov, *Ocherki*, 16, 18–21; V. I—n [Vladimir Iokhel'son], "Olekminskie skoptsy: Istoriko-bytovoi ocherk," pt. 2, *Zhivaia starina* (1894), 313–14.

99. Bychkov, *Ocherki*, 50. On peasant land ownership rights, see V. I—n [Iokhel'son], "Olekminskie skoptsy," pt. 2, 314.

100. Bychkov, *Ocherki*, 53–54, 57–58.

101. Bychkov, *Ocherki*, 19, 26; also Gur'ev, *Sibirskie skoptsy*, 26–30. On variations in wealth, see also V. I—n [Iokhel'son], "Olekminskie skoptsy," pt. 2, 315–16.

102. For the "progressive" view, see V. I—n [Vladimir Iokhel'son], "Olekminskie skoptsy," pt. 1, *Zhivaia starina* (1894), 203; pt. 2, ibid., 306.

103. Latyshev, "Prodolzhenie," l. 16; Latyshev, "To chto," l. 1 (quote).

104. Latyshev, "Nachalo," l. 56ob.

105. Among the Melitopol defendants, 82 percent were related to at least one other person; among defendants in the six post-1905 trials, 80 percent were. Among the inhabitants of the Siberian settlements of Troitsk (on the Aldan River) and Spasskoe, from the time of their establishment until just after 1905, 54 percent and 41 percent, respectively, had one or more relatives in the same village (GMIR, f. 2, op. 5, d. 250). The percentage for Markha over the same period was 54 (GMIR, f. 2, op. 5, d. 244).

106. Bychkov, *Ocherki*, 43, 51–52, 61–62. For social services in Markha, see "Imennye spiski," l. 27.

107. G. P. Men'shenin, "Ssyl'nye skoptsy v Iakutskoi oblasti" (1900), GMIR, f. 2, op. 5, d. 273, l. 12ob.

108. Bychkov, *Ocherki*, 55–60.

109. Bychkov, *Ocherki*, 59–60. On attractive houses, see also V. I—n [Iokhel'son], "Olekminskie skoptsy," pt. 2, 302.

110. Bychkov, *Ocherki*, 47. Same comment about absence of children's cries: V. I—n [Iokhel´son], "Olekminskie skoptsy," pt. 2, 303.

111. Bychkov, *Ocherki*, 48.

112. Bychkov, *Ocherki*, 2, 5 (quote).

113. V. I—n [Iokhel´son], "Olekminskie skoptsy," pt. 1, 199–201, 203; pt. 2, 309.

114. For list of decrees that did not help the Skoptsy, see Men´shenin, "Ssyl´nye skoptsy," l. 20–24.

115. For verses and mention of the decrees, see A. F. Sanin, "Bytie skopcheskie strady" (with letter from P. P. Zverev to V. D. Bonch-Bruevich, June 10, 1929), GMIR, f. 2, op. 5, d. 11, l. 8.

116. "Imennoi Vysochaishii ukaz, dannyi Senatu: Ob oblegchenii uchasti lits, osuzhdennykh za religioznye prestupleniia" (June 25, 1905), no. 26480, in *Polnoe sobranie zakonov Rossiiskoi Imperii*, ser. 3 (St. Petersburg: Gosudarstvennaia tipografiia, 1908), 25:559–61. Paragraph 8 (p. 560) refers to para. 17–20 of Art. 19 in Manifesto (August 11, 1904), no. 25014, in ibid. (St. Petersburg: Gosudarstvennaia tipografiia, 1907), 24:866–67.

117. Art. 147 (po Prod. 1908 g.) (on Skoptsy); Art. 148 (on other sectarians), in *Ustav o pasportakh* (1903 ed.), in *Svod zakonov Rossiiskoi Imperii*, ed. I. D. Mordukhai-Boltovskii, 5 vols. (St. Petersburg: Deiatel´, [not before 1913]), 5:18. Art. 178 (on Skoptsy), in *Ustav o ssyl´nykh* (1909 ed.), ibid., 247. For restrictive interpretation, see memo from Ministry of Internal Affairs, Department of Spiritual Affairs, to Irkutsk Governor-General (May 15, 1913), RGIA, f. 821, op. 133, d. 234, l. 35–36.

118. Telegram to Ministry of Internal Affairs, St. Petersburg, from Irkutsk, signed by 36 Skoptsy (January 29, 1913), RGIA, f. 821, op. 133, d. 233, l. 174–77.

119. Telegram from director of Ministry of Internal Affairs, Department of Spiritual Affairs, to Iakutsk (May 16, 1913), RGIA, f. 821, op. 133, d. 233, l. 194.

120. Sanin, "K bytiiam," l. 47–50.

121. Latyshev, "To chto," l. 100b. (quote); Latyshev, "Prodolzhenie," l. 210b.

122. Latyshev, "To chto," l. 110b.–130b., 140b.

123. Men´shenin, "Ssyl´nye skoptsy."

124. G. P. Men´shenin, "Zametki bolee vydaiushchie sobytiia [*sic*] i raznogo roda sluchai iz zhizni v Rossii i Sibiri" (1900), GMIR, f. 2, op. 5, d. 272, l. 30b.–4, 5–60b.

125. Copy dated March 8, 1905, of "Ufimskaia palata ugolovnogo i grazhdanskogo suda, Vypiska iz prigovora [Men´sheninykh]" (September 23, 1874), GMIR, f. 2, op. 5, d. 225, l. 1–2.

126. Men´shenin, "Zametki," l. 80b., 100b., 11–120b. (quote, 12).

127. Men´shenin, "Zametki," l. 120b.–130b., 130b.–150b. (quote, 140b.). See photo of Men´shenin's father, Prokopii Ioakimov Men´shenin, in front of a hay wagon, page 101: GMIR, f. 2, op. 29, d. 122 (Snimki iz zhizni skoptsov Veliuiskogo okruga, Iakutskoi oblasti). Men´shenin's grandfather was not the only murder victim among Skoptsy exiles, another sign that the community was plagued by the same vices and dangers that beset their ordinary neighbors. For mention of murder, see "Imennoi spisok skoptsam

Spasskogo seleniia, Olekminskogo okruga, Iakutskoi oblasti" (1902; notes as late as 1909), GMIR, f. 2, op. 5, d. 250, passim.

128. Men'shenin, "Zametki," l. 18–190b. On writing and trades: ibid., l. 8 and 120b.; command of writing uncertain: letter from G. P. Men'shenin to L. N. Tolstoi (March 31, 1898), GMIR, f. 2, op. 5, d. 120, l. 18.

129. Of the 200 residents of Spasskoe in 1894, 54 percent were described as illiterate, 28 percent as semiliterate, and 18 percent as literate: V. I—n [Iokhel'son], "Olekminskie skoptsy," pt. 2, 304.

130. "Olekminskoe okruzhnoe politseiskoe upravlenie, udostoverenie G. P. Men'sheninu" (August 21, 1895), GMIR, f. 2, op. 5, d. 169. Men'shenin, "Zametki," l. 170b. (quote).

131. Men'shenin, "Zametki," l. 21–22 (quote, 22).

132. Letter from G. P. Men'shenin to L. N. Tolstoi (December 10, 1897), GMIR, f. 2, op. 5, d. 120, l. 12.

133. Men'shenin, "Ssyl'nye skoptsy," l. 5–10, 38.

134. V. I—n [Iokhel'son], "Olekminskie skoptsy," pt. 2, 302.

135. Bychkov, *Ocherki*, 47.

136. Men'shenin, "Ssyl'nye skoptsy," l. 11.

137. V. I—n [Iokhel'son], "Olekminskie skoptsy," pt. 2, 303. Also Bychkov, *Ocherki*, 47.

138. Men'shenin, "Ssyl'nye skoptsy," l. 11–110b.

139. Men'shenin, "Ssyl'nye skoptsy," l. 110b.–12 (quote), 14–140b., 16.

140. Latyshev, "To chto," l. 7–10.

141. Men'shenin, "Ssyl'nye skoptsy," l. 160b., 17 (quote). Cf. Gur'ev, *Sibirskie skoptsy*, 44, 63–75.

142. Men'shenin, "Ssyl'nye skoptsy," l. 37.

143. Men'shenin, "Ssyl'nye skoptsy," l. 18–180b. (assimilate), 370b. (settlement).

144. G. P. Men'shenin, "Gnusnye dela vystupiat na svet, khotia by i vsei zemlei ikh zavalivali" (September 2, 1899), GMIR, f. 2, op. 5, d. 271; and Men'shenin, "Zametki."

145. "Olekminskoe okruzhnoe politseiskoe upravlenie, okruzhnoi ispravnik, udostoverenie G. P. Men'sheninu" (December 21, 1891), GMIR, f. 2, op. 5, d. 168, l. 1; (August 21, 1895), ibid., d. 169, l. 1.

146. Short biography of Arkhip Fedorov Sanin, included with letter from A. F. Sanin to V. D. Bonch-Bruevich (January 8, 1914), GMIR, f. 2, op. 5, d. 356, p. 24. Sanin is mentioned in N. Volkov, *Sekta skoptsov*, ed. and intro. N. M. Matorin, 2d ed. (Leningrad: Priboi, 1931), 108, where he is described as "the Skoptsy historian and poet."

147. Believers also retold the "Passion" in their own words, but following the original style. See, e.g., notebook in different hands: "Poslaniia gospoda nashego Iisusa Khrista" (May 1888), GMIR, f. 2, op. 5, d. 292.

148. "Bytie skopcheskie strady: Sochinenie Arkhipa Fedorova Sanina" (1902), GMIR, f. 2, op. 5, d. 352, l. 60b. For a variation, see "Bytie skopcheskie strady," l. 3.

4. *Testimony of Faith*

1. Letter from N. P. Latyshev to V. D. Bonch-Bruevich (September 14, 1915), GMIR, f. 2, op. 5, d. 47, l. 40b. (izvilina).

2. Yelena V. Barchatova, Introduction, in *A Portrait of Tsarist Russia: Unknown Photographs from the Soviet Archives* (New York: Pantheon, 1989), 7–37.

3. *Skopcheskoe delo: Protsess Kudrinykh i drugikh 24 lits, obviniaemykh v prinadlezhnosti k skopcheskoi eresi: Stenograficheskii otchet*, stenographer A. Ia. Lipskerov, ed. A. P. Sokolov (Moscow: Ioganson, 1871), 7, 65–66, 109 (quote, 65). On another social group that documented its existence on film, see *Merchant Moscow: Images of Russia's Vanished Bourgeoisie*, ed. James L. West and Iurii A. Petrov (Princeton: Princeton University Press, 1998).

4. N. M. Iadrintsev, *Russkaia obshchina v tiur'me i ssylke* (St. Petersburg: Morigerovskii, 1872), 257. The essay in question was A. P. Shchapov, "Umstvennye napravleniia russkogo raskola" (*Delo*, 1867), rpt. in *Sochineniia A. P. Shchapova*, 3 vols. (St. Petersburg: Pirozhkov, 1906), 1:590–647. See above, Chapter 2.

5. Police inventories mention N. V. Reutskii, *Liudi bozh'i i skoptsy: Istoricheskoe issledovanie* (Moscow: Grachev, 1872); N. A. Gur'ev, *Sibirskie skoptsy, ikh ekonomicheskoe i pravovoe polozhenie* (Tomsk: Orlov, 1900); A. S. Prugavin, *Monastyrskie tiur'my v bor'be s sektantstvom: K voprosu o veroterpimosti*, 2d ed. (Moscow: Posrednik, [1906]); F. V. Livanov, *Raskol'niki i ostrozhniki* (St. Petersburg: Khan, 1872); *Missionerskii sbornik* from 1912. See, "Obvinitel'nyi akt po delu o sekte skoptsov" (Kharkov: "Khudozhestvennyi trud," n.d.), RGIA, f. 821, op. 133, d. 233, l. 160b.–17 (pp. 6–7); "Obvinitel'nyi akt" (Orenburg, October 2, 1910), RGIA, f. 821, op. 133, d. 233, l. 1360b. (p. 4); "Obvinitel'nyi akt" (Riazan), Moskovskaia Sudebnaia Palata (March 17, 1915), RGIA, f. 821, op. 133, d. 234, l. 85 (p. 7).

6. "Obvinitel'nyi akt" (Kharkov), l. 240b., 26; "Obvinitel'nyi akt" (Riazan), l. 83–84 (pp. 3, 5). On Serafim of Sarov, see Gregory L. Freeze, "Subversive Piety: Religion and the Political Crisis in Late Imperial Russia," *Journal of Modern History* 68 (1996), 312–29.

7. Letter from N. P. Latyshev to V. D. Bonch-Bruevich (September 21, 1913), GMIR, f. 2, op. 5, d. 28, l. 7.

8. G. P. Men'shenin, ed., *Poeziia i proza sibirskikh skoptsov* (Tomsk: Levenson, 1904).

9. "Protokol doprosa: Stepan Kornoukhov" (February 1, 1911), GMIR, f. 2, op. 5, d. 194, l. 1.

10. "Protokol doprosa: Dar'ia Daletskaia" (February 2, 1911), GMIR, f. 2, op. 5, d. 183.

11. Examples from Ufa: "Protokol doprosa: Nikifor Daletskii" (January 30, 1911), GMIR, f. 2, op. 5, d. 182. Nikolai Rabeev claimed Dmitrii Likhachev had one: "Protokol doprosa: Nikolai Rabeev" (February 2, 1911), GMIR, f. 2, op. 5, d. 204. Mentioned also in the Kharkov trial: "Obvinitel'nyi akt" (Kharkov), l. 16–170b., 250b., 30.

12. "Protokol doprosa: Andrian Ivanov" (January 31, 1911), GMIR, f. 2, op. 5, d. 188; "Obvinitel'nyi akt" (Kharkov), l. 170b. (Razinkova testimony).

13. "Protokol doprosa: Stepan Kornoukhov."

14. Ufa data from various files in GMIR. Records from the other post-1905 trials do not indicate literacy. On Spasskoe, citing the census: V. I—n [Vladimir Iokhel´son], "Olekminskie skoptsy: Istoriko-bytovoi ocherk," pt. 2, *Zhivaia starina* (1894), 304–6.

15. Letter from G. P. Men´shenin to V. D. Bonch-Bruevich (May 10, 1909), GMIR, f. 2, op. 5, d. 61, l. 10b.; letter from Latyshev to Bonch-Bruevich (September 21, 1913), l. 7.

16. M. Gorkii, "O pisateliakh-samouchkakh" (1911), in *Sobranie sochinenii* (Moscow: Khudozhestvennaia literatura, 1953), 24:99–137. Mark D. Steinberg, "Worker-Authors and the Cult of the Person," in *Cultures in Flux: Lower-Class Values, Practices, and Resistance in Late Imperial Russia*, ed. Stephen P. Frank and Mark D. Steinberg (Princeton: Princeton University Press, 1994), 168–84; idem, "Workers on the Cross: Religious Imagination in the Writings of Russian Workers, 1910–1924," *Russian Review* 53 (1994), 213–39.

17. Men´shenin, *Poeziia i proza*, 1–10 (introduction); 5 ("fanatik").

18. Letter from G. P. Men´shenin to V. D. Bonch-Bruevich (August 21, 1916), GMIR f. 2, op. 5, d. 76, l. 1–20b.

19. Letters from Tolstoi to G. P. Men´shenin (December 31, 1897; March 11, 1898), in L. N. Tolstoi, *Polnoe sobranie sochinenii* (Moscow: Khudozhestvennaia literatura, 1954), 70:223–25, 303–6; (November 3, 1908), in ibid. (1956), 78:246.

20. A. I. Klibanov, *Iz mira religioznogo sektantstva: Vstrechi, besedy, nabliudeniia* (Moscow: Politicheskaia literatura, 1974), 23. Letter from Men´shenin to Bonch-Bruevich (August 21, 1916), l. 2. Note in L. N. Tolstoi, *Polnoe sobranie sochinenii* (Moscow: Khudozhestvennaia literatura, 1933), 72:447.

21. Letter from G. P. Men´shenin to L. N. Tolstoi (March 21, 1898), GMIR, f. 2, op. 5, d. 120, l. 16. For the passage from Matthew 19:12, see L. N. Tolstoi, *Polnoe sobranie sochinenii* (Moscow: Khudozhestvennaia literatura, 1933), 27:7.

22. Letter from G. P. Men´shenin to L. N. Tolstoi (December 10, 1897), GMIR, f. 2, op. 5, d. 120, l. 13.

23. Letters from Tolstoi to Men´shenin (December 31, 1897; March 11, 1898), 225 quote).

24. Letter from Men´shenin to Tolstoi (March 21, 1898), l. 14.

25. Letter from Men´shenin to Tolstoi (March 21, 1898), l. 15–17.

26. Salutations, in order: Men´shenin to Tolstoi (n.d.; reply received March 21, 1898), GMIR, f. 2, op. 5, d. 120, l. 14; Tolstoi to Men´shenin (March 11, 1898), replying to first letter, in *Polnoe sobranie,* 70:303; Men´shenin to Tolstoi (March 31, 1898; May 26, 1899), GMIR, f. 2, op. 5, d. 120, l. 18, 20.

27. Quoted in English from 1905 edition, in Eberhard Müller, "Opportunismus oder Utopie? V. D. Bonč-Bruevič und die russischen Sekten vor und nach der Revolution," *Jahrbücher für Geschichte Osteuropas* 35 (1987), 512. See Stepniak, pseud. of S. M. Kravchinskii, *The Russian Peasantry* (New York: Harper & Brothers, 1888), 291, 337, 372–74.

28. Müller, "Opportunismus," 510–15; also the ill-tempered critique in A. I. Klibanov, "V. D. Bonch-Bruevich i problemy religiozno-obshchestvennykh dvizhenii v Rossii," in V. D. Bonch-Bruevich, *Izbrannye sochineniia*, vol. 1: *O religii, religioznom sektantstve i tserkvi* (Moscow: Akademiia nauk, 1959), 25. On radicals' attitude to popular religiosity, see also Reginald E. Zelnik, "'To the Unaccustomed Eye': Religion and Irreligion in the Experience of St. Petersburg Workers in the 1870s," *Russian History* 16:2–4 (1989), 299.

29. Vladimir Bonch-Bruevich, "Sredi sektantov," *Zhizn': Literaturnyi, nauchnyi i politicheskii zhurnal*, no. 5 (London: Sotsialdemokraticheskaia organizatsiia "Zhizn'," 1902), 179.

30. Vladimir Bonch-Bruevich, ed., *Materialy k istorii i izucheniiu russkogo sentantstva i raskola*, vol. 1 (St. Petersburg: Vol'f, 1908). See M. I. Shakhnovich, "V. D. Bonch-Bruevich: Issledovatel' religiozno-obshchestvennykh dvizhenii v Rossii," *Ezhegodnik Muzeia istorii religii i ateizma* 7 (1963), 296–97.

31. See D. Filosofov, "Izuchenie russkogo sektantstva," *Russkaia mysl'*, no. 12 (1910), 195–200.

32. I. A. Amenitskii, "Doklad po voprosu o priglashenii v sudebnoe zasedanie po delu Ivanovykh i dr. obviniaemykh po 95 st. Ug. Ul. v kachestve eksperta g. V. D. Bonch-Bruevicha," GMIR, f. 2, op. 5, d. 138. For the clerical evaluation, see "Uchebnyi komitet pri Sviateishem Sinode: Otnoshenie v Ufimskii Okruzhnoi Sud" (July 7, 1912), GMIR, f. 2, op. 5, d. 224, l. 2 (quote). Confirming his eventual appearance: Ufa Circuit Court, letter to V. D. Bonch-Bruevich (November 5, 1912), GMIR, f. 2, op. 5, d. 102.

33. "Pis'ma L. N. Tolstogo o skopchestve," in Bonch-Bruevich, ed., *Materialy k istorii*, 1:69–73. See Antonella Salomoni, "Un luogo per Matteo 19:10–12: Lev Nikolaevič Tolstoj e lo *skopčestvo*," *Asmodée/Asmodeo* 1 (1989), 114.

34. Letters from Men'shenin to Bonch-Bruevich (May 10, 1909), l. 20b. (Tolstoi); (March 28, 1910), GMIR, f. 2, op. 5, d. 66, l. 20b. (photos from Iakutsk).

35. Letters from G. P. Men'shenin to V. D. Bonch-Bruevich (January 20, 1910), GMIR f. 2, op. 5, d. 64, l. 1–2 (honesty); (April 13, 1910), GMIR, f. 2, op. 5, d. 65, l. 10b. (spreading the word); (November 16, 1910), GMIR, f. 2, op. 5, d. 70, l. 1 (urging haste); (November 12, 1909), GMIR, f. 2, op. 5, d. 62, l. 2 (quote).

36. Letter from Men'shenin to Bonch-Bruevich (March 28, 1910), l. 1.

37. Letter from Men'shenin to Bonch-Bruevich (March 28, 1910), l. 1. Bonch-Bruevich had already published the text of "Poslanie ko vsem skoptsam," in *Materialy k istorii*, 1:206–16. This text (based on a manuscript in the Academy of Sciences) differs from the one in Nadezhdin, reprinted in V. S. Tolstoi, "Skoptsy," *Chteniia*, bk. 4, pt. 5 (1864), 66–90. On the status of the various texts, see A. Remezov, "Kritika: V.V. Rozanov, *Apokalipsicheskaia sekta* (St. Petersburg, 1914)," *Bogoslovskii vestnik*, no. 5 (1914), 188.

38. "Tri skopcheskie rukopisi," *Sovremennik*, bk. 3 (1913), 334–41, rpt. in Vladimir Bonch-Bruevich, *Iz mira sektantov: Sbornik statei* (Moscow: Gosudarstvennoe izdatel'stvo, 1922), 205.

39. Letter from Men'shenin to Bonch-Bruevich (January 20, 1910), l. 1.

40. Letters from G. P. Men'shenin to V. D. Bonch-Bruevich (August 21, 1916), l. 2; (September 1, 1920), GMIR, f. 2, op. 5, d. 78, l. 30b.–4.

41. Letter from Men'shenin to Bonch-Bruevich (August 21, 1916), l. 2. Appeals to Men'shenin to intercede with the authorities: letters from Iakov Pavlovich Zverev to G. P. Men'shenin (November 15, 1911; December 31, 1911), GMIR, f. 2, op. 5, d. 115, 116.

42. Letter from N. P. Latyshev to V. D. Bonch-Bruevich (October 1914), GMIR, f. 2, op. 5, d. 32, l. 3.

43. Letter from Iakov Pavlovich Zverev to Men'shenin (November 15, 1911), l. 1.

44. Letter from A. F. Sanin to V. D. Bonch-Bruevich (April 15, 1913), GMIR, f. 2, op. 5, d. 95, l. 1.

45. Letter from Men'shenin to Tolstoi (May 26, 1899), l. 20 (referring to Kiriukhin as "P. S. K."). Kiriukhin identified and interventions described, in Tolstoi, *Polnoe sobranie*, 72:447.

46. Reply acknowledged in A. F. Sanin to V. D. Bonch-Bruevich (May 24, 1913), GMIR, f. 2, op. 5, d. 96, l. 1.

47. "Bytie skopcheskie strady: Sochinenie Arkhipa Fedorova Sanina" (1902), GMIR, f. 2, op. 5, d. 351, l. 60b.; and A. F. Sanin, "Vo chto veruiut skoptsy" (October 13, 1913), GMIR, f. 2, op. 5, d. 354, pp. 1–37.

48. Letter from Sanin to Bonch-Bruevich (May 24, 1913), l. 1–10b. (quote, 1). Note at beginning of letter in Bonch-Bruevich's hand indicates a negative reply.

49. Letter from Sanin to Bonch-Bruevich (May 24, 1913), l. 2, 20b.

50. Letter from A. F. Sanin to V. D. Bonch-Bruevich (January 8, 1914), GMIR, f.2, op.5,d.356, l. 27 (p. 21).

51. Letter from Sanin to Bonch-Bruevich (May 24, 1913), l. 2, 20b.

52. Letter from G. P. Men'shenin to N. P. Latyshev [late 1910], GMIR f. 2, op. 5, d. 122, l. 1–10b.

53. "Imennye spiski skoptsov i skopcheskikh selenii Iakutskoi oblasti, Olekminskogo okruga" (1902; notes as late as 1909), GMIR, f. 2, op. 5, d. 250, l. 230b.

54. N. P. Latyshev, "To chto ia khotel by peredat' chitaiushchemu miru" [between 1906 and 1913], GMIR f. 2, op. 5, d. 263, l. 1–140b.

55. Letter from N. P. Latyshev to G. P. Men'shenin (November 18, 1910), GMIR, f. 2, op. 5, d. 119, l. 10b.–2.

56. Letter from N. P. Latyshev to V. D. Bonch-Bruevich (before December 18, 1912), GMIR, f. 2, op. 5, d. 28, l. 2. The account appeared in *Russkoe slovo*, a newspaper favored by moderately educated people. Thanks to Boris Kolonitskii for this designation.

57. Letter from N. P. Latyshev to V. D. Bonch-Bruevich (December 27, 1912), GMIR, f. 2, op. 5, d. 29, l. 3. On Men'shenin's role, see also Klibanov, *Iz mira religioznogo sektantstva*, 24.

58. The notebooks are in GMIR, f. 2, op. 5: (1) "To chto" (cited in Bonch-Bruevich, "Tri skopcheskie rukopisi," 206); (2) "Nachalo moego povestvovaniia" (1910), d. 261, l. 1–580b.; (3) "Prodolzhaia nachatoe mnoiu opisanie" (January 4, 1915), d. 264, l. 1–6; and (4) "Prodolzhenie" (December 26, 1915), d. 265, l. 1–57.

59. Letter from Latyshev to Bonch-Bruevich (September 14, 1915), l. 4.

60. Letter from N. P. Latyshev to V. D. Bonch-Bruevich (December 7, 1914), GMIR, f. 2, op. 5, d. 31, l. 10b.

61. Latyshev, "To chto," l. 1, 5.

62. Latyshev, "Nachalo," l. 2–3 (quotes), 5. More on complacency of Romanian Skoptsy: ibid., l. 160b.–17.

63. Latyshev, "Nachalo," l. 5–50b., 80b.–9.

64. Latyshev, "Nachalo," l. 250b.–260b., 160b. (quote).

65. Latyshev, "Nachalo," l. 10, 12, 130b.–16.

66. Latyshev, "Nachalo," l. 27–270b.

67. Latyshev, "To chto," l. 10b.

68. Latyshev, "To chto," l. 2. Uses the word "kastratsiia."

69. Latyshev, "Nachalo," l. 35–350b.

70. Latyshev, "Prodolzhenie," l. 3–4.

71. Latyshev, "Prodolzhaia nachatoe mnoiu opisanie," l. 50b.

72. Latyshev, "To chto," l. 2.

73. Latyshev, "Nachalo," l. 270b.–28.

74. Latyshev, "Nachalo," l. 30, 330b., 350b., 47–470b.

75. Latyshev, "Nachalo," l. 30, 29 (quotes).

76. Latyshev, "Nachalo," l. 46–460b.

77. Latyshev, "To chto," l. 3–30b.

78. Latyshev, "To chto," l. 30b.–5.

79. Latyshev, "To chto," l. 50b., 7 (quotes), 8–80b.

80. Latyshev, "To chto," l. 7.

81. N. P. Latyshev, notebook, Osa on the Ural River (1934), GMIR f. 2, op. 5, d. 266, l. 16–160b.

82. "Imennye spiski," l. 230b.

83. Latyshev, "To chto," l. 140b.; reverse of photo, "Skoptsa otets Latyshev Petr Ivan. i syn Latyshev Andrei Petr.," GMIR, f. 2, op. 29, d. 388; letter from Latyshev to Bonch-Bruevich (December 27, 1912), l. 4.

84. Letters from Latyshev to Bonch-Bruevich (December 27, 1912), l. 3 (calls himself "malogramotnyi"); (September 14, 1915), l. 7; Latyshev, "To chto," l. 140b. (quote).

85. Letters from N. P. Latyshev to V. D. Bonch-Bruevich (October 1914), l. 3 (talent); (December 29, 1912), GMIR, f. 2, op. 5, d. 28, l. 6 (alive).

86. Letter from Latyshev to Bonch-Bruevich (October 1914), l. 4.

87. Letter from Latyshev to Bonch-Bruevich (September 14, 1915), l. 3.

88. Letter from Latyshev to Bonch-Bruevich (December 7, 1914), l. 2, 40b.–5. See also "Tetrad' 'glagolov' skoptsov," GMIR, kollektsiia I, op. 6, d. 2, l. 41 ("I'm called a philosopher and evangelist").

89. Letter from Latyshev to Bonch-Bruevich (September 14, 1915), l. 1–10b.

90. Letter from Latyshev to Bonch-Bruevich (September 14, 1915), l. 4–5.

91. Latyshev, "Prodolzhenie," l. 56.

92. Letter from N. P. Latyshev to V. D. Bonch-Bruevich (April 18, 1913), GMIR, f.2, op.5, d.30, l. 2ob.

93. Letter from Latyshev to Bonch-Bruevich (September 14, 1915), l. 6. The expression "to preach God's Cause" (besedovat' za Bozhie delo), includes the term "beseda," meaning conversation, which was used by Orthodox as well as sectarian folk to describe informal prayer meetings. In this context it can also mean preaching.

94. Letter from Latyshev to Bonch-Bruevich (April 18, 1913), l. 3ob.

95. Letter from Latyshev to Bonch-Bruevich (April 18, 1913), l. 3ob.

96. Letter from Latyshev to Bonch-Bruevich (December 27, 1912), l. 3.

97. Letter from Latyshev to Bonch-Bruevich (before December 18, 1912), l. 2.

98. Latyshev, "Prodolzhenie," l. 17 (return date); letter from Latyshev to Bonch-Bruevich (December 27, 1912), l. 4.

99. Letter from Latyshev to Bonch-Bruevich (December 27, 1912), l. 1–2. For the text of the letters he was reading, see "Pis'ma L. N. Tolstogo o skopchestve."

100. Letter from Latyshev to Bonch-Bruevich (April 18, 1913), l. 2.

101. Letter from Latyshev to Bonch-Bruevich (October 1914), l. 3–4.

102. Letter from Latyshev to Bonch-Bruevich (October 1914), l. 3 (indicating reply on November 20, 1914).

103. Letter from Latyshev to Bonch-Bruevich (December 7, 1914), l. 1–1ob., 3ob.–4ob.

104. Letter from Latyshev to Bonch-Bruevich (December 7, 1914), l. 3–3ob.

105. Letter from Latyshev to Bonch-Bruevich (September 14, 1915), l. 1–3ob.

106. Letter from Latyshev to Bonch-Bruevich (September 14, 1915), l. 6. "Glas vopiiushchego v pustyne narodnoi" (The voice of one crying in the [people's] wilderness). Matthew 3:3, amended by him.

107. Letter from Latyshev to Bonch-Bruevich (September 14, 1915), l. 6ob.–7.

108. Letter from Latyshev to Bonch-Bruevich (December 7, 1914), l. 5ob.

109. Latyshev, "Nachalo," l. 55, 56–56ob.

110. Latyshev, "Nachalo," l. 51.

111. Latyshev, "Prodolzhenie," l. 51ob.–52, 53ob.

112. Latyshev, "Prodolzhenie," l. 11, 15, 16; Latyshev, "Nachalo," l. 58.

113. Latyshev, "Prodolzhenie," l. 13ob.–14.

114. Latyshev, "Nachalo," l. 52ob.

115. Latyshev, "Prodolzhaia nachatoe mnoiu opisanie," l. 1, 2ob.–4, 6ob.

116. Letter from Latyshev to Men'shenin (November 18, 1910), l. 1ob. Similar image: Latyshev, "Prodolzhaia nachatoe mnoiu opisanie," l. 4ob.

117. [Anonymous], "Predsmertnaia ispoved'" (postmarked August 3, 1911), GMIR, f. 2, op. 5, d. 295; [Anonymous], "Biografiia obezdolennoi i muchitel'noi zhizni," GMIR, f. 2, op. 5, d. 279. Author not identified, but handwriting is the same in both cases, as are the details of the accounts.

118. Gur'ev, Sibirskie skoptsy, 68. For use of "bereft" (obezdolennye) to describe the

poor in general, see Adele Lindenmeyr, *Poverty Is Not a Vice: Charity, Society, and the State in Imperial Russia* (Princeton: Princeton University Press, 1996), 10.

119. Aleksandr Bychkov, *Ocherki iakutskoi oblasti*, pt. 2: *Skoptsy v ssylke* (Irkutsk: Makushin, 1902), 2.

120. G. P. Men'shenin, "Ssyl'nye skoptsy v Iakutskoi oblasti" (1900), GMIR, f. 2, op. 5, d. 273, l. 10b., 24.

121. [Anonymous], "Predsmertnaia ispoved'," l. 1.

122. [Anonymous], "Biografiia," l. 1–3 (quote, 1).

123. [Anonymous], "Predsmertnaia ispoved'," l. 10b.–2, 60b.–7.

124. [Anonymous], "Biografiia," l. 4–40b. (shame of passport); [Anonymous], "Predsmertnaia ispoved'," l. 50b. (fanatics use law). On treatment of Skoptsy women who married out of the sect, see Gur'ev, *Sibirskie skoptsy*, 70.

125. V. I—n [Iokhel'son], "Olekminskie skoptsy," pt. 2, 319.

126. [Anonymous], "Predsmertnaia ispoved'," l. 3, 100b.

127. [Anonymous], "Predsmertnaia ispoved'," l. 40b.; [Anonymous], "Biografiia," l. 30b.

128. [Anonymous], "Biografiia," l. 50b.

129. [Anonymous], "Predsmertnaia ispoved'," l. 7, 80b.

130. [Anonymous], "Predsmertnaia ispoved'," l. 9–90b., 10.

131. [Anonymous], "Biografiia," l. 6–60b.

132. Letter from Latyshev to Bonch-Bruevich (before December 18, 1912), l. 2.

133. Latyshev, "Prodolzhaia nachatoe mnoiu opisanie," l. 30b.–4.

134. Letter from Latyshev to Bonch-Bruevich (April 18, 1913), l. 20b.

135. "Tetrad' 'glagolov' skoptsov," l. 17.

136. "Tetrad' 'glagolov' skoptsov," l. 35.

137. "Tetrad' 'glagolov' skoptsov," l. 45–46.

138. "Tetrad' 'glagolov' skoptsov," l. 41–420b.

139. Latyshev, "Nachalo," l. 580b.

140. Latyshev, "Prodolzhenie," l. 180b.–22.

141. Letter from Latyshev to Bonch-Bruevich (September 14, 1915), l. 7–70b.

142. Letter from Latyshev to Bonch-Bruevich (September 14, 1915), l. 70b.

143. Latyshev, "Prodolzhenie," l. 34–380b.

144. Latyshev, "Prodolzhenie," l. 44–440b.

145. Latyshev, "Prodolzhenie," l. 450b.–470b.

146. See Aleksandr Etkind, *Khlyst: Sekty, literatura i revoliutsiia* (Moscow: Novoe literaturnoe obozrenie, 1998).

5. Light and Shadow

1. John Shelton Curtiss, *The Russian Church and the Soviet State, 1917–1950* (Boston: Little, Brown, 1953), 14.

2. On church position and clergy's move to the right before October 1917, see Curtiss, *Russian Church,* 21–35.

3. Joshua Rothenberg, "The Legal Status of Religion in the Soviet Union," in *Aspects of Religion in the Soviet Union, 1917–1967,* ed. Richard H. Marshall Jr. (Chicago: University of Chicago Press, 1971), 62–63. On the early decrees, see "K istorii otdeleniia tserkvi ot gosudarstva i shkoly ot tserkvi v SSSR: Dokumenty i materialy," in *Voprosy istorii religii i ateizma: Sbornik statei,* vol. 5 (Moscow: Akademiia nauk, 1958), 3–49.

4. Text in Marshall, ed., *Aspects of Religion,* 437.

5. Rothenberg, "Legal Status," 65.

6. Stefan Plaggenborg, "Volksreligiosität und antireligiöse Propaganda in der frühen Sowjetunion," *Archiv für Sozialgeschichte* 32 (1992), 110.

7. See Laura Engelstein, "The Dream of Civil Society in Tsarist Russia: Law, State, and Religion," in *Civil Society before Democracy: Lessons from Nineteenth-Century Europe,* ed. Philip Nord and Nancy Bermeo (Lanham, Md.: Rowman and Littlefield, 2000).

8. Rothenberg, "Legal Status," 68–71; Joan Delaney, "The Origins of Soviet Antireligious Organizations," in Marshall, ed., *Aspects of Religion,* 104–14. On formulation of policy in these years, see *Arkhivy Kremlia,* vol. 1: *Politbiuro i tserkov',* *1922–1925 gg.,* ed. N. N. Pokrovskii and S. G. Petrov (Novosibirsk: Sibirskii khronograf; Moscow: Rossiiskaia politicheskaia entsiklopediia, 1997).

9. Plaggenborg, "Volksreligiosität," 100–102. On desacralization of the monarchy, see Gregory L. Freeze, "Subversive Piety: Religion and the Political Crisis in Late Imperial Russia," *Journal of Modern History* 68:2 (1996), 308–50. Cf. William B. Husband, "Soviet Atheism and Russian Orthodox Strategies of Resistance, 1917–1932," *Journal of Modern History* 70:1 (1998), 74–107.

10. Curtiss, *Russian Church,* 61, 230; on change, see also Rothenberg, "Legal Status," 82.

11. Law on religious associations of April 8, 1929; amended January 1, 1932: Marshall, ed., *Aspects of Religion,* 438–45.

12. Delaney, "Origins," 117. See also Daniel Peris, *Storming the Heavens: The Soviet League of the Militant Godless* (Ithaca: Cornell University Press, 1998).

13. Curtiss, *Russian Church,* 237, 240, 243, 251–54; Rothenberg, "Legal Status," 81.

14. See Aleksandr Etkind, "Russkie sekty i sovetskii kommunizm: Proekt Vladimira Bonch-Bruevicha," *Minuvshee,* no. 19 (1996), 275–82, 284–85, 298; Kathy Rousselet, "Utopies socio-religieuses et révolution politique dans les années 1920," *Revue des études slaves* 69:1–2 (1997), 257–71; Eberhard Müller, "Opportunismus oder Utopie? V. D. Bonč-Bruevič und die russischen Sekten vor und nach der Revolution," *Jahrbücher für Geschichte Osteuropas* 35 (1987), 526–27, 529, 532–33.

15. Letter from G. P. Men'shenin to V. D. Bonch-Bruevich (December 28, 1917), GMIR, f. 2, op. 5, d. 77, l. 2.

16. "Tetrad' 'glagolov' skoptsov," GMIR, kollektsiia I, op. 6, d. 3, l. 163ob.–164. A note by Latyshev added in 1934 indicates the words referred specifically to the Soviet regime: ibid., 164.

17. This line of argument is pursued by Aleksandr Etkind in various publications, for example: "Russkie sekty," 309. On the convergence, see also Claudio Sergio Ingerflom, "Communistes contre castrats (1929–1930): Les enjeux du conflit," in Nikolaï Volkov, *La secte russe des castrats*, trans. Zoé Andreyev, ed. Claudio Sergio Ingerflom (Paris: Les Belles Lettres, 1995), xi–lxiii.

18. Boris Kolonitskii, "Antibourgeois Propaganda and Anti-'*Burzhui*' Consciousness in 1917," *Russian Review* 53:2 (1994), 193–95.

19. Husband, "Soviet Atheism."

20. Letters from G. P. Men'shenin to V. D. Bonch-Bruevich (September 24, 1920), GMIR, f. 2, op. 5, d. 79, l. 1–4; (March 25, 1921), GMIR, f. 2, op. 5, d. 80, l. 1ob. (quote).

21. Letter from G. P. Men'shenin to V. D. Bonch-Bruevich (June 16, 1922), GMIR, f. 2, op. 5, d. 81, l. 1ob.

22. Letter from G. P. Men'shenin to TsKRKP/b/, addressed to V. D. Bonch-Bruevich in the Kremlin (July 15, 1924), GMIR, f. 2, op. 5, d. 121, l. 3–3ob.

23. Letter from N. P. Latyshev to V. D. Bonch-Bruevich (November 25, 1920), GMIR, f. 2, op. 5, d. 37, l. 1ob.–2. On the trope of illumination, see Igor Halfin, "From Darkness to Light: Student Communist Autobiography during NEP," *Jahrbücher für Geschichte Osteuropas* 45:2 (1997), 210–36.

24. Letter from Latyshev to Bonch-Bruevich (November 25, 1920), l. 3ob.

25. Letter from Latyshev to Bonch-Bruevich (November 25, 1920), l. 1–1ob., 3ob.

26. Letter from Latyshev to Bonch-Bruevich (November 25, 1920), l. 2–2ob.

27. Letters from G. P. Men'shenin to V. D. Bonch-Bruevich (October 30, 1924), GMIR, f. 2, op. 5, d. 82, l. 5–6ob.; (n.d.), GMIR, f. 2, op. 5, d. 84 [1926], l. 1–2ob.; (November 18, 1926), GMIR, f. 2, op. 5, d. 84, l. 5–6. On Zverev, see P. P. Zverev, "Zaiavlenie na prediavlenie mne obvinenie, no st. 138 U.K." (May 27, 1926), GMIR, f. 2, op. 5, d. 249, l. 2–6 (quote, 2); "Zaiavlenie Tomskoi gruppy ssyl'nykh skoptsov" (June 14, 1926), GMIR, f. 2, op. 5, d. 366, l. 1; letter from P. P. Zverev to V. D. Bonch-Bruevich (September 8, 1929), GMIR, f. 2, op. 5, d. 12, l. 1. (Zverev remembers leaving Siberia in 1908, but Latyshev gives the date as 1906; see above, Chapter 3.)

28. See *Kurskaia pravda*: GMIR, f. 2, op. 5, d. 40, l. 11. Family story in letter from N. P. Latyshev to V. D. Bonch-Bruevich (March 25, 1929), GMIR, f. 2, op. 5, d. 40, l. 9–10ob. (quote, 9).

29. In the years following 1905, when many forms of casual violence became endemic to Russian life, thugs were known to attack the members of Baptist congregations. See Heather Coleman, "The Most Dangerous Sect: Baptists in Tsarist and Soviet Russia, 1905–1929" (Ph.D. diss., University of Illinois, 1998). If the Skoptsy experienced similar attacks, none complained of them in the letters or court testimony I have seen.

30. Letter from Latyshev to Bonch-Bruevich (March 25, 1929), l. 9ob.

31. Letter from N. P. Latyshev to V. D. Bonch-Bruevich (November 25, 1928), GMIR, f. 2, op. 5, d. 38, l. 3ob.

32. Letter from Latyshev to Bonch-Bruevich (March 25, 1929), l. 90b.

33. Letter from G. P. Men'shenin to V. D. Bonch-Bruevich (September 27, 1927), GMIR, f. 2, op. 5, d. 85, l. 3 (tsarizm-popovshchina).

34. Letter from G. P. Men'shenin to V. D. Bonch-Bruevich (June 6, 1928), GMIR, f. 2, op. 5, d. 86, l. 5–60b.

35. Letter from G. P. Men'shenin to V. D. Bonch-Bruevich (October 15, 1929), GMIR, f. 2, op. 5, d. 87, l. 5–6.

36. Letter from Latyshev to Bonch-Bruevich (November 25, 1928), l. 3.

37. Letter from N. P. Latyshev to V. D. Bonch-Bruevich (October 9, 1929), including letter to Latyshev from fellow Skopets (March 1, 1929), GMIR, f. 2, op. 5, d. 39, l. 3–30b.

38. Letter from Latyshev to Bonch-Bruevich (March 25, 1929), l. 9–100b.

39. Letter from N. P. Latyshev to V. D. Bonch-Bruevich (September 14, 1915), GMIR, f. 2, op. 5, d. 47, l. 2.

40. Letter from V. D. Bonch-Bruevich to G. P. Men'shenin (November 6, 1928), OR-RGB, f. 369, k. 173, ed. khr. 31, l. 6.

41. Letter from V. D. Bonch-Bruevich to N. P. Latyshev (December 1929), GMIR, f. 2, op. 5, d. 133, l. 10b.-2 (pp. 3–4).

42. Letter from Bonch-Bruevich to Latyshev (December 1929), l. 2 (p. 4).

43. Letter from Bonch-Bruevich to Men'shenin (November 6, 1928), l. 6.

44. Letter from Bonch-Bruevich to Latyshev (December 1929), l. 2 (p. 4).

45. V. I—n [Vladimir Iokhel'son], "Olekminskie skoptsy: Istoriko-bytovoi ocherk," pt. 1, *Zhivaia starina* (1894), 203, 199.

46. N. A. Gur'ev, *Sibirskie skoptsy, ikh ekonomicheskoe i pravovoe polozhenie* (Tomsk: Orlov, 1900), 23–30. For a similar view see [Nikolai Nadezhdin], *Issledovanie o skopcheskoi eresi* (n.p.: Ministerstvo vnutrennikh del, 1845), 348 (rich vs. poor).

47. See "Obvinitel'noe zakliuchenie po delu Lomonosova i dr." (December 29, 1929), GMIR, f. 2, op. 5, d. 166, l. 1–2. Also Petr [A.] Gnezdilov, *Chernyi korabl': Sudebnyi protsess Saratovskikh kulakov-"skoptsov"* (Saratov: Sektor pechati N.-V. Kraevskogo Soveta SVB, 1930); Evg. Gorskii, *Izuvery: Leningradskaia sekta skoptsov* (Moscow: Bezbozhnik, 1930); I. Malyshev, "Skopcheskoe izuverstvo," *Bezbozhnik*, no. 6 (1931), 11; and idem, "Izuvery," *Bezbozhnik*, no. 23 (1931), 12–13.

48. Nadezhdin, *Issledovanie*, 69, 284, 349, 361–62.

49. Gnezdilov, *Chernyi korabl'*, 21.

50. "Obvinitel'noe zakliuchenie," l. 10b. (quote); *Ugolovnyi kodeks RSFSR* (Moscow: Iuridicheskoe izdatel'stvo, 1926), 18 and 38.

51. "Nikolai Mikhailovich Matorin," in *Ateisticheskii slovar'*, 2d ed. (Moscow: Politicheskaia literatura, 1985), 259.

52. Speech quoted in Gorskii, *Izuvery*, 32–38.

53. N. Matorin, "K voprosu ob ideologii skopchestva," *Antireligioznik*, no. 6 (1930), 43–44.

54. Letter from Bonch-Bruevich to Men'shenin (November 6, 1928), l. 6.

55. Letter from Bonch-Bruevich to Latyshev (December 1929), l. 2 (p. 4).

56. Letter from V. D. Bonch-Bruevich to P. P. Zverev (April 5, 1929),GMIR, f. 2,op. 5, d. 134, l. 1–20b.

57. Letter from Bonch-Bruevich to Zverev (April 5, 1929), l. 1–20b. On Baptists, see V. D. Bonch-Bruevich, ed., *Materialy k istorii i izucheniiu russkogo sektantstva*, vol. 6: *Presledovanie baptistov* (Christchurch, Eng.:Tchertkoff, 1902).

58. Letter from V. D. Bonch-Bruevich to G. P. Men'shenin (November 25, 1929), OR-RGB, f. 369, k. 173, ed. khr. 31, l. 3.

59. Invitation: telegram to V. D. Bonch-Bruevich from N. Matorin (November 24, 1929), GMIR, f. 2, op. 5, d. 59.Attack: N. M. Matorin,"Predislovie" (December 28, 1929), in N.Volkov, *Sekta skoptsov*, ed. and intro. N. M. Matorin, 2d ed. (Leningrad: Priboi, 1931), 3.

60. On Volkov, see A. M. Reshetov, "Otdanie dolga," pt. 1: "Pamiati sotrudnikov Instituta etnografii AN SSSR, pogibshikh v boiakh za rodinu," *Etnograficheskoe obozrenie* 4 (1995), 7–9; also Ingerflom, "Communistes contre castrats." Also see N. Volkov, "Avtobiografiia" (May 25, 1938), ARAN, f. 142, op. 5, d. 249, l. 38; idem, "Avtobiografiia" (January 10, 1940), ARAN, f. 142, op. 5, d. 5, l. 122. Date of joining Party given as 1920 in Reshetov; 1921 in archival sources.

61. "SSSR Soiuz voinstvuiushchikh bezbozhnikov, Leningradskii oblastnoi sovet, v Biuro kollektiva Akademii nauk SSSR" (September 10, 1930),ARAN, f. 222, op. 2, d. 76, l. 17.

62. N.Volkov, *Sekta skoptsov*, ed. and intro. N. M. Matorin (Leningrad: Priboi, 1930). E. Kagarov,"Otzyv o trude N. N.Volkova,"ARAN, f. 142, op. 5, d. 149, l. 220b. (quote). See also N. Volkov, "Khristovy voiny tsaria nebesnogo," *Bezbozhnik* 3 (February 1930), 6–8.The substance of the original book was included in a later version, including some new, politically topical material, under the title *Skopchestvo i sterilizatsiia: Istoricheskii ocherk* (Moscow:Akademiia nauk, 1937). For a French translation of the 1930 edition, see Volkov, *La secte russe des castrats*.

63.Volkov, *Skopchestvo* (1937), 59–60.

64.Volkov, *Sekta skoptsov* (1931), 114–15; *Skopchestvo* (1937), 91, 93.

65.Volkov, *Skopchestvo* (1937), 59; *Sekta skoptsov* (1931), 111–14.

66.Volkov, *Sekta skoptsov* (1931), 102.

67.Volkov, *Sekta skoptsov* (1931), 86; also *Skopchestvo* (1937), 82.

68.Volkov, *Sekta skoptsov* (1931), 79–85.

69.Volkov, *Sekta skoptsov* (1931), 82.

70. Kagarov, "Otzyv," l. 220b. See also D. Zelenin, "Otzyv o rabote N. N.Volkova" (July 28, 1935),ARAN, f. 142, op. 5, d. 249, l. 20–21.

71. Yuri Slezkine, *Arctic Mirrors: Russia and the Small Peoples of the North* (Ithaca: Cornell University Press, 1994), 263. For the denunciation of Matorin's political crimes, see "Ot redaktsii," *Sovetskaia etnografiia*, no. 6 (1936), 3–4. He was accused of "Trotskyist-Zinovievite" deviation, "lack of Bolshevik vigilence and rotten liberalism," and "counterrevolutionary falsification of Marxism-Leninism" (quotes, ibid., 3).

72.Volkov, "Avtobiografiia" (May 25, 1938).

73. "Data i prichina uvol´neniia" (January 7, 1948), ARAN, f. 142, op. 5, d. 249, l. 149ob. Art. 47-D of the Code of Labor Laws included conviction for criminal acts as the basis for dismissal: see *Kodeks zakonov o trude* (Moscow: Profizdat, 1938), 16.

74. Reshetov, "Otdanie dolga," pt. 1, 7–9. Reshetov differs from the archival sources concerning dates of arrest (1947 and 1948, respectively) and dates of death (March 7, 1953, and March 4, 1953). Cf. ARAN, f. 13, op. 1, introduction, p. 3.

75. Letter from N. P. Latyshev to V. D. Bonch-Bruevich (February 12, 1932), GMIR, f. 2, op. 5, d. 42, l. 4–8.

76. Letter from N. P. Latyshev to V. D. Bonch-Bruevich (April 25, 1932), GMIR, f. 2, op. 5, d. 42, l. 14–16.

77. Letter from V. D. Bonch-Bruevich to N. P. Latyshev (July 13, 1932), GMIR, f. 2, op. 5, d. 135, l. 1.

78. Letter from N. P. Latyshev to V. D. Bonch-Bruevich (February 23, 1933), GMIR, f. 2, op. 5, d. 43, l. 1–10b. Many peasants wrote letters to higher authorities complaining of local abuses and the misbehavior of their neighbors: see Sheila Fitzpatrick, *Stalin's Peasants: Resistance and Survival in the Russian Village after Collectivization* (New York: Oxford University Press, 1994), 256–58, 295.

79. Letter from D. D. Chistiakov to N. P. Latyshev (August 24, [1933]), GMIR, kollektsiia I, op. 6, d. 4, l. 1. Annotated by Latyshev, l. 10b.

80. Letter from Chistiakov to Latyshev (August 24, [1933]), l. 1–10b.

81. N. P. Latyshev, "Nachalo moego povestvovaniia" (1910), GMIR, f. 2, op. 5, d. 261, l. 50–50ob.

82. Letter from N. P. Latyshev to V. D. Bonch-Bruevich (December 16, 1933), GMIR, f. 2, op. 5, d. 43, l. 8–10.

83. Letters from Latyshev to Bonch-Bruevich (December 16, 1933), l. 8–10; (December 10, 1933), GMIR, f. 2, op. 5, d. 43, l. 13.

84. Letter from N. P. Latyshev to V. D. Bonch-Bruevich (October 20, 1933), GMIR, f. 2, op. 5, d. 43, l. 17–20.

85. Letter from Latyshev to Bonch-Bruevich (December 10, 1933), l. 13–13ob.

86. Letter from Latyshev to Bonch-Bruevich (October 20, 1933), l. 19.

87. N. P. Latyshev, notebook Osa on the Ural River (1934), GMIR, f. 2., op. 5, d. 266, l. 17.

88. Latyshev, notebook (1934), l. 17–18.

89. Latyshev, notebook (1934), l. 18ob.

90. Letter from N. P. Latyshev to I. V. Stalin, sent to Bonch-Bruevich (December 22, 1938), GMIR, f. 2, op. 5, d. 49, l. 3. Sheila Fitzpatrick reports that among the numerous letters written by peasants and sent to the peasant paper, *Krest'ianskaia gazeta*, in 1937–38, hardly any mention Stalin, let alone praise him: *Stalin's Peasants*, 295–96.

91. "Tetrad´ 'glagolov' skoptsov," GMIR, kollektsiia I, op. 6, d. 2, l. 42.

92. Letter from Latyshev to Stalin (December 22, 1938), l. 3–30b.

93. Letter from Latyshev to Stalin (December 22, 1938), l. 4–40b.

94. Letter from Latyshev to Stalin (December 22, 1938), l. 50b., 60b.

95. Letter from Latyshev to Stalin (December 22, 1938), l. 8–8ob.

96. Letter from Latyshev to Stalin (December 22, 1938), l. 8ob.–9.

97. Letter from Latyshev to Stalin (December 22, 1938), l. 9–9ob.

98. Letter from Latyshev to Stalin (December 22, 1938), l. 10–10ob.

99. Letter from Latyshev to Stalin (December 22, 1938), l. 12ob.

100. Letter from N. P. Latyshev to V. D. Bonch-Bruevich (March 6, 1939), GMIR, f. 2, op. 5, d. 50, l. 5–8ob.

101. Letter from Latyshev to Bonch-Bruevich (March 6, 1939), l. 5–6.

102. Letter from Latyshev to Bonch-Bruevich (March 6, 1939), l. 8–8ob. "Dust and rot" (prakh i tlen ') is a variation on "dust and ashes" (prakh i pepel) from Genesis 18:27 and Job 30:19.

103. Letter from Latyshev to Bonch-Bruevich (March 25, 1929), l. 9ob.–10. Until 1932, peasants viewed Kalinin as a figure to whom one could appeal: see Husband, "Soviet Atheism," 89.

104. Letter from Latyshev to Stalin (December 22, 1938), l. 10ob.

INDEX